D1508314

PLAYING
FOR KEEPS

PLAYING FOR KEEPS

**How the World's
Most Aggressive and
Admired Companies Use
Core Values to
• Manage • Energize
• and Organize
Their People, and
• Promote • Advance
• and Achieve
Their Corporate Missions**

Frederick G. Harmon

John Wiley & Sons, Inc.
New York • Chichester • Brisbane • Toronto • Singapore

Copyright © 1996 by Frederick G. Harmon
Published by John Wiley & Sons, Inc.

Library of Congress Cataloging-in-Publication Data:
Harmon, Frederick G.
    Playing for keeps : how the world's most aggressive and admired
companies use core values to manage, energize, and organize their people
and promote, advance, achieve, their corporate missions / Frederick
G. Harmon.
        p.   cm.
    Includes index.
    ISBN 0-471-59847-X (Cloth : alk. paper)
    1. Management.   2. Employee motivation.   3. Values.   4. Work
ethic.   5. Value added.   I. Title.
HD31.H3452   1996
658.3′14—dc20   95-45410

TO EVERYONE ATTEMPTING
TO ELEVATE VALUES AT WORK

ACKNOWLEDGMENTS

I owe special thanks to Garry Jacobs, a principal in the consulting firm Mira International of Napa, California. Garry and I have shared, debated, and created management concepts for more than 20 years. The book we wrote together in 1985, *The Vital Difference: Unleashing the Powers of Sustained Corporate Success*, introduced several of the key concepts in this book. Beyond that, Garry and his consulting partner Robert Macfarlane read every word of my manuscript. Their thoughtful suggestions enriched every chapter.

My wife Nancy provided enthusiastic encouragement tempered with very practical advice. My brother John helped keep me focused when, at times, I became distracted by details along the way. My son John completed the early library research that helped me select companies to include as examples.

From start to finish, Sue Holmes provided invaluable help. She set up my interviews, kept our files, checked facts in the manuscript. Kathy Yarrusso kept my consulting business running smoothly while I was away interviewing or writing the book.

John Mahaney, my first editor at John Wiley & Sons, helped define the book's focus. When John moved on, his enthusiastic successor, Janet Coleman, completed the project with energy and dispatch.

My clients provided many practical opportunities to extend my knowledge and test my ideas. I thank all of them for the assignments that significantly expanded my understanding of values in action.

I also extend my appreciation to James W. Krause, president of North Central Management Associates, Inc., Excelsior, Minnesota; Andrea Cunningham, CEO of Cunningham Communication, Inc., of Santa Clara, California; and George Havens, honorary chairman of the Jayme Organization, Inc., of Cleveland, Ohio. Each of them arranged interviews with executives who made a significant contribution to the book.

Finally, I am grateful to the executives who agreed to interviews about their work with values. From beginning to end, I found the difficulty in writing about values was to make them real, not just concepts. I thank these executives for whatever success I have achieved with that challenge.

CONTENTS

CONTENTS

CONTENTS

INTRODUCTION

In the 1940s and 1950s, U.S. mastery of quantitative techniques created an aura of invincibility. An ability to manage by the numbers became the hallmark of success. By the 1970s, Europe and Japan had caught up. By the middle 1980s, techniques that were once an American monopoly were available everywhere.

Competitive pressures inspired a search for newer techniques. By the late 1980s, the focus had shifted to qualitative improvement. Values, the generator of qualitative improvement, slowly moved to the forefront. Many raised in the era of quantitative supremacy rejected the new ideas as a fad. Others eagerly embraced them as a quick fix. Over time, a more realistic attitude has emerged.

Qualitative improvement programs focused on values such as Quality, Customer Service, and Diversity have become a staple of progressive management. They have spread rapidly across America and are now circling the globe. Some companies claim the programs produce phenomenal results. Others complain of phenomenal costs.

Even among the most successful, few have combined quantitative and qualitative into a seamless design. A fuller integration of the numbers and values will be a major challenge to 21st-century management. How to meet that challenge is the central focus of this book.

People use—and more commonly abuse—the term "values" every day. I use it reluctantly, because we have no better term for the qualitative aspects of a business. The word has lost vitality. It falls frustratingly short when describing our greatest opportunity to create and sustain corporate success.

Stripped of current connotations, what is a value? It is simply something we regard as valuable. What is the true source of value in a company? It is not, as commonly supposed, the company's assets, net worth, or annual earnings. In any company, value grows out of the quality of the individual actions that sustain performance.

That focus has logical implications different from today's practice. For one, values initiatives can have only one goal. They are worth the effort only when they enrich individual actions. It follows there is only one practical way to measure the success of values initiatives: To what extent do they improve operations? Do they produce better products? Promote faster service? Expand staff capacity? Do they add flexibility and focus to the organization? How do they specifically enhance the use of time, machinery, and capital?

This is not the common understanding of corporate values today. Some managers still dismiss values as superfluous. Others consider them desirable appendages to the company's real work. Both views miss an obvious truth. Values are the vibrant core of institutional life in all for-profit and not-for-profit enterprises.

Commitment to values lifts performance—personal and corporate. I learned that as a senior executive. However, my knowledge was more intuitive than reasoned. My more recent work as a consultant and writer has deepened my understanding. In the past decade, I've collaborated on a book on sustaining corporate growth. I've written another on personal success. In researching the first book, I interviewed dozens of people at every level in pace-setting American companies. For the second, I listened while successful people reflected on their rise in corporate life.

The subtext of all these conversations was values. Standout companies and exceptionally successful individuals share a commitment. Sometimes consciously, more often by instinct, they pursue values in their work.

My consulting work has reinforced another important lesson: Understanding a power of success is one thing, knowing how to use it is another. That's why this book focuses more on the doing than on the knowing. The issue today is seldom the value of values. The issue today is how to bring them to life—or renew them—in specific corporate environments.

Over the past decade, I've discussed corporate values with hundreds of people. I learned effective approaches and techniques in the interviews that form the practical foundation of the book. My conceptual understanding matured in more interactive forums. I regularly give lectures and conduct strategic planning sessions for entrepreneurs, senior and middle level corporate managers, and individual contributors.

In these sessions, people have thrown at me every conceivable question about the theory, application, and implementation of corporate values. Thanks to their challenges, I am now able to present a step-by-step system for values implementation. Thanks to the interviews, I can provide concrete examples of each step. I have also tried to answer 33 of the most common questions from these sessions.

Companies and managers often believe it takes superhuman leadership to achieve values-driven activities. The evidence suggested the opposite. The stories in this book focus on ordinary people who became exceptional by setting new directions through values. The keys are commitment, systems, consistency, and application. With these, any company or individual can follow a values-driven path to success.

PART I

CORE VALUES: THE ONCE AND FUTURE FRONTIER

Five Key Questions

- What are core values?
- Why are they important?
- How do they impact performance?
- Why is there such interest in values today?
- How are values-driven companies different?

CHAPTER 1

BEHIND THE NUMBERS

What is the source of all profit? Certainly not the numbers. The numbers are only symbolic representations of corporate performance. In any company, the real source of profit is thousands of individual actions by individual employees. Add value to each of those acts and you add profit. The aim of corporate values is to add that value. In every act. All the time.

Profit is determined by ten thousand individual acts. The quality of those acts determines the quality of the profit.

Generating more profit from a company, department, or individual contributor depends on adding value to individual acts carried out by that company, department, or contributor. Everybody understands this intuitively. Yet this obvious truth is seldom present when managers direct attention toward what is important.

"Let's begin with the numbers." All management meetings begin with the numbers. The numbers are the single best indicator of how the business is doing. The numbers are so real. So real, it's hard to remember they are abstractions, macro reflections of the quality of thousands of individual acts.

When well-executed acts significantly exceed poorly executed acts, the numbers "look good." When poor exceeds good, they "look bad." *Look* is the right word. The numbers are always images of reality, never reality itself.

Next on the agenda at that typical meeting: A review of the production schedule for the next month. Are we meeting the schedule? If we are, move on. No time to ask how to add more value to the thousands of individual acts that sustain the schedule every day.

Next: Progress on putting together next year's budget. Will we make our sector's profit targets? So far, yes in 80 percent of our units, no in 20 percent. OK, where are we going to make our cuts?

Maybe we should discover where profits are draining away through wasted energy and misspent resources? No time. Make the cuts. Move on. Remember the good news. Eighty percent can make the financial target. Maybe there's more profit hidden in the individual acts carried out in those operations? "If it ain't broke, don't fix it." Move on.

Next: That nasty personnel situation. She's talking about suing. Human resources says she may have a case. Who's going to talk with her? HR is having a small dinosaur on this one. They want everybody to attend that managing diversity course. How are we going to fit *that* into the schedule?

Ten minutes left. Enough time to look at the CEO's new flavor of the month: customer service. Anyone got any good stories to pass up the line? Any candidates for this month's Customer Service Star Award? How are we doing on our customer complaint index? Scores are worse. Find out who's screwing up and why.

Get it all done, team, or we'll all hear about it at performance review time. Remember our Four Commandments: Make money, grow fast, watch the numbers, stay out of trouble with corporate.

The people at this meeting focused on what they think matters most. Experienced managers, they know how to manipulate symbols to move their sector forward. Accustomed to symbols, they overlook reality. At a minimum, reality has ten

4

times the power of its symbols. People focused on reality will always outperform people focused on symbols.

THE VIEW FROM THE TRENCHES

To see the reality of the ten thousand acts, look at what's happening while the managers sit in their meeting. Out on the plant floor, production on the new line stopped more than an hour ago. R&D and production are waiting for the managers to get a decision on that small mistake hidden somewhere in the specifications. In the office, a secretary is typing an overdue proposal for new business. In her hurry, she mistypes "Mr." instead of "Ms." The company will lose the job. Also lost will be more than 40 hours of preparation time.

With the managers tied up in their meeting, their overworked associates are bouncing a prospective customer around on the telephone. Asked by the third person to "please hold," he is thumbing through his telephone directory looking for the name of a competitor. The company's top sales producer, furious over the lack of prompt support from the back office, has declared a Mental Health Day. He's working on his putting at the golf course. He can afford it. The company cannot.

None of these small acts—or hundreds of others like them—will appear on next month's statement of financial results. They will not appear in the budget or in the managers' performance appraisals. Yet together they form an invisible sieve, draining profit dollar by dollar.

Happily, hundreds of other equally small acts are accumulating profits. A sales representative drove 135 miles this morning to deliver a replacement part to a customer. Sometime next year, the customer will place an extra order. In the back office, three secretaries are meeting informally to balance their work so they can meet their deadlines. This cooperation gets three customer inquiries handled a day early and convinces the senior secretary to turn down another job. Replacing her would have cost $6,000 above budget in temp and recruitment costs.

Harry in maintenance has just uncovered a potential problem with machine number 3. He's installing a $38 part that will avoid a $12,000 replacement plus three weeks of downtime this summer. Chris is training recruits on safety procedures. Accidents that won't happen will lower next year's insurance costs. Mary's careful review of accounts receivable uncovers an invoicing error that will mean $950 in extra revenue.

Like their negative counterparts, none of these acts—or hundreds of others like them—will appear on next month's statement. They will not surface in the budget or in the managers' performance appraisals. Yet together they form an invisible bank account, collecting profit dollar by dollar.

THE BASIC CELL OF PERFORMANCE

The small individual act is the basic cell of all performance. Everything we call management ends there. The more complete or even perfect the act, the higher the level of performance. The greater the number of complete acts handled by a company, department, or individual contributor, the better the level of performance.

In skilled companies, completing the act 75 percent or even 85 percent of the time is routine. Routine is also the best word to describe the performance of most companies. The gap, the incompleteness of routine acts, shows up clearly when there is a failure.

Trace the source of the most recent failure where you work and you will find a gap between idea and execution of an individual act. An unclear communication. A critical element late. A lost document. A delayed response. A lack of discipline. A phone call not returned. An instruction given with disrespect. A dishonest performance appraisal. A policy ignored.

The secret behind outstanding companies, departments or contributors is simply that they work harder at adding value to their individual acts. The sum total of those value-added acts produces greater profit. Managing for profit means constantly working on the structure, systems, and skills that enable people throughout the organization to add more value to their individual acts.

People overlook this common truth in favor of more grandiose visions. Complex models are easier to understand than what is around us every minute. In the common analogy, the fish is not conscious of the water until the water drains away. Similarly, most managers overlook individual acts until something goes wrong. Good managers respond with a burst of energy, rewriting or creating policies, improving systems and skills to prevent similar mistakes. The best managers focus consistently, without waiting for mistakes, on helping their teams add quality to individual acts.

This, and nothing else, is value-added management.

Managers are too easily beguiled by attempts to improve performance through strategy, reorganization, or technique. True, all three can be useful. An effective strategy focuses on marketplace reality and aligns operations with that reality. A sensible reorganization cuts obsolete functions, improving the balance between resources and results. The best techniques encourage fresh thinking about routine operations. Yet none of these three produces better results on its own. Their power to generate constructive change lies in their capacity to direct or redirect individual small acts.

Originality is a poor predictor of the success of that bold new strategy. Far more important is the strategy's capacity to inspire individuals to add more value to their individual acts. Organizational reengineering is a popular management technique of the moment. Where its purpose is solely to add efficiency, it is useful but not dynamic. When designed to help people deliver more value in their individual acts, the new technique releases enthusiasm as well as efficiency.

The conclusive test of any strategy, reorganization, or technique is how well it enables people to add more value to their individual acts.

WHAT MANAGERS REALLY MANAGE

In any serious analysis, managers manage neither results nor numbers. They manage the quality of individual acts. What does a sales manager really do? She manages almost no sales herself. Her schedule consists of managing individual acts that will help others in putting numbers on the board.

She spends an hour showing an inexperienced salesman how to add value to his presentation. She runs a sales meeting, describing the new incentive program and explaining the benefits of a new product. She meets with a dissatisfied customer. By listening intently, she regains a measure of the customer's goodwill. She meets with a satisfied customer, learning how her products could be easier to use. She counsels a young saleswoman on how to handle a harassing customer. She rewrites a letter to the production department three times, making it more positive so the department leader will take her suggestions seriously. She handles her paperwork carefully, ensuring the accounts department has no unanswered questions about her reports.

Yet at the end of the quarter, her boss will not measure her by how well she carries out any of these actions. He will measure her almost exclusively on sales against quota. In a more sophisticated system, the sales department will break down her quota by new customers versus old, new products versus old, and by region. The company will measure her expenses as a ratio of sales and her success in retaining salespeople. The quality of her individual acts—the very acts that will produce or lower profit—will appear only at the margins of her evaluation.

While fluent in managementspeak, her boss really believes how she treats her people or the integrity of her communications is soft stuff. He knows how to deal with soft stuff: pretend it doesn't exist until there is a problem. Stay with what counts.

Mentally paraphrasing football coach Vince Lombardi, her boss doesn't think making your numbers is the most important thing. He believes it is the only thing. In the 1980s he would have said so. In the 1990s he's more circumspect. Asked directly, he will voice support for respect, integrity, "and the rest of that Boy Scout stuff." In his reviews with the sales manager, however, he pays attention to what matters—the numbers.

What if her boss went beyond the numbers? What if he asked her to think about which of her recurring acts had the most power to increase profit? What if he then asked her to find ways to add more value to the way she and her team carried out each of those critical acts? What if they worked out ways together to measure her progress? What if he then regularly reviewed that progress in addition to her numbers every month? Think of the impact on her performance.

What if her boss then asked all sales managers in his region to add the same value to their work? Think of the impact on profit in his region. What if all the support people backing up the region's salespeople then agreed to add the same value to their recurring individual actions? Spread that idea throughout a company. Think of the impact on the company's profit.

Glimpse the result of thousands of individual acts energized by adding the same value or quality, and you glimpse the potential of what people today commonly call *Core Values.*

HIDDEN GOLD

Look behind the numbers, and values appear like gold nuggets on the ground.

For example, today everyone sees the profit-making power of a value called Customer Service.* This awareness expanded in the last decade, when hurricane-force competition awakened managers everywhere. Unleashed competitive energy reshaped whole industries, sweeping away jobs, security, and expectations. Change triggered a desperate search for hidden profit, leading managers to look behind the numbers.

Less than a mile into this unfamiliar territory, the explorers

---

*Specific Values are capitalized in the book to distinguish them from the activity or trait they describe. Thus the aim of a Quality program is to produce better quality in products.

hit a vein of pure gold: profitability grows out of satisfying the customer. The discovery was old news to companies that had worked this mine for decades. Yet the unexpected strike justifiably excited the exploring managers. Perhaps for the first time, they were consciously touching the power of a core value.

Thousands of companies abandoned exploration on the spot. They set up permanent camps called Customer Service and began mining nuggets of profit. Blinded by the yield from one value, they lost sight of even greater treasures nearby. Over time, the more alert discovered an adjacent rich field called Customer-Driven Quality. As news of this discovery spread, exploration again slowed for all except the most adventurous.

Yet the profit-generating capacity of Customer Service or even of Customer-Driven Quality is only a beginning. It is the power of the steam engine compared with atomic energy. For any company or any manager, dozens of values silently wait, each with potential to unleash profit and accelerate careers. To revisit the explorer analogy, even the most adventurous are only ten miles into a continent of untapped resources.

PHYSICAL VALUES

To generate more profit from basic levels of operations, anyone can apply the leverage of physical values. Waiting here are such everyday workhorses as Cleanliness, Orderliness, and Speed. There are also obvious profit makers such as Efficient Use of Money and Materials. Quality (of product, service, or work) is another widely acknowledged profit builder. Safety pays regular dividends by reducing waste and lifting morale. More subtle physical values include Maximum Use of Time, and Effective Use of Space.

In the late 1980s, General Electric Company CEO Jack Welch transformed the physical value of Speed into a competitive weapon. Said Welch: "Speed exhilarates and energizes. Whether it be fast cars, fast boats, downhill skiing, or a business process, speed injects fun and excitement into an otherwise routine activity." In business, "speed tends to propel ideas and drive processes right through functional barriers, sweeping bureaucrats and impediments aside in the rush to get to the marketplace."[1]

After adopting Speed as a value, GE pared production time for locomotives to forty-six days from ninety-two. Burdened with a less efficient plant and higher labor costs, General Motors began to lose ground to its speedier rival.[2]

Speed clearly spells profit in product development. An economic model created by management consultants McKinsey & Company documents the difference. McKinsey's research shows high-tech products that come to market six months late but on budget earn 33 percent less profit over five years. In contrast, coming out on time and 50 percent over budget cuts profits by only 4 percent.[3]

While important, accelerating product development only taps the surface potential. A companywide commitment to Speed uncovers profit everywhere. Speed closes expensive gaps between marketing and production. When Speed is a common value, both departments must develop coordinated systems to reduce wasted time and money. A commitment to Speed means marketing quotes must go out in one day. That requires work schedules with maximum flexibility and minimum down time. Speed means inventory must be more precisely calibrated, lowering expenses. The accountants must stay on top of their backlog, increasing cash flow by sending out invoices faster. A commitment to Speed requires work simplification, revealing the hidden costs of duplication and obsolete systems. Human resources must develop faster recruiting systems, lowering the direct and indirect costs of temporary workers.

When people first notice a new value, they seek to compartmentalize it. Customer Service was once housed exclusively in Customer Service departments. Quality Control departments handled all quality issues. Less familiar values are still introduced in this way. In adopting Speed as a value, many executives see it solely as a tool to improve product development. What they miss is its potential to link activities and functions across the organization.

Executives complain about the high cost of interdepartmental squabbling. Turf wars drain productivity and profits everywhere. ("Why can't these people get along? We compete with each other more than we fight outside competition.") At the heart of most of these civil wars is the battle for resources—time, people, money, equipment. Values are not a panacea for conflicting ambitions and clashing egos. However, when a company commits to the same value everywhere, rivalries are channeled in a positive direction. Sharing resources is only sensible when everyone is trying to live the value.

A comprehensive commitment to Speed links continuous improvement everywhere. Before manufacturing can produce more rapidly, research and development must provide perfect specifications. Manufacturing must discuss schedule changes with sales and marketing to ensure no delays to customers. Better coordination between production and purchasing is necessary to ensure the right materials are available on time. The systems department must improve software to provide faster, more detailed control information. Finance and accounting must find ways to provide quicker "flash" figures to help all departments stay on track. Human resources and purchasing must work together on the installation of the latest stress-reduction furniture, equipment, lighting, and training.

Any company or individual can speed up in an emergency. Adopting Speed as a value means converting today's special emergency pace to tomorrow's routine without burning people out. With that common goal, cross-functional teams quickly become an obvious way to get work done. Teamwork promotes better understanding of the views of others. Personal animosity is submerged in pursuit of the common goal.

MULTIPLYING PROFIT

As the Speed example illustrates, any company comprehensively committing to *just one value* will quickly see a dramatic increase in profitability. Add other values, and profit multiplies.

For good or ill, values shape every act at work. For most, this shaping is unconscious. Even for conscious values, emphasis differs among individuals and departments. One department values Speed and strives to deliver speedy responses, risking an occasional mistake. Another values Accuracy; its responses are perfect but slow. Each group complains about the other. Each can defend its value at the expense of the other.

Common commitment to both values will lead to a higher synthesis. Warring departments first must look inward for ways to strengthen their weaker value. Next, they must work together to improve both Accuracy and Speed. When the company elevates a third value—Respect for Each Other—it energizes the process still further. To live all their values, groups must work together to increase speed and accuracy while honoring each other's contribution and views.

When Speed, Accuracy, and Respect increase, wasteful conflicts diminish. Access to fast, accurate information lifts productivity everywhere. Workers who are more productive use fewer resources in serving customers better, generating more profit. A spirit of Respect encourages people to pick up the slack for others when necessary. When one of the values is missing, the void neutralizes each of these positive developments totally or in part. Productivity, profitability, and growth suffer. When present, conscious values shape the cohesion, integrity, efficiency— and above all, the profitability—of any company.

ORGANIZATIONAL VALUES

Beyond the physical level, increased profit grows out of organizing and coordinating work at higher levels of efficiency. Here the levers are such organizational values as Empowerment, Decisiveness, Discipline, Systematic Functioning, Coordination, Integration, Communication, and Teamwork.

While Speed is presently popular, Decisiveness, arguably an even more potent value, has lost favor. This is a missed opportunity. Many of today's executives are veterans of the Wars Against Authority in the 1960s and 1970s. Suspicious of abuses of power, they confuse decisiveness with autocratic behavior. For profit's sake, any company needs important decisions made sooner, not later. Few executives lose their jobs for wrong decisions made too early. Far more end up on the street after dithering over decisions that required prompt action.

Too many managers seek perfect consensus on important decisions. When they can't achieve this, they delay, hoping something will turn up. Eventually, they run out of time. Under pressure, they implement their decision autocratically, duplicating the style they so despise.

Delayed decisions eat into profitability at every level. The board delays discussing succession with a venerable CEO, and the company stagnates for years. The marketing vice president delays launching a new product, and a competitor steals the market. The purchase order for new equipment that could lower costs by more than 2 percent sits unsigned on the manufacturing vice president's desk for three months. Why the delay? He's reluctant to offend a long-time supplier.

Most common of all, failure to face employee performance problems drains profits and morale throughout the company. After years of enduring unproductive performance, management decides to cut its losses. Even then, the company lowers profits by hiring an expensive consultant to recommend what is by now obvious to everyone.

The cost of each delay multiplies silently. A delay in purchasing equipment leads to production delays, meaning more overtime. Even with the overtime, sales momentum slows. Lost or delayed sales reduce cash flow, leading to higher interest costs. The cash squeeze reduces funds available to purchase inventory, slowing future production. Converting each of these negatives to a positive requires improving performance on one value—Decisiveness.

Managers who choose Decisiveness as a core value view their work in a more complete perspective. Greater awareness of the cost of delays leads to more brisk decision making. Far from being autocratic, true decisiveness requires *appropriate* consultation before decisions. When you are truly decisive, you consult in advance so you don't have to reverse decisions later. Setting deadlines in advance for each step builds confidence in the final result.

Even with the best process, someone will disagree. Even when there is agreement, there is risk of failure. However, a systematic, appropriately time-sensitive process will reduce the sure cost of delays while improving the odds for success.

Look for the value of Decisiveness in the next person you choose for a critical assignment or job!

PSYCHOLOGICAL VALUES

In any organization, people are the limitless resource. Everyone knows intuitively that inspired people generate more profit. Every business magazine describes those superhuman people in Company X who are always willing to go "above and beyond." These folks love working in teams to serve customers. Every year they come up with hundreds of new ideas to reduce costs. They express pride and energy in routine actions. Company profit soars on the wings of their enthusiasm.

How do you get people like that? "Dynamic leadership" is the common incomplete answer. True, it takes leadership to attract, keep, and inspire good people. Before anything exceptional happens, however, those special people must hear the leader's message. The quality of people's hearing depends on the psychological values present. Really dynamic leadership consists of instilling and maintaining those inspirational values.

Psychological values generate profit by harnessing the higher aspirations of individual employees. Inspired employees work longer, harder, and with more attention to the details that make or lose profit. Lacking a crisis, leaders need clear psychological values to inspire others to action.

Psychological values include the highest attributes of organizational life. Trust, Integrity and Respect for the Individual are qualities that grow in values-driven companies.

Increasingly today, Respect honors the value of Diversity. Moving beyond mere satisfaction, psychological values today aim to *delight* both customers and associates. Near the pinnacle of values: Service to Society.

In an era of downsizing and corporate scandals, people view Trust as an abstract, impractical value. Yet trust is basic to all business success. What happens when a company loses the trust of its customers? People become skeptical, suspicious, cynical. Attractive prices and good quality no longer matter. People buy elsewhere. What happens when you don't trust your boss or your associates? Energy is squandered in protecting your back.

What happens when trust is present? The Walt Disney Company promises an exciting show in a safe, courteous theme park. On faith, millions of people pay a premium price to visit Disney parks because they trust Disney.

Everything in business depends on trust. People's faith in the government, not gold, is the true backing for our monetary system. Stock market booms and crashes create or destroy wealth in hours. These movements reflect only rising or falling trust in the future of our system.

Lack of trust is corrosive and contagious. Fed up with years of broken promises, a condominium association fired its management firm. At the first meeting with the new managers, members challenged every statement made by the new firm. "We've only been on the job six weeks, give us a chance," pleaded the company's vice president. Experience overcame reality. Distrust was palpable. The accusations continued unabated.

On the macro level, lack of trust poisons political life. The presumption of innocence is an obsolete concept in the court of public opinion. New presidents and their administrations used to get a honeymoon period before distrustful attacks began. Now the honeymoon doesn't last until Inauguration Day.

In such a climate, any company that people trust touches a wellspring of goodwill and profitability. People trust the safety of Volvo cars, the performance of Northwestern Mutual Life Insurance policies, the reliability of Maytag appliances. Each company commands a premium for its product. Each works unstintingly to preserve the always fragile trust on which its profitability rests.

At every level, trust builds sales. The first day on the job, every salesperson learns that it's more profitable to sell existing customers than get new ones. To keep customers, Merck & Company, Inc. salespeople learn to protect the company's trust value, Credibility. Doctors trust Merck because Merck ensures that all sales materials and presentations are correct. Merck tests its salespeople on how well they explain the negative side effects of its drugs. Merck's profitability, among the highest in its industry, attests to the power of Trust.

When employees trust management, there are fewer tensions and disputes to lower productivity. When management trusts employees, overhead and control systems are more cost effective. AT&T Universal Card Services Corporation trusts its frontline associates to answer customer requests, even requests for credit extensions. Customer representatives handle 95 percent of customer requests on the spot. Trust speeds customer service and reduces the costs of supervision and approval systems.

A FORMULA FOR NON-STOP GROWTH AND PROFIT

Speed, Decisiveness, and Trust are three examples of an available three dozen values. Taken together, such values form the essence, the foundation, the building blocks of successful acts, activities, and organizations. Every value ignored is a missed opportunity. Every value pursued is a path to profit.

Any manager can apply each of these values to virtually every act. The impact of applying values across the board to every act will multiply the productivity and profitability of any company. The conscious application of all these values will upgrade the quality of every act. This upgrading will have an exponential impact on corporate results.

Too many managers think of values as those highly desirable but unattainable ideals. Not at all. We all manage multiple values over a multitude of acts every hour of every day, at home and at work. We do this to ensure that acts are accomplished safely, neatly, efficiently, and accurately in a well-organized, pleasant, and timely manner.

Every company does the same. Transformed into a fully conscious process, continuously raising the qualitative context of acts in a company is a formula for nonstop growth and profits that continuously ascend from peak to greater peak.

CHAPTER 2

THE OTHER SIDE OF
THE BALANCE SHEET

Mastery of the numbers lifted American business to unequaled heights. Then competition forced a reappraisal. Were the numbers the only path to profit? What about Customer Service? Quality? Respect for Each Other? Looking behind the numbers, managers discovered a huge, unutilized asset that isn't listed on the balance sheet. Even "America's toughest boss" became a convert.

Paying attention to Core Values scarcely qualifies as an overnight sensation.

E. I. du Pont de Nemours & Company, Inc. has elevated Safety within its plants for nearly 200 years. At Maytag, Reliability has shaped performance for a century. Managers at Northwestern Mutual Life Insurance have focused for decades on Service to Policyholders.

While not revolutionary, today's emphasis on values is expanding the way people look at work. The effort to elevate the quality of individual acts is becoming more clearly defined every day. Two of the most publicized efforts are the Total Quality Management and Customer Service campaigns of recent years.

The focus on values extends further. Corporate leaders are sponsoring programs to manage the value of Diversity. Punctuality consultants show companies how to add timeliness to thousands of individual acts. Courses on business ethics train

19

managers to submit everyday business decisions to ethical standards.

Every popular value has its own gurus. These teachers promote the power of specific values. They provide techniques for carrying their chosen value down to individual acts. The best of their programs promote multiple values. To serve customers well, you have to be Punctual. You must provide high Quality in your products. You need to operate your business in a systematic way.

Gurus often drift into single-mindedness. They try to bring everything under their chosen value. In doing so, they strain necessary balance in a company. When everything is Total Quality, Respect for People becomes a means rather than an end. Elevating several equal values is more likely to build balanced growth.

Earlier management practice developed exciting new concepts to promote profit and growth. Leading companies adopted the concepts, encouraging imitation. Over time, form dominated content. Managers emphasized the control potential of what had been liberating ideas. Strategic Planning in the 1940s and 1950s and Management By Objectives in the 1960s and 1970s are two examples. The effective content in these concepts is now mainstream management; their rigid form is obsolete.

The risk of too narrow a focus reappears in the newer techniques. Many benchmarking teams search primarily for concrete, quantitative information in their on-site visits. When limited by that narrow vision, teams act like industrial tourists, shooting snapshots of reality. How much more valuable to pay detailed attention to the practices behind the numbers.

ANXIETY AND ASPIRATION

Today's interest in values stems from anxiety and aspiration. Anxiety grew when the numbers-first 1980s produced too many crash landings. The 1990s opened with a search for ways to measure business success beyond the numbers. During the 1980s, the numbers on the financial statements—and the resulting bonuses—went up dizzily. Before long, however, many former paragons were explaining some lurid individual acts behind the numbers. Many managers turned to values to add balance to the short-term thinking that led to excess.

Aspiration plays a role, too. "When we began to benchmark ourselves against strong companies," one senior executive told me, "we were looking for two or three ways they performed better. We discovered it wasn't one or two techniques. It was the way they did everything that made the difference." Inspired by such research, companies launched processes to do everything better by adding more value to individual acts.

Enthusiasm grows as admired leaders speak out on the qualitative side of the ledger. Levi Strauss & Company CEO Robert D. Haas says his company used to talk about hard stuff and soft stuff. "The soft stuff was commitment to the work force. The hard stuff was what really mattered: getting pants out the door." Haas suggests today the soft stuff and the hard stuff are two parts of a complete whole. "A company's values—what it stands for, what its people believe in—are crucial to its competitive success. Indeed, values drive the business."[1]

AMERICAN MANAGEMENT

It wasn't always that way at Levi Strauss or elsewhere. For more than 40 years, the quantitative ledger drove U.S. management practice. World War II brought quantitative techniques to the forefront. Young planners using new analytical tools in Washington could project accurate cost/benefit decisions faster than experienced generals in the field.

After the war, these same young planners applied their quantitative tools to industry. From its Ford Whiz Kids of the forties to its merger kings of the eighties, the United States led the world in crunching numbers in new ways. Adapting techniques pioneered by the military, businesspeople developed a widely admired style that became known as American Management.

Barely 25 years ago, a French best-selling book predicted America would shortly dominate all world business because of its quantitative management systems. This so-called American Management changed the way executives organized and led their companies in every Westernized country.

For 40 years, Americans either developed or were first to put in place a host of new management techniques. Each technique strengthened the quantified side of the ledger. The more enduring of those contributions include ROI, MBO, PERT, Strategic Planning, Zero-Based Budgeting, employee morale surveys, and market research. As computers developed speed and flexibility, the numbers were available faster with more detail.

Americans became so skilled at following the numbers that many forgot there was anything to business besides numbers. Qualitative management was always as important as the numbers, but it was a lot harder to measure. Besides, why worry too much about *how* you were producing the results when the overriding goal was to produce better numbers? Companies and individuals judged success by a single criterion: more. More autos, more refrigerators, more leveraged buyouts, more profits.

Americans first noticed gaps in the vaunted American management style during the Vietnam War. Purely quantitative indicators such as Pentagon body counts actually projected a distorted view of reality. Then, in the 1980s the burgeoning Japanese economy proved the power that flows from consistency in such values as Quality and Customer Service. Something was clearly missing in U.S. methods.

THE BEDROCK OF MANAGEMENT

Values are the bedrock of management. Values such as Quality, Customer Service, Credibility, Trust, Respect for People always underpin a healthy balance sheet whether managers understand their importance or not. What's new today is that Americans are relearning to mobilize the resources within this qualitative side of the ledger. The currently accelerating management evolution is unifying the qualitative with the quantitative in a new synthesis.

Representative of the new synthesis is Activity-Based Accounting (ABC). At its best, ABC links the cost of individual acts with a value such as Customer Service or Efficiency. This is a significant shift in emphasis from the older, more sterile view of the numbers as an end in themselves.

INSPIRING ENTHUSIASM IN PEOPLE AT EVERY LEVEL

Interest also grows from increased understanding of the limits of the quantitative ledger. Quantitative management retains little power to enthuse workers below management level.

> "I read about your company in the paper," I mentioned to the woman at the checkout counter in the supermarket. "Your earnings were up 19 percent this quarter."
>
> "Really?" she replied. "That's nice."
>
> If I want to spark her genuine enthusiasm, I ask about one of the many special service award buttons she wears proudly on her jacket. Or I can ask about the "Quality and Value" award won recently by her branch.

AMERICA'S TOUGHEST BOSS

To compete, American companies must liberate the energy of their workers. The key to this lies in a better balance between their quantitative and qualitative ledgers. Quantitative success pleases and reassures workers. Qualitative success releases their pride and enthusiasm. Both are necessary. Both must be in balance before America can compete fully in the dawning global boom.

General Electric CEO Jack Welch is famous for acting on this challenge well before his peers. *Fortune* magazine once called Welch "America's toughest boss." He earned that title for his relentless pursuit of profit. GE named Welch CEO in 1981. In every year since, GE's sales, earnings, and revenue per share have topped the previous year.

Boldly combining hard and soft, Welch is creating a new model—the 21st century global corporation. GE's record leaves many large American companies feeling outclassed in speed and agility. In shareholder value, to cite one key indicator, GE raced to the top. A decade ago, GE ranked seventeenth among publicly traded companies. Today, it ranks first.

Welch sees values as a sequential step in the struggle to increase profits, productivity, and growth. "You've got to be hard to be soft," he says. "You have to demonstrate the ability to make the hard, tough decisions—closing plants, divesting, delayering—if you want to have any credibility when you try to promote soft values. We reduced employment and cut the bureaucracy and picked up some unpleasant nicknames, but when we spoke of soft values . . . people listened."[2]

First or Second in Every Market

In 1981, Welch set a goal to rank number one or number two globally in every market in which GE competes. Achieving that goal required a new management system at GE. James Baughman is Managing Director, J. P. Morgan Company. Baughman led GE's Corporate Management Development activities in the years Welch was introducing his system at GE. Baughman says three values—Speed, Simplicity, and Self-Confidence—were central in creating that system.

Converting to the new mind-set was difficult. "Not everybody wants to be quick," says Baughman. "We had whole departments that were paid to make things complicated." Welch and Baughman understood that mere words would attract little attention to values at numbers-driven GE. Implementation required a visible commitment. Welch also needed to show a closer link between the values and his quantitative goals. How would the new values help GE stay number one or number two in every market?

Baughman led a process that hammered out an eighteen-page white paper linking the GE values with Welch's vision for the company. The document circulated through every business team for two years, until some 20,000 people had discussed or reviewed it. People thought it was too long. Baughman condensed it to 10 pages and asked for more comments. In 1985, Welch published the values and the business strategies to support them in a single document.

Welch had a goal to be number one or number two. He had a vision of GE as greater than the sum of its parts. He bought and sold companies to fit that vision. He launched structural changes to liberate Speed, Simplicity, and Self-Confidence. His big strategic moves impressed the business press and Wall Street. However, by the late 1980s, his message was still only faintly audible to those at the bottom of the organization.

GE's employees were raising a host of questions about the new processes, values, and priorities. Says Baughman: "We were still not penetrating down to the shop floor or the office floor with walking the talk. We were still only talking the talk as far as it was impacting GE."

WORK-OUT AND BEST PRACTICES

Welch responded with Work-Out, a Baughman idea for a companywide program bringing together local teams of managers and workers from all levels. Work-Out aims to surface new ways to speed up, simplify, and promote self-confidence. Any topic can be—and was—raised: how to improve jobs, environment, productivity, quality of products and services, and customer satisfaction. The setting resembled a three-day town meeting where everybody submitted ideas.

The name Work-Out is a triple pun, according to Baughman. You have to get the nonsense *work out* of the company. You *work out* at the gym when you want more muscle and agility. You try to *work out* a problem, issue, or misunderstanding among coworkers.

As Work-Out sessions became routine, Welch's revolution took fire at the operating level. The results showed in decreased cycle times and improved product quality. The ratings went up on customer satisfaction, or "delight," as GEers call it.

"LOW-HANGING FRUIT"

Work-Out enlisted ideas and energy throughout the organization. Work-Out's rules required executives to adopt simple, commonsense ideas on the spot. Baughman calls this "harvesting the low-hanging fruit." In speeches and informal talks, Welch emphasized the link between his new values and GE's profitability, productivity, and growth. Walking the talk, Welch discarded tradition whenever tradition stalled progress. He talked about Simplicity in language everyone could understand.

Living self-confidence, Welch delegated new authority to leaders of his 13 core businesses. He went so far as to grant each business authority to set up its own compensation system. His actions dramatized his philosophy: run your business as you want with two requirements. First, stay number one or number two globally in your market. Second, create a climate that liberates people by promoting the right values. At GE, quantitative and qualitative had become a single focused path to success.

WORKING VERSUS DECORATIVE VALUES

Endorsements by such respected leaders as Welch and Haas sparked wider interest in the qualitative side of management. As interest has grown, so has confusion. We have no word better than "values," yet that word lacks precision. " 'Values' has so many different meanings," complains a 30-year-old knowledge worker. "Religious values, economic values, political values, social values."

In this book, the term "corporate values" refers specifically to *operational qualities used by organizations to maintain or enhance performance.* This definition includes physical values such as Speed and Safety, organizational values such as Coordination and Decisiveness, and psychological values such as Honesty and Respect for Others.

Companies use each of these values to elevate the qualitative side of work. Each value requires a different strategy to live at work. However, one similarity unites them all. Until they are living at the workplace, they are decorative values, pretty statements of intent. Decorative values are rhetorical exercises. They are separate from real work. Yet, as Jack Welch showed, put values to work and they can lift performance everywhere.

Today, many executives settle for decorative values. They express an even greater mystical faith in words than in the numbers. They believe words like *Customers First* or *Quality Is Everybody's Job* will be enough to produce the results. Some even justify such absurdities by citing their deep faith in people. "Once you tell our folks what you want, they'll deliver every time," they tell me with pride. If that is the case, why do they set sales quotas? Why not hang posters that say "Sell More"? When challenged, they reply: "That, of course, is different."

Everywhere in Corporate America, you find carefully crafted statements of noble aims. Expensively printed posters, banners, and brochures proclaim "Our Values." The cost of decorative values goes well beyond printing bills. When not supported by action, empty rhetoric fosters negativity and cynicism.

A backlash awaits people who talk too expansively about empty, decorative values. Employees, consumers, and the press are always quick to detect a gap between high prose and low performance. Employees see through the facade first. In the jargon of the day, they say management is not "walking the talk."

Too much glib talking and not enough strenuous walking clearly worsens the cynicism in many companies today. "I have a problem with the word values," says one 31-year-old salesman. "It's the in word for management. They put this poster on the wall and it's, look, here it is. They have these wonderful words on the wall but they have no reality in the workplace."

But don't believe this salesman is immune to the power of values. He rejects Corporate America's values hyperbole, but he deeply identifies with the values of a community organization where he is active. He credits his volunteer work with teaching him "to look at the greater good of the organization rather than the greater good of myself."

This young man's experience dramatizes the difference between decorative and working values. When values are real, they inspire service. When they are decorations, they are ignored or inspire contempt.

Reputation Grows from Inside Out

If employees catch on fast, the press and the public are often quick to follow. A values statement is always a poor cover for inferior performance. Andrea Cunningham is president and CEO of Cunningham Communication, Inc., of Santa Clara, California. "When people talk about the hostile press, it's nonsense," she says. "The press is just saying aloud what other people are saying privately." Ninety-nine times out of 100, she adds, there is a real problem behind complaints.

External perception is a reflection of internal reality. A sincere commitment to enhance values always shows on the outside. Alan Towers, president of Alan Towers Associates, a New York public relations firm, has studied the competitive value of corporate reputations. At companies such as McDonald's Corporation, Walt Disney, Merck, General Electric, Johnson &

Johnson, and Xerox, "reputation creates competitive advantage," he says.[3]

DON'T FAKE IT

In introducing values, when in doubt, don't pretend. Decorative values are not neutral. They cause harm. Either be willing to work on the genuine article or dismiss the current talk of values as a fad. Sounding out-of-date will do you less harm than acting like a hypocrite.

For those willing to work, there is a clearly marked path to success. Values implementation is a known process. There are logical, sequential steps. For decades, people elevated values unconsciously, following the example of a committed founder or leader. Today the process is conscious. With the necessary commitment, anyone can lead.

VALUES BEGIN ANYWHERE

The departmental level is a promising place to start. Most departments are small enough to produce fast results, big enough for those results to attract attention. I once helped a department leader identify and elevate performance on values within her unit. Her work caught the attention of the CEO, who soon launched a companywide program. Within three years the department leader received two promotions with large raises. Was her success a coincidence? I've seen too many successes follow a commitment to values to trust coincidence. My advice is always: "Don't wait for someone else to start. Begin today where you are."

HORIZONTAL THINKING

When leaders pay more attention to the qualitative side, they expand a company's vision in at least three ways—horizontally, vertically, and historically.

Horizontally, values link diversified business units around common themes. *Business Week* calls health-care giant Johnson & Johnson "a model of how to make decentralization work." Yet within a decentralized structure, the J&J credo commits all J&J's managers to common values. *Business Week* noted: "Like different people with kindred values, J&J companies have common standards but unique personalities."[4]

VERTICAL FOCUS

Vertically, values link the CEO and the frontline worker through shared commitment. At every level, executives and workers carry out thousands of routine actions every day. The quality of those actions affects every person they touch. Throughout the company, employees can handle any request in a bored, routine, efficient, effective, pleasant, or delightful way.

In poorly disciplined companies, individuals decide the response mostly on their own. More disciplined companies rely on supervision, time clocks, policies, and procedures—in short, negative discipline from above. Today, smart leaders are learning to use a common commitment to values to release the positive discipline that grows from within the individual.

GE lore recalls a worker with 25 years seniority who stood up after a vigorous Work-Out session to express his views. "Today is the first day you asked for my brain at work," he said. "The sad part is you could have had these ideas any time you asked."

IN COMPETITION WITH HISTORY

Long-established values challenge leaders to a creative competition with their ancestors. In the past decade, DuPont became a leader in providing family benefits to employees. The company expanded the quality of child care and elder care available for its workers. DuPont was adapting its safety value to current needs. In addition to physical safety, the company now provides employees with mental safety through freedom from worry.

PRODUCTIVITY THROUGH A NEW LENS

Until recently, productivity campaigns focused exclusively on the quantitative ledger. Reduce the workforce but not production. Hold wages down. Take out layers of supervision. Use time/motion studies to speed processes. Invest in labor-saving equipment. Pain and stress increased everywhere. There is a widespread sense that such techniques are reaching their limit.

New efforts to improve productivity must go beyond the quantitative ledger. Millions around the world are eager to work for wages far below U.S. standards. That was true even before new labor pools opened in Eastern Europe and China. Technology now permits lower-paid service workers in another country to process applications for a U.S. insurance company. Capital and know-how move around the world with the speed of a fax.

As the power of Quantitative management slows, Qualitative management retains its full capacity to unleash America's real strength, the inventive energy of every worker. When energy is focused solely on narrow economic goals, our diversity leads to division, with each group pursuing its own gain. Yet when energy is linked to a higher aspiration, productivity grows naturally among individuals, departments, organizations, or countries.

A WIDER VISION

Competing in a global economy requires a wider vision. The traditional view reduces any business result to a single number. That limitation encourages unidimensional thought about business. Yet on a personal level, we all assess results in a more sophisticated fashion.

The unidimensional result of an airline trip is to arrive at our destination. Yet we rate the airline on far more. How long was the line at check-in? Did the plane arrive on time? How was the food? Were the seats comfortable? Did the flight attendants greet people cordially? How long was the wait for luggage?

Airlines get us where we're going 99.9 percent of the time. If we personally rated airlines only on that criterion, we would be 99.9 percent satisfied. What really makes the difference is not the unidimensional result but the multi-faceted, qualitative result. It is here that values work their magic.

Airlines that elevate values such as Punctuality, Comfort, and Graciousness even a bit beyond the norm earn our gratitude and our business.

Everyday personal experience should lead us easily to the more complex, qualitative ledger in business. That it does not attests to the strong hold the quantitative still has over all business concepts and practices.

While companies strain for more quantitative gains, the profit potential in the qualitative remains largely untapped. That's what prompted "America's toughest boss," among many others, to begin talking so fervently about values.

PART II

TOWARD VALUES-DRIVEN LEADERSHIP: ISSUES AND STRATEGIES

Five Key Issues

- What is values-driven leadership?
- How do you create a values-driven management system?
- How can values strengthen your corporate personality?
- How can you use values to energize your process?
- How do you keep a proper balance between the numbers and values?

CHAPTER 3

THE COMMONPLACE MIRACLE

ServiceMaster literally carves its values in stone. "If you don't live it, you don't believe it" is the company's rallying cry. Founder Marion Wade launched 50 years of nonstop growth the day he brought his personal values to work. The key lesson: commitment to values fuels growth and multiplies profits.

Values touch emotions. When we are at the far end of deeply felt, well-executed values, we always feel their power. Their force doubles when we find ourselves at that tether end because we are in trouble.

My wife Nancy is a hard-to-please consumer. Full of enthusiasm, I once told her that companies were adopting Customer Delight as a new value. She replied that mere customer satisfaction would be a stretch for most companies she deals with.

"What about ServiceMaster?" I protested.

"Ah, well, ServiceMaster," she said, "they're exceptional."

ServiceMaster earned my wife's respect the hard way—in a crisis. On a late Friday afternoon in September a water pipe burst in our condominium apartment. By the time Nancy got the news, our master bedroom and bathroom were ankle deep in water. There was shallower flooding in a second bedroom and the hall. Worse, small streams of water were seeping down the walls of three apartments below.

Nancy is the director of a school for young children. Particularly at the start of a school year, she can barely spare a moment for an emergency phone call. Our miniflood occurred at closing time, one of the most hectic periods of the school day. True to form, I was away on a business trip.

Selecting at random from phone-book ads, Nancy dialed a firm specializing in fire and water damage. Jane Gandee, co-owner of the ServiceMaster of Alexandria (Virginia) franchise, answered the phone and calmly set about restoring order.

> Jane dispatched an emergency truck, quieted neighbors, called our insurance company. She honored every commitment on schedule. The flooded bedroom of a neighbor with physical disabilities presented special problems, which Jane's team handled with speed and tact. Jane personally delivered drying fans to a neighbor. The technicians who arrived in our apartment were efficient and courteous. They took time for follow-up phone calls between their visits. When the bill arrived, it was less than we expected. Jane settled the one disputed item in our favor in one phone call of fewer than two minutes.

Friends told us our experience was indeed exceptional. Those who had survived similar problems told of calling other companies and then waiting in frustration and anger. When the service people finally showed up, they lacked skills and were cantankerous to boot.

What made the difference? No single action stood out. Yet consistent execution added up to exceptional performance. At the basic level, ServiceMaster people expressed efficiency in approach and action. At a higher level, they showed concern to ease our anxiety. Values were visible throughout.

> The most obvious was Customer Service, with supporting values like Promptness, Courtesy, and Empathy. A technician called when he was behind schedule 15 minutes. Jane

36

answered questions before we thought to ask them. The ServiceMaster staff was candid about losses and disruption, yet they assured us our apartment would be back to normal before long.

HOW TO BE EXCEPTIONAL

Nancy could have called any of a half-dozen companies. For any company she chose, the clear, single-dimensional result would have been to restore four apartments to their previous condition as quickly as possible. Indeed, ServiceMaster **satisfied** us by achieving this single result. We judged them **exceptional**, however, because they went so far beyond one result.

In a crisis-driven business, technicians are always on the run. It's understandable they sometimes fall behind schedule or fail to have the right equipment. Companies hire them for technical skills, not for consoling stressed customers. An abrupt manner is often the hallmark of a competent technician. In a hectic period, uniforms get soiled, trucks stay dirty, equipment gets misplaced. All of this is so understandable that today it is the common expectation. ServiceMaster was exceptional because it achieved its single-dimensional result in a multifaceted way that exceeded these common expectations.

For the weakest companies in any field, inefficiency, poor attitudes, and breakdowns in operating systems mean premature death. Many of those that survive do so through their commitment to a single-dimensional rallying cry. It is their pride and accomplishment that *we do whatever we must to get the job done!* Usually they satisfy their customers. Their workers make decent pay. The company shows a modest profit. However, margins are always close to the edge. Expansion often spells trouble.

These are routine companies. Their growth is slow and uneven. No delighted customer will ever tell others they are "exceptional." Their workers will judge achievement by the size of the pay packet. Their owners will judge success by sales and the amount left over in the bank account at the end of the year.

Such routine companies are usually more nearsighted than inefficient. Focused on a single result, they miss the profit potential hidden in the small acts they carry out every day. Intent only on getting the job done, they waste physical energy in every transaction. Systemic improvements are happy accidents rather than habitual targets. Productivity gains grow from physical rather than mental energy. Stress levels are always high.

DOING THE COMPLETE JOB THE FIRST TIME

Although still a small company, ServiceMaster of Alexandria has grown beyond the routine. True, it does what it has to do to get the job done. However, its focus is wider—it looks at the complete job.

> The complete job means handling every task efficiently. It means orderliness, cleanliness, effective maintenance of equipment. Most unusually, it means empathizing with the customer's anxiety. That requires providing reassuring information without confusing details. The string of complete acts extended from the way Jane answered the first phone call to the final billing.

ServiceMaster people did not consciously shift from value to value. There was no sense of "now I am being Efficient; next I must be Customer Focused." Rather, actions were a seamless web of often barely visible values. When the technician called to say he would be late, he was expressing at least three values. We could feel his commitment to Promptness, to Customer Service, to Systematic Functioning.

Although intrigued by my wife's appreciation, I wondered whether we were benefiting from plain good luck. Maybe our disaster occurred when the company had extra people available. Maybe their strive-to-please attitude reflected a desperate desire for business. There is nothing like hard times to spur people to action.

Compelled by curiosity, I visited the people who own and operate this ServiceMaster franchise. What I found was far removed from the typical small family business. The quality of the service we received grew from conscious thought. It was the result of this small company's commitment to two targets: growth and values.

The owners, Jane Gandee and her husband Greg, come from families of entrepreneurs. However, the ServiceMaster franchise was the first business they operated on their own. They started with an annual revenue base of $30 thousand in 1986. By 1995, they were approaching revenues of $1.4 million.

HEAVY EMPHASIS ON VALUES

I learned our experience wasn't really "exceptional" at all. For the Gandees, no individual action is small enough to take for granted. They teach their technicians how to enter a home and introduce themselves, how to discuss the job, answer questions, perform the work, collect the payment, and move on to the next job.

"We keep going back until we satisfy the customer," says Jane. "We guarantee it." Detailed definitions of excellence support that goal. A human being picks up the company's telephone 24 hours a day. The customer will receive a call back within 15 minutes. On emergency work, a technician will arrive within two hours. In times of natural disasters such as heavy rains, the Gandees and their technicians work around the clock to maintain these standards.

"It's a constant battle," says Jane, "but we never give up." You can't let the customer's crisis become humdrum, she adds. "Oh, five inches of water? I saw 10 inches last week. You have to continue to remind yourself that this is their home, their furnishings. That's the new ceiling they paid to have fixed last summer."

The Gandees must always be ready to handle a variety of crises. Fires and floods are common examples. Interwoven with unpredictable, rush activities, the company must coordinate its regular commercial cleaning contracts.

Complicated schedules mean discipline. ServiceMaster people must show up on time and keep moving. To stay in business, the Gandees must get consistent performance from workers who often start with low skill levels and distrustful attitudes.

Theoretically, you can teach anyone the rudiments of the commercial cleaning of floors and carpets in a week. The job sounds simple: go into an office, clean the carpets or the rugs, and leave. Yet the Gandees provide close supervision for everyone on the job for at least six weeks. When you look deeper into any supposedly simple task, there are always dozens of costly risks.

"There are people out there with $20,000 or $30,000 sofas. All you have to do is pull the wrong cleaning chemical off the truck and. . . ." Jane leaves the rest of that catastrophe to the imagination. Dealing with fire and water damage is even more complex. For these jobs, close supervision continues for up to 12 weeks.

A PRIMARY LESSON

For managers at any level, there is a lesson in the Gandees' success. Consistent performance on Core Values leads to big success even in small places. Greg and Jane started with three employees including themselves. They were willing to work hard. Although they did not create the ServiceMaster values, they used the values to give direction to their hard work.

Shared values can have that impact in any small department or company. Values energize people. Then they give focus and direction to their released energy. The Gandees' success also illustrates the power that grows when you align values with the most important everyday priorities of the company or department.

The Gandees' dedication impressed me. Yet I understood that their achievements were built on something beyond themselves. There were too many traces of a pattern, too much order and system to their accomplishment. The root source of their success lay elsewhere. At that source, I found people who knew how to extend values not just in one business but in hundreds.

FOUR OBJECTIVES

I walked into the ServiceMaster world headquarters in Downers Grove, Illinois, expecting to find a commitment to values. I was not disappointed. Directly in front of me, I saw chiseled into a marble serpentine wall four statements strongly proclaiming the company's commitment to both quantitative and qualitative achievement:

1. To honor God in all we do
2. To help people develop
3. To pursue excellence
4. To grow profitably

Lofty goals, carved for everyone to see. Yet experience compelled me to keep a healthy skepticism. To what extent were these fine words the decorator values I'd seen in so many corporate entrances around the country? Sure, the Gandees took them seriously. However, I always expect more cynicism in any corporate headquarters than in the field.

"IF YOU DON'T LIVE IT, YOU DON'T BELIEVE IT."

However, even in visible commitment, ServiceMaster goes all out. Colorful banners with slogans hung everywhere in the open, two-story lobby. You can't miss the founder's most famous motto: "If you don't live it, you don't believe it." In time, I saw the building, a converted warehouse, as a physical metaphor for the ServiceMaster work ethic. A functional exterior houses a bright and inspirational interior.

Everyone at ServiceMaster calls the statements in the lobby the four objectives. From the CEO to the Gandees' technicians, everyone knows them by heart. Human beings, not saints, work at ServiceMaster. Not everyone honors each value every day. However, commitment is exceptionally high. Behind that commitment is a conscious process, put in place over decades. When the Gandees purchased a franchise, they bought this process as well.

TO HONOR GOD IN ALL WE DO

The first objective grabs your attention. Few companies claim the supreme deity as the judge of their performance. "Because of this starting point we have a view," says ServiceMaster Chairman C. William Pollard, "a value system that influences how we operate our business, how we treat our employees, how we serve our customers."

At every level, ServiceMaster people talk eagerly about honoring God in their work. I'm always skeptical of mixing religious fervor with business. I've seen too many scoundrels claim the Lord's blessing for their greed and chicanery. Still, Service-Master people impressed me with their sincerity. I liked the trouble they took to define God inclusively. The company works with Shinto Buddhist partners in Japan. It has Muslim partners in the Middle East. In Alexandria, Muslims on the staff feel comfortable enough to join with the Christian Gandees in weekly prayer.

Could an atheist or an agnostic work for ServiceMaster? They could and they do, replies Chairman Pollard. However, they have "no right to exclude me because I want to talk about God."

Whatever the source of its inspiration, ServiceMaster enjoys enviable financial success. The company's customer level revenues exceeded $4 billion in 1994, the 24th con-

42

secutive year of growth in revenue and profits. During that period, the company doubled in size every three and one-half years. "The Lord helps those who help themselves," commented *Fortune* in placing ServiceMaster at the top of its 1980s Stars of the Service 500.[1]

ServiceMaster people trace the start of their growth to a tragic moment in the life of founder Marion Wade. In 1944, after 15 years in business, Wade and six employees were barely scratching out a living in his home-mothproofing company. Then, while Wade was mothproofing a closet, the material he was using exploded in his face. At first, Wade's doctors believed he would be blind.

During a slow, inactive recovery period, Marion Wade reflected on the contrast between his Sunday beliefs and the realities of his workdays. He returned to work resolved to "serve God in the marketplace."

Although its exact phrasing evolved later, the first of the four ServiceMaster objectives was in place. Wade's employees, men he had met at church, responded instinctively to his new approach. After Wade's return, the company began the rapid growth that has continued for five decades.

Today, ServiceMaster provides cleaning and maintenance services to more than 1,300 health care institutions and 500 colleges, universities, and public school districts. It serves 100 major industrial facilities. Its Consumer Services Division, which includes the Gandees' franchise, serves nearly five million homeowners with a variety of specialty services from housecleaning to pest control and lawn care.

TO HELP PEOPLE DEVELOP

Getting this job done, says Chairman Pollard, requires "dealing with people in entry-level positions, unskilled, many times uneducated, and more often than not unnoticed." The most important contribution of ServiceMaster, Pollard believes, is to train, motivate, and develop these people. This is the core of the second qualitative objective of ServiceMaster—to help people develop.

ServiceMaster of Alexandria's emphasis on training consciously reflects this second qualitative objective. At the Downers Grove corporate training center, ServiceMaster trains more than 1,200 managers a month. The company estimates it is providing some form of on-the-job or formal training to as many as 100,000 people a year.

Management training mixes practical skills with empathy. When Pollard joined the company 19 years ago, he spent time cleaning floors in hospitals. He pushed a mop not to become an expert, but to understand what it feels like to do this job every day.

MORE THAN HONORABLE SLOGANS

ServiceMaster CEO Carlos Cantu believes the company has an obligation that goes beyond empowering people. It must provide them with the skills necessary to deliver customer service. The company rejects the common term *human resources*, believing it suggests employees are a means rather than an end. The company's "People Services" staff works to express the Service-Master qualitative objectives in every aspect of their jobs. Why this explicit emphasis? "Because we can't afford to have our values become just honorable slogans," says one senior vice president, Richard A. Armstrong.

PURSUING EXCELLENCE

Driven by its third qualitative objective, excellence, the company was well into the Total Quality Management movement as early as the mid-1970s. To keep its TQM program aligned with its values, ServiceMaster customized its quality language. At ServiceMaster the definition is a simple aspiration: *Quality is truth.*

Pursuing excellence means constantly studying how to handle work more efficiently. The company's research laboratories generate the excitement over a faster, cheaper solvent that you would find over a faster, cheaper chip in Silicon Valley. Defining excellence constantly challenges everyone. Pollard recalls an unusual definition by workers in one hospital. Their standard for excellence in cleaning was seeing the clear outline of a ceiling light on the polished floor.

Pursuing excellence means staying close to people on the front line. When business booms in Alexandria, Jane works the phones overtime. Greg puts on his work clothes and goes out on a job. The system is more formal at headquarters, but the result is the same. Every manager spends a minimum of one day a year carrying out frontline work.

For example, Pollard spent one We Serve Day helping a pest-control technician with his assignments. Sandy Jett, senior vice president for administration, vividly remembers his day at a ServiceMaster day-care center. Jett worked just like everyone else—almost. "I changed seven diapers in a row and every one of them was dirty. I thought it was a setup," he says, laughing.

TO GROW PROFITABLY

The first three qualitative objectives integrate with and support the fourth objective, which is quantitative: to grow profitably. Everywhere, the target is a 20 percent increase in revenues every year. The Gandees stay up late trying to figure out how to win their seventh annual 20 percent award.

In 1994 they won the National Eagle Award, given annually to the ServiceMaster franchise with the largest dollar growth.

People at headquarters work late to meet their growth targets, too. Executive compensation packages include a component known as Additional Provisional Compensation, which constitutes up to 50 percent of an individual's total compensation. However, the APC bonus doesn't kick in until the company has exceeded the year's growth targets.

Rewards for profitable growth extend to frontline employees. At Merry Maids, the home cleaning service, hourly work teams earn a percentage of the team's revenues rather than a minimum wage.

Profitable growth is an essential to the whole ServiceMaster equation. "If we're not growing," says Senior Vice President Armstrong, "then our ability to provide opportunities to grow and develop is limited." Or, as Chairman Pollard puts it: "Growth is not an option, it's a mandate."

As the objective insists, growth must be profitable. Ken Hansen, a former CEO, institutionalized his gift for numbers into the company's system of tight cost controls. Today, people at every level strain to keep on top of their numbers.

In Alexandria, Jane and Greg review and sign every check. At headquarters, executives follow Rolling Quarters with equal attention. This financial system provides everyone with rolling updates of financial results and projections every 15 days. Every week ServiceMaster monitors payroll, its biggest cost item.

THE MONITORING SYSTEM THAT NEVER SLEEPS

Profitable growth is a seductive target, especially when linked to individual compensation. From Wall Street to Main Street, unscrupulous managers manipulate employees and cheat customers in pursuit of profitable growth. Could that happen at ServiceMaster? Unlikely, insists Bill Pollard. Or at least not while the objectives provide a system of checks and balances.

"You don't have the option of saying 'Today I'm going to honor God and I don't care about making money,'" says Pollard. "Or 'Today, I'm going to make money and I don't care about helping people develop.' They have all got to fit together in your management responsibilities. If they don't fit, then maybe something's wrong with the decision."

Pollard insists that the constant talk about the four objectives creates a monitoring system that never sleeps. "We're all over the world today. If somebody out there is really manipulating people, not treating them right, despite the fact you have these objectives on the wall and everybody talks about them, there is going to be a little explosion. If someone still doesn't correct it, there will be an even bigger explosion. That's one of the best internal control mechanisms we have."

CATCHING VALUES

Committed people such as Pollard and Armstrong absorbed the values over years. What about managers who grew up in other corporate cultures? Could they adapt to the ServiceMaster approach?

ServiceMaster faced that challenge in a big way in the late 1980s and early 1990s. Between 1986 and 1993, the company rapidly expanded its consumer services activities by acquiring companies like TruGreen, ChemLawn, Terminix, and Merry Maids. How could ServiceMaster extend its objectives to so many acquisitions over such a short time?

"You can't impose values," Pollard insists. "You can't inoculate for them. You can't indoctrinate people. Values have to be caught." Catching the values is a process that begins before acquisition and goes on for years.

"You can't just buy a company with numbers," says Pollard. Yet in most acquisitions the purchaser's team spends most of its time with lawyers and accountants. While acquiring TruGreen, its lawn-care business, the ServiceMaster team spent 80 percent of its acquisition time talking with the company's service workers.

Carlos Cantu, the current CEO, is an example of the benefits of this approach. He joined ServiceMaster when it acquired Terminix in 1986. "When Terminix was on the auction block, we met with many companies," he says, "but only ServiceMaster placed as much emphasis on people as they did on financial statements. That made a difference, and it made the joining of our companies that much easier."

THE COMMONPLACE MIRACLE

Values are the commonplace miracle. We all know at least one retailer who goes above and beyond, one service company whose service consistently delights, one manufacturer whose quality stands out. When we think about it all, we are quick to explain exceptional performance: A founder's example; a long tradition; especially dedicated workers; inspirational leadership; a Quality program; teamwork courses; competitive pressure. Even when strung together, such partial answers mask the truth.

Consistently outstanding performance is the result of a conscious or unconscious process supporting values. As that process matures, it becomes more conscious. A well-developed process can extend to thousands of people carrying out millions of individual actions in hundreds of locations. When strong enough and well enough developed, the process can extend quickly to people in newly acquired corporate cultures.

The customer at the tether end of the ServiceMaster process remembers the result. For that customer, the result was anything but routine. The power of the process is exactly the opposite. ServiceMaster, like any values-centered company, works every day to transform its high values into small, routine actions. It is precisely this transformation that makes values-centered performance seem so "exceptional" to customers.

CHAPTER 4

THREE MODES OF LEADERSHIP

Survival-driven leaders focus on physical needs close to home. Under market-driven leaders, the customer is the driving force. Values-driven leaders discover opportunity in every activity. Of course, market is important. So also are people, organization, products, and finance. Sustaining growth requires upgrading values in all components of the business.

We have been looking at values as something separate from the routine of business. Yet the routine is indispensable. While people were elevating values, who was pushing sales? Who was controlling costs? Who was creating the next generation of products? Do values have anything at all to do with producing the monthly figures, collecting the receipts, paying the bills?

In most companies, values are only partially visible or even invisible. We have to study them separately to see them clearly. In stark relief, their elements emerge more fully. To have any real impact, leaders must fully integrate values into the core of the business.

We defined values as operating qualities. We said their purpose is to maintain and enhance performance. This definition requires an integral relationship with the business of the company. Values are at once a part of and a dimension of every part of the whole. In the same way, mind is a part of the body and also a part of every cell in the body.

A SENSE OF SEPARATION

Mentally separate values from the core of operations and you limit their rich potential. Yet even in companies where values are important, there is often a sense of separation. When you go to investigate values in Corporate America, your first stop is always the human resources department. Go to the same company to learn about quantitative results and you start at the Finance or Strategic Planning department.

The division goes even deeper. Values efforts focus on process. Values coordinators spend much of their time analyzing and improving processes. They often have little technical knowledge of the content of the process. People developing the quantitative side are usually technical experts, heavy on content, lighter on process.

For values to work, there must be content: hard results. Also there must be well-functioning networks of continuously developing processes. It is the processes that carry values and feedback about values throughout the organization. Processes are essential to create values-centered actions. Yet without solid content, values are a flavor of the month. Values champions must show how to execute routine actions in an effective, values-driven way. Busy line executives will rightly demand results, not just process.

INTEGRATION AT MANY LEVELS

Values efforts must support operating needs of the organization. Values can elevate any routine system even as that system relays financial and coordinating information. With the right values, a financial reporting system becomes more user friendly or customer oriented. It takes only a little imagination but a lot of commitment to get this done. Once achieved, however, the revitalized system strengthens and coordinates both sides of the ledger. Haven't we always done this? Certainly. With values-driven leadership, however, it is a conscious action.

Many companies mentioned in this book consciously integrate values and the numbers at many levels. At ServiceMaster, Bill Pollard told us, "You don't have the option of saying 'Today I'm going to make money and I don't care about helping people develop.' They have all got to fit together in your management responsibilities." Such integration of numbers and values is still exceptional. In the future it will be routine.

At first, values implementation usually remains separate from the major functioning of the company. Over time, however, it naturally occurs to managers to seek more integration. If it does nothing else, integration lessens the workload of monitoring two systems.

Serious values efforts quickly create a need for greater coordination. How long can the customer service system remain separate from a value like Customer Delight? Once the company integrates the system and value, it won't be long before it brings evaluation and pay into line with the value. The computer revolution is also making it far easier to track separate sets of information in one system. A decade from now it will be normal to find companies with values fully integrated at the core of operations.

To understand differing degrees of values integration, we must first look at three modes of leadership. Each of these modes is present in every company. They must coexist or the company will swing wildly out of balance. The force and shape of leadership depend on which mode predominates. Also the leadership mode shapes the degree of integration between numbers and values.

SURVIVAL-DRIVEN LEADERSHIP

The central force in *survival-driven leadership* is satisfying the needs and desires of those working in the business. Owners look at their businesses as extensions of themselves. "I don't have a business. I've just created a job for myself," the owner of a barbershop once told me. I glanced around the small shop. On the surface it looked like a business. There were other people working there. There were systems to collect money and disburse payments. There was a product, admittedly ephemeral, the haircut. More tangible products were on display—lotions and hairdressings for sale to customers. However, his attitude revealed the key ingredient of survival-driven leadership. He was there primarily for the money. A good year was one in which he paid all his bills and paid himself a decent salary. His employees operated under no illusion either. It was a job, not a career or a path of self-development.

Survival-driven leadership has its strengths. Even within its limitations, it is a mode found in every company, even the most developed. When the company fails to satisfy the basic physical needs of employees, higher-level motivations quickly falter.

The barber did provide some of the basics of leadership. He established and enforced rules for his employees. He had some outreach to his market. He learned the names and interests of his customers. His business provided a socially useful function. It contributed taxes and jobs to the community. However, the business's practices and procedures were routine. One day at work was much like another. The environment brightened or faded almost exclusively according to the personalities of that day's customers.

That barbershop was a microcosm of most work on most days in most companies. The shop's major function was to sustain the physical needs of owner and employees. It provided some sustenance to their emotional needs, making them feel useful and part of a small community. It indirectly provided some mental growth. Conversations in the barber chair extended the knowledge of both customers and barbers. However, this growth was a by-product rather than a direct ingredient of the work itself.

Even this type of work can be made more challenging by introducing higher attitudes. In another city, I regularly had my hair cut in the shop of a world-champion barber. To this individual, there were no simple haircuts. Every session was a practice for the competitions he entered around the world. I knew that during every brief period in his chair, I would learn something about the latest styles and competitions. I remember his sense of mission, his willingness to train younger barbers at his own expense. His standards were high. He would periodically check on and offer suggestions to his employees.

In the first barber's chair we talked sports and politics. In the world champion's chair there were only discussions about his competitions. His shop was always busy. Customers knew they were part of something special. Employees were always wide awake. I always left the first shop feeling relaxed and a bit sleepy. I left the second shop alert and invigorated by the enthusiasm in the atmosphere. The same business, but a different order of energy and leadership.

In both shops, however, survival-driven leadership predominated. The world champion's shop represented the aspirations of that barber/owner as surely as the first represented those of his counterpart. For both men, the customer was principally a means, not an end. For one the aspiration was physical comfort and security. The other owner was driven by a need to excel as well as provide for his physical needs. The second barber brought a mental and emotional energy to his work. Neither, however, focused on the customer.

MARKET-DRIVEN LEADERSHIP

At a higher order, there is *market-driven leadership*. Here, the customer is the driving force of the business. This mode dominates the entrepreneurial sensations, those companies that go from the garage to $100 million in a decade. Every issue of *INC* magazine features such success stories. Market-driven leadership, like survival-driven leadership, is always present in any sustained or sizable success.

It is difficult for companies dominated by survival-driven leaders to gain the traction to become fast sprinters. Once the owners and workers satisfy their needs, there is little to stimulate growth. In market-driven companies, there are always new opportunities for growth. A new customer appears. An old customer is unhappy. A competitor introduces a product and gains sudden prominence. The philosophy of the market-driven company is do whatever you must do to please the customer. Since the customer's evolving needs are endless, the challenge is endless.

Market-driven leaders attract deserved admiration. Consultants praise them. When they offer stock, investors quickly subscribe. To many, this mode is so desirable that it becomes a permanent apex of business. Nothing, says the conventional wisdom, replaces a clear focus on the customer. However true, this view limits perspective. The market is important, but it is not everything.

As the company grows, the gap between market-driven owner and survival-driven workers often widens. One such owner regularly vents his frustration about workers who are unwilling to serve his customers. His complaint: workers refuse to come in on a seventh day after three seven-day weeks in a row. Their lack of "ambition" baffles and angers him. It blocks the further flowering of his market-driven ambition. He does not see that what really holds him back is a lack of other values—Development of People and Systematic Functioning.

Market-driven leaders create jobs. Beyond that, they account for much of the legendary dynamism of American business. However, like survival-driven leaders, they tend to meet barriers at critical stages of their growth. Often these barriers show up as spiraling costs. Profit margins, once robust, begin to narrow. The attention lavished on one or two aspects of the business leaves serious gaps in others.

> I have visited market-driven companies where the pace is so fast there is little time to dispose of obsolete machinery or clean the plant. There is even no time to send out invoices for work already completed. The weight of these uncompleted activities accumulates. Before long, the owner makes regular trips to the bank to cover cash-flow shortages. The once exuberant owner feels trapped by the "stuff I hate." There is no longer time for the joyful conquest of yet another market pinnacle.

While this story is common, it is neither universal nor inevitable. The market-driven owner can sustain a steady focus on the customer once she introduces other values to expand perspective. She must also personally attend to or get others to attend to other parts of the business. Market-driven leaders who build strong teams in many aspects of the business often become legends.

At Microsoft company parties, they sometimes show a photograph of the entire customer service department at one point in the mid-1970s. The picture shows Bill Gates alone on a telephone. Imagine the personal and professional growth required for Gates to evolve as the CEO of a company with sales of $5 billion a year. Very early on, perhaps right from the start, Gates adopted a market-driven mode. However, in the fiercely competitive software industry, he could never forget the imperatives of survival-driven leadership. Keeping both motivations, he evolved to another level, carrying his company with him.

VALUES-DRIVEN LEADERSHIP

At a still higher level, *values-driven leadership* gives even fuller expression of the limitless human power within a company.

Survival-driven leadership focuses on the physical needs of the leader and employees. Market-driven leadership touches an emotional wellspring, linking the aspiration of leader and employees with customers. The values-driven company runs on high-octane mental energy. Actions that are instinctive in early modes now become systematized and routine. Customer service is a by-product in the survival-centered company. In the market-driven company it is an emotional obligation. At the values-driven company it becomes quieter, a reflection of "the way we work around here." Every mode is expressed in that phrase, but the values-driven approach dominates.

While there is a clear evolution, every mode is present in every company all the time. This is a condition for continued health and robustness. A market-driven company that ignores the physical and emotional survival needs of its workers loses its capacity to expand. Any survival-driven company must please the customer at a basic level or go out of business.

Each level of evolution subsumes the others. Every values-driven company is certain to have explicit customer and employee values. This ensures that earlier modes are expansively represented in any advance. Some well-known companies forget this lesson.

Downsizing erodes confidence in future survival for both workers and managers. This uncertainty drains enthusiasm for market-driven approaches. In such companies, evolution toward values-driven leadership will depend on new definitions of the social contract between employees and the company. Management can replace traditional job security only with new approaches that equip people for greater economic independence. The emerging people value in progressive companies will focus on training workers for careers that may include other companies.

All modes are necessary, all the time. The difference is the emphasis found in any company at any time. This is not to say all are equal in potential or worth. A company driven primarily by the ego needs of owners and workers will quickly exhaust its opportunities for expansion. For the primarily market-driven company, the challenge is to widen its perspective. It takes nothing away from the importance of the market to insist that future growth depends on consciously balancing other parts of the business. Keeping pace with an expanding market requires greater capacity to manage cash. You must hire and train more skilled workers. You must develop the capacity to introduce more successful products.

A WIDER VISION

Values-driven leadership sees the company from this wider vision. Of course, market is important. So also are people, organization, products, and finance. Sustaining growth requires upgrading values in each of these components.

While there is a clear evolutionary nature to the modes, one is not morally superior to another. This concept is operational, not moral or ethical. Those traits are more appropriately applied to individuals than to organizations. The single mother supporting her family through survival-driven work is more ethical than the executive following his company's values to gain money for weekend excesses.

Values-driven leadership contains more seeds of growth than either of the other two modes. It strengthens and completes the development begun by quantitative leadership. Values open the door to a comprehensive vision, uniting quantitative and qualitative. Values-driven leadership seeks to apply values to every aspect of the business. Values are not something separate but at the center of every activity. Individual acts, energized by values, become Complete Acts. Complete Acts combine into Complete Systems. Complete Systems reinforce one another, creating structures strong enough to sustain either crisis or opportunity as the moment requires. The numbers no longer can do this alone except in short bursts.

In the companies represented in this book, we see this integration again and again. Consciously or unconsciously, more activities come under the sway of a few values. "We don't know much about creating a vibrant culture," 3M's Dick Lidstad told me. "We just know how to maintain one." That's what it feels like when values-centered leadership is securely in place.

Northwestern Mutual Life Insurance Company has led insurance companies on *Fortune's* Most Admired list for a decade. The company has been consistently pursuing the same values for more than 100 years. You can feel that commitment everywhere. You sense it in the way the company recruits and treats its people, in how its staff members handle requests from policyholders. It's there in the training course, the library, the dining room. Former Northwestern Mutual CEO Donald Schuenke told me, "It's invisible, like the air we breath, but just as important."

THE CENTRAL THEME OF THIS BOOK

The central theme of this book is that any company can consciously accelerate its growth by values-driven leadership. We no longer need 100 years or even 10. Now that the elements are unfolding with such clarity, it is possible to jump-start the process at any point. This, of course, is the secret of any process to accelerate human progress. We see it most clearly in education. There we take basic knowledge gathered over centuries and pass it along to the next generation in a dozen years. Without that speed, civilization could not advance.

How do we know we can accelerate values-driven leadership? The start-ups tell us. American Steel and Wire and AT&T Universal Card both created values-centered cultures in only a few years. The latter moved so fast that the company won the national Malcolm Baldridge Quality Award in its third year in business. Successful values processes also show what can be done. True, the failure rate for concentrated efforts to improve values such as Quality, Customer Service, Diversity, and Speed is high. However, the successes show what can be done. What one company can achieve, any company can achieve. Most failures arise from a lack of will rather than from faulty knowledge.

We know how to instill values. We know how to do it at speeds that were unthinkable in the past. What has been missing is the knowledge of how to coordinate the qualitative and quantitative hands of management. Values-driven companies integrate this knowledge into the whole fabric of management. It's the elusive secret at the heart of that frustrating "just the way we work around here."

We have long known how to extract power and profit from quantitative energy. Only two major issues remain to do the same on the qualitative side. We need a comprehensive integral design. And we need practical techniques for converting that design into results. Later sections of this book focus on those missing elements.

CHAPTER 5

THE NEXT
MANAGEMENT SYNTHESIS

Values-driven planning unites the quantitative and qualitative ledgers. It creates unity of purpose. It links the highest conceptual level to "the way we do business around here."

The next management synthesis will unite qualitative with quantitative. Values lift performance in every part of the company. Balance throughout the company creates a platform for sustained growth. We now require a practical synthesis that creates an integrated whole.

Many such systems are already evolving. There is already too much conscious movement toward qualitative goals for leaders to miss the logic of integration for long. Chapters 5 through 8 describe possible approaches in what will shortly be a rich diversity of solutions.

If unity is the goal, the fastest progress will come from revitalizing quantitative systems through values. Three traditional pillars of quantitative management are strategic planning, budgeting, and performance review and appraisal. With varying success, all are functioning in any reasonably evolved company.

For all their importance, the three systems are losing vitality in most companies. Jack Welch threw out the corporate planning system that GE had pioneered in the 1950s. Filling the big books with numbers and carefully calibrated assumptions had become a meaningless exercise.

Welch had a luxury not shared by many CEOs. When he closed his strategic planning department in the early 1980s, every GE manager understood planning as a discipline. Welch could rely on managers adhering to a logical system of decision making even as he liberated them from bureaucratic routine. As the years go by, GE has fewer managers schooled in this approach. It is a safe bet that one of Welch's successors will find a need to reinvent corporate planning in a new and more dynamic form.

A FANTASY GAME OF NUMBERS

Budgeting, another critical activity, is an agony in most organizations. At its worst, it is a fantasy game of numbers created by financial people based on assumptions about next year. At a higher level, the game is more participative. Self-appointed detectives from the finance department search for buffers hidden in the preliminary budget numbers submitted by line managers. At a further advanced level, it is a serious debate about allocation of future resources. At a still higher level, the budget is a numerical statement of next year's plan.

Performance review and appraisal, as practiced in most companies, is another bane of the management job. Companies preach teamwork, then set people against one another in the appraisal system. Company policy on appraisals often requires a departmental average of three. Giving Mary a four means someone must get a two. When you tie appraisal specifically to money, the tension gets worse. Management argues that without guidelines, appraisal-rating inflation will push salaries to uncompetitive levels.

Underpinning the appraisal system is the antiquated job-description system. It's terrible, but managers don't see alternatives. Modern business practice encourages flexibility, yet most job-description systems are rigid. One of management's biggest complaints about unions is that they set rigid work rules. Yet human resources departments spend weeks every year updating job descriptions that slot supervisors and managers into tight boxes.

Most job descriptions are out of date within weeks of publication. Few of them make any allowance for the teamwork so essential in modern corporate practice. Yet for all the hyperbole, most companies can't manage in chaos. People need to know what to do and what others expect of them.

Any system uniting qualitative and quantitative must deal with the realities behind these systems. Companies need to plan their activities, especially in times of rapid change. They need budgets to keep control of resources, particularly cash flow. Employees need to know what others expect and how well they are doing their jobs. The present formats containing these truths are straining at the seams. Companies still adhere to these forms because of the importance of the need they serve and the absence of anything better.

INTEGRATED STRATEGIC PLANNING

Welch was not alone in declaring strategic planning an obsolete form years ago. Michael Kami helped design planning systems at International Business Machines Corporation (IBM) and Xerox in the 1960s and 1970s. By the early 1980s, Kami was an independent consultant urging managers to abandon traditional planning formats. He advocated instead a new form of strategic planning that was "fast, fluid and flexible." Strategic Management, as Kami and others call this evolving form, seeks to focus all of a company's resources and systems behind clearly identified goals.

New designs flowing from Strategic Management reinvigorated strategic planning. In some applications, Strategic Management integrated planning with Organizational Development. Elsewhere it unified strategies around such concepts as competitive advantage. Everywhere, it represented a more comprehensive vision of the company and its relationship to its market.

A still more integrated model of strategic planning unites quantitative and qualitative. It offers a rich potential for companies stuck in an obsolete planning mode. It can generate a burst of renewed energy for companies seeking to move Strategic Management to an even higher plane. By introducing values at every step in the process, integrated strategic planning creates unity of purpose. It links the highest conceptual level to the Complete Acts that daily elevate "the way we do business around here."

THREE BASIC CONCEPTS

Integrated strategic planning begins with strategic thinking. In this stage, planners identify and define three basic concepts that set the direction of the company: Vision, Mission, and Core Values (Figure 5.1). While working on these three concepts, it's easy to become confused by jargon. You can look at 50 statements and discover what is called a Mission in one company would describe a Vision or Values in another. This overlapping reflects how much the qualitative and quantitative are merging in many companies.

It doesn't matter what you call your statements. It doesn't matter whether you have one, two, or three. It doesn't matter whether your words sing (of course, it helps when they do). What matters most is that you describe your aspiration, explain what business you are in, and define the operating qualities you use to elevate performance.

For clarity, I recommend first considering the three concepts separately. Later, you can merge them and eliminate overlapping ideas. It is not difficult to put words together if you know who you are, what you want, and how you should behave. If you don't know, however, confusion will surely follow. The more difficult the task, the more urgently you need to get started.

Figure 5.1
Integrating Values and Mission in Strategic Planning

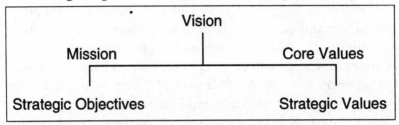

BEGIN WITH VISION

The journey begins with a *Vision*. A Vision is a crisp, clear word picture of the organization's aspiration. An effective Vision captures the imagination of people throughout the organization. It is a unifying force at every level of the values-driven company. A Vision stretches beyond today and well into tomorrow.

Vision highlights the importance of the work the company does. It is as individualistic as human dreams. If companies have a soul, then Vision describes it. Idealistic or materialistic, the Vision unlocks human aspiration and aims it at a higher level of achievement.

The Vision of the National Aeronautics and Space Administration (NASA) is to explore the universe. Jack Welch's vision for GE is to be number one or number two globally in every market where the company competes. AT&T Universal Card aspires to be "our cardholder's number one service relationship." The statement of the Leo Burnett Company quotes founder Leo Burnett: "Our primary function in life is to produce the best advertising in the world, bar none."[1]

Vision touches hidden wellsprings of unity in any organization. It reminds people why they signed on with the outfit in the first place. I always begin any board retreat with a review or creation of a Vision statement. Directors often bring highly personal agendas to any board meeting, particularly a planning retreat. Putting the Vision statement first encourages deeper reflection on the relevance of those personal agenda items.

WHAT IS OUR BUSINESS?

Mission, the second core concept, answers the critical question: What business are we in? Whereas Vision describes the future, Mission illuminates the here and now. Vision is an image of unrealized future potential. It sets a grand goal, an ultimate direction and purpose. Mission is a more specific definition of purpose. It directs energies through the present and immediate future.

Mission is the heart of the quantitative process. Yet it consists of words, not numbers. It should, however, be concrete. The Avis Rent-A-Car statement says in part: "Our business is renting cars."[2] Some Mission statements are short. Disney World's Mission is "to make guests happy." Others describe in detail specific market niches and products. Whatever the length, the effective Mission statement explains in the fewest possible words what business we are in.

Mission grows from Vision and Core Values. NASA's first Mission defined the first step in its Vision to explore the Universe. It was "to place a man on the moon and bring him back successfully by the end of the decade." The Mission of the Leo Burnett Company is "to create superior advertising."[3]

When the business changes, Mission changes too. A new opportunity, threat, or acquisition triggers a Mission review. Levi Strauss & Company once considered itself a manufacturer that sold to retail stores. Now it sees its Mission as a marketer in collaboration with its customers. That distinction changed both the company's self-perception and its method of operation.

HOW WILL WE ACHIEVE OUR MISSION?

Core Values, the third key concept, are to the qualitative side of the business what Mission is to the quantitative. Values define how we will achieve our Mission. Values reinforce Vision and translate it to more concrete detail. As the word *Core* implies, previous crises, opportunities, or the vision of thoughtful leaders have embedded the values in a company's operations.

Like the human personality, a healthy corporate personality expresses many positive values. However, for most individuals or companies a few values stand out because they effortlessly shape everyday decisions. Safety at DuPont. Teamwork at Northwestern Mutual. Respect for People at Levi Strauss. Speed at GE.

Successful companies can easily identify a number of Core Values, but there are always a few that a company holds above the rest in concept and practice. As Vision and Mission limit and define, so must Core Values. An endless list of positive traits quickly loses vitality. Like Vision and Mission, Core Values must set direction at every level. They must communicate as clearly as Mission what managers must protect and enhance to ensure future success. This requires choice between what matters most and what is merely important.

This necessary choice often breeds confusion. Many executives act as if once they identify three or four Core Values, they can never choose another. The opposite is true. Selection of Core Values actually prompts attention to other values. Core Values define what the company has already accomplished. They highlight the relationship between values and success. The marketplace, the environment, competition, and internal challenges dictate the need for new values at every turn. As integrated strategic planning moves to the next level, the place and utility of these emerging values becomes clearer.

Introducing values at the highest level adds new energy to a process that has primarily served the quantitative ledger. Planning should not only be about how many, but also about how well. Placing values at the core signals that the end product of the plan will not be simply numbers. Values touch people's aspirations. Even in survival-driven companies, people need to find meaning in their work. Including Core Values makes aspiration and Vision more concrete. This subtle shift at the heart of the planning process elevates the qualitative to justified equality. Maintaining that perspective becomes easier in later planning steps.

STRATEGIC GOALS

In survival-driven and early market-driven leadership, Vision, Mission, and Values are largely the inspiration of the leader. There is no need for written words. Charles Schwab opened his original San Francisco brokerage office with a dozen people. There were no statements on the wall. People copied the leader's actions, followed his directions, treated customers the way he did. Today, Charles Schwab & Company, Inc. has more than 200 branches. The company has under way highly sophisticated efforts to elevate its Service Quality value everywhere. Size has made a formal system urgent. (See Chapter 6 for details.)

Defining Vision, Mission, and Values should be as participative as possible. We seek the essence of the company in these three statements. That essence goes far deeper than the executive suite or the boardroom. Long-term service employees have a surer feeling for the company's Core Values than do newly arrived superstar executives. The Vision ideally should represent everybody's aspiration. The Levi Strauss statement begins: "We all want. . . ." That's more than politeness. At the retreat that set Levi Strauss's aspiration statement in motion, every senior executive sat next to a member of an ethnic minority group. Elsewhere, the GE statements took two years to approve. Hundreds of people discussed every word. A company that explicitly honors Speed, GE showed the importance of participation.

The second stage of an integrated planning process focuses on Strategic Objectives and Strategic Values. The quantitative side of this step—Strategic Objectives—is in place in most companies. Well-managed companies regularly assess current performance and set quantified targets for improvement. Early in the process managers reappraise the environment, market, competition, and the strengths and weaknesses of their operations. From this analysis, they produce the objectives for the next planning cycle. The step remains unchanged in integrated planning.

However, introducing Strategic Values at this point adds a new dimension—and energy—to the process. When a major company raises its quality standards, its suppliers understand that value now has strategic significance for them. When customers reduce inventories by Just-in-Time methods, Speed and Systematic Functioning soon become critical success factors. When competitors introduce easier-to-use products, Simplicity becomes essential to preserve market share. When a new technology makes existing manual processes obsolete, Development of People assumes a new urgency.

Unlike Core Values, Strategic Values represent new challenges, not embedded achievement. Often they represent more specific and current expressions of a Core Value. When the Core Value is Customer Service, the current market challenge may require focusing on Accuracy. Such organic development usually becomes second nature in values-driven companies.

Often, the internal or external environment requires elevating a new value. This can represent an exceptional opportunity. Similar challenges in the past created each of the original Core Values. Accepting the current challenge begins the process of adding another value to the core. Strengthening the core widens the platform for future growth. Continuous improvement spurs continuous growth.

Raising performance on Strategic Values from ordinary to peak levels unleashes enthusiasm. As people accept the new values, they assimilate them into their work. Before long, the once-new Strategic Values become routine. They shape the activities, systems, processes and skills of individual jobs. Slowly they mature into Core Values. In time, these new Core Values become an integral part of a more dynamic corporate personality.

Traditional planning focuses on Strategic Objectives. It asks an important but limiting question: What are the quantitative goals we need to grow the business? Raising Strategic Values to equal prominence opens other horizons. What are the qualitative improvements that also will spark and sustain growth? Either approach creates opportunities. Combined, they create new capacities within the organization. Those capacities in turn generate strategies to promote growth and profitability.

CHAPTER 6

VALUES-DRIVEN STRATEGIES FOR GROWTH

*Tiny store or global giant, every company has five components: a **Market** to sell to, a **Technology** to deliver its products, **People** to carry out its work, **Capital** to fund operations, and **Organization** to tie the other four together. Grow the components and the company will grow. The fastest way to grow a component? Introduce or upgrade a value.*

Strategic Objectives and Values define priorities for a company's future growth. Successful implementation of these priorities requires answers to two new questions: What are the most effective strategies to achieve these goals? And what exactly do we mean by growth? In integrated strategic planning, growth is a wider concept than expansion of sales and profits. This more comprehensive approach aims to create strategies that will grow every aspect of the business as well as the company as a whole.

Every company from the corner video store to the *Fortune* 500 consists of five basic components: Market, Technology, People, Capital, and Organization.[1] No company exists without all of them. In a healthy company, the five are dynamic and in balance. In a troubled company, they are spinning out of balance. In a seriously ill company, components are way out of balance. In extreme cases, many components show little signs of life.

69

It's natural for marketing people to believe Market drives the business. Finance people logically insist we can't live without Capital. Human resources managers speak out for the limitless power of People. Any CEO knows that a defective Organization can abort the most brilliant plan. Production workers claim the company's profitability depends on their Technology. All are correct. However, it distorts reality to insist one component is more important. When even one component lags too far behind, trouble is on the way. That warning applies equally to the tiny video store or the billion-dollar corporation.

Achieving Strategic Objectives and Strategic Values requires strength in every component. In shaping the future, a planning team should test every component. It should develop strategies to increase the capacity of all components (Figure 6.1). Often, however, the corporate personality gets in the way. Companies favoring one component lose balance. They set ambitious Objectives. They even want to improve performance on Strategic

Figure 6.1
Integrating Values and Mission in Strategic Planning

Values. However, they work at improving only one or two components. Over time, other components steadily weaken. Eventually, ambitious Objectives mean nothing.

Chrysler Corporation nearly went out of business in the early 1980s. For decades, Chrysler took pride in its Technology. It boasted of its quality engineering. That, rather than Market or Organization or Capital, was the leading component. Engineers dominated Chrysler from the time Walter Chrysler, the Lee Iacocca of his day, pulled the company back from the brink in the 1920s.

Chrysler engineers successfully resisted the company's early entry into the small-car market. Their case was simple: "You can't fit Chrysler engineering into a small car." That's the decision making you get when you're certain one component is more important than the rest. By the time everyone could see the crisis, weakness was visible in every component.

Balanced components play a critical role in any comprehensive growth strategy. When a company grows, exactly what is it that does the growing? It is not just sales, profits, numbers of branches, or production levels. Growth results from capacity to produce more work. That increased capacity grows from the expansion of every component.

Growth becomes visible through increased sales volume and dollars. Yet sustained sales expansion depends on increased capacity to produce (Technology). Growth requires increased capacity to mobilize Capital. Growth depends on an expansion of the knowledge, skills and capacities of People. Without expanding human capacity, growth in Market, development of Technology, and management of Capital are not possible for long.

Sustained growth also depends on continuous development of the Organization. How else can the company handle more customers, products, people, capital? A dynamic Organization component supports growth through continuous improvement of structures, streamlining of systems, and coordination of activities.

TO SPUR GROWTH AND PROFITABILITY

Strategic Objectives and Strategic Values aim to spur growth and profitability. To do this, they must expand the potential of each component. Simply concentrating on one or two components—strengthening financial resources and marketing capacity, for example—limits potential and leads to further imbalance.

Properly applied, any Strategic Value can energize any component. A more comprehensive approach uses values to raise qualitative performance within *every* component. Speed, for example, can energize Organization by cutting bureaucratic delays. It improves Market by lifting customer satisfaction through faster service. Faster product development gives the company's Technology a competitive edge. Sustained Speed requires greater efficiency, reducing frustration among the company's People. Promptness in collections and maintenance improves cash flow, strengthening component Capital.

The same pattern emerges when managers apply any value—Orderliness, Innovation, Development of People—to all components. In integrated strategic planning, this interaction produces dynamic strategies to build the capacity of every component. Those strategies expand every component's ability to withstand stress and sustain growth.

MISSED OPPORTUNITIES

Survival-based leadership, with minimum commitment to Strategic Values, focuses minimum attention on development of the five components. The market-driven company elevates one component, Market, to a special status. It emphasizes values that energize that component, values such as Speed, Accuracy, Responsiveness. Meanwhile, it misses opportunities to develop other components. Technology-driven companies do the same for their favored component.

Even companies that develop two components to a high level can be myopic. This is the story behind those wonderfully idealistic firms that adored their customers, spoiled their employees, and then went broke. They exhibited high values. They applied them diligently. However, they focused only on the popular components of the day, Market and People. One-sided efforts led to imbalance. Imbalance restricted growth. With too wide an imbalance, components started collapsing. Products didn't get out the door. Disorganization reigned. Cash flow sputtered and then stopped. For the idealistic as well as the hard-nosed, balance is necessary for survival and growth.

More mature companies often speak constantly about one or two components: "The keys to our success are rigorous attention to our customers and staying on the cutting edge of technology." That's boilerplate from more than one CEO speech. Don't be misled. Companies that survive and grow have learned the importance of developing all five components. In these companies it is not just Market or Technology that drive growth. All components are drivers.

FIVE ENGINES FOR GROWTH

Any component can lead the pack. Discover a hidden niche for your products, and Market leads. Create the product that everyone wants, and Technology sets the pace. Bring in a half-dozen people with urgently needed skills, and feel the energy in the People component. Get a bank loan for the latest equipment, and Capital revolutionizes the balance. Reorganize the company or introduce three new systems, and Organization moves to the forefront.

For decades, development of new technology drove the growth of new businesses. The other four components struggled to keep up. More recently, competitive pressures and new delivery systems energized relationships with customers. Today, managers must fortify other components to support expanding approaches to the market.

For thoughtful managers, acceleration in one component signals a need to strengthen other components. "To exploit this sales opportunity, we're going to need training . . . and cash . . . and more production capacity . . . and a better way to organize shipping and receiving." Yet formal planning often misses what is intuitive for experienced leaders.

An integrated approach to planning develops the potential of all components. Strategic Objectives and Strategic Values are versatile tools to build the capacities of components in a balanced and harmonious way. In this comprehensive effort, every component yields the strategies that guide and underpin growth. The key question: How must we develop this component to meet this Strategic Objective or Value?

For example:

The Five Components	Quantitative Strategies	Qualitative Strategies
Market	Expand sales force	Raise quality of Service or Speed of response
Technology	Increase R&D budget; buy new equipment	Upgrade Innovation, Teamwork; improve Coordination with marketing
People	Recruit new people	Develop People through training; increase Delegation to encourage Initiative
Organization	Add computers to raise productivity; set up new department to focus on new objective	Improve systems for Coordination between departments

The Five Components	Quantitative Strategies	Qualitative Strategies
Capital	Raise additional funds through bank loan	Improve Effective Use of Time to raise productivity of existing resources; simplification of systems to Speed cash flow

When something energizes a component, any leader faces a choice. She can resist change, trying to maintain the components in the existing balance. She might insist, "I know it's an opportunity, but we can't increase production. We don't have the people or the capacity." Or she may pursue the opening by sheer will, forcing underdeveloped components to respond. Judging by the high levels of stress reported in American corporations, this is a common response today.

Threats, promises, and human energy temporarily move performance to higher levels. After a time, however, stress within every component leads to breakdowns. People get sick or quit. Mistakes occur with alarming regularity. Overtime and temporary help drain cash. Customers no longer trust the managers' promises. Teamwork succumbs to organizational rivalry. Unless the leader intervenes, such performance can quickly become "the nature of our business."

TURNING WEAKNESS INTO STRENGTH

Fortunately, the manager has a third choice. She can use values-driven leadership. Bringing her team together, she can create strategies to strengthen their weakest component by elevating one of their values. Is this too idealistic a notion? This is exactly how Gloria Venski, in the policy benefits division at Northwestern Mutual, solved her problem. The department's workload was rapidly expanding. Her unit temporarily couldn't support one component—Market—with its Customer Service value. Work stacked up. Customers were unhappy. One choice was to add more people, contradicting the company's value of keeping costs down. Another choice was to keep driving her people, overriding Northwestern's commitment to its people.

Instead, Gloria Venski asked her people for help in strengthening the component—Organization—that was holding them back. Elevating the company's Teamwork value in a weak component changed the dynamics. A crisis became an opportunity. She replaced with teams an organization of specialists working in separate boxes. She empowered the teams to make decisions. A situation that had formerly drained people suddenly energized them. Now no one would ever want to go back to the old form of organization. A weak component has become a strength.

In the process, Venski's unit reinforced a Core Value, Customer Service. The decision in a values-driven company like Northwestern Mutual is never which value to abandon. Nor is it which component to ignore. The decision is how to strengthen a lagging component by elevating a value. That is values-driven leadership. Not coincidentally, the manager in our example received a promotion soon after taking this approach.

At the departmental level or in an entire company, any serious effort to elevate a value eventually creates strategies to strengthen every component of the business.

WATCHING THE FOUNDER

Charles Schwab & Company has passed through many stages of values implementation. Twenty years ago, the founder's example was the values program. Holly Kane Mayette started with Chuck Schwab in his first discount brokerage office with 10 other people. Today she is vice president and manager of Schwab's San Francisco branch. She sat next to Schwab and watched the way he handled customers. If the situation was gray, "he would always side with the customer." Long before he published his Vision and Values, "it was always understood." Formalization came, says Kane

Mayette, "because of our rapid growth. We were hiring at such a rate that everyone needed to know that's what we're all about."

By the early 1990s, the company had a smoothly functioning business model. Even so, Chuck Schwab and his team wanted to raise Service Quality within a business already the envy of the industry. Assets have been pouring into Schwab at a rate of $30 billion a year. For all securities markets, 1994 was a shaky year. Yet Schwab opened 736,200 new accounts. Since 1989, Schwab's earnings have multiplied at a compound rate of 62 percent.

Before 1975, there were no discount stockbrokers. Brokers took a fixed commission for buying and selling securities. Then came May 1, 1975. On that day, now known on Wall Street as May Day, the Securities and Exchange Commission abolished fixed commissions. Brokers could charge what they liked. With a $100,000 investment from his uncle, 36-year-old Chuck Schwab opened a discount brokerage office in San Francisco.

In traditional terms, Schwab's firm sold nothing. It offered no advice. It placed orders for knowledgeable investors at discount prices. That business still accounts for 75 percent of Schwab's annual profits. However, the company is rapidly diversifying. As *Business Week* notes, ". . . Schwab lays out a sumptuous banquet of low-cost and imaginative investment programs."[2] Included are no-fee mutual funds, computerized stock trading, and specialized banking services.

Rapid growth tests commitment to values in any company. The quantitative ledger drives all before it. Record sales, record profits, record assets! More clients, more transactions, more new hires! Who can worry about values at a time like this? Only leaders with good memories.

PERSONAL VALUES AS A COMPANY STANDARD

Chuck Schwab espoused a high vision and four values for his company. His vision was to provide investors with "the most useful and ethical brokerage services in America." His personal values, Fairness, Respect, Continuous Improvement and Trust, became the company standard.

For 20 years, millions of transactions with thousands of customers have tested Schwab's Vision and Core Values. The overall record is exemplary, but not perfect. In 1988, Schwab discovered some reps had overstepped their trading authority, resulting in a stiff fine by the Securities and Exchange Commission. As a consequence, Schwab learned a hard but valuable lesson. It tightened its compliance everywhere. Schwab's computer system checks accounts for irregularities. Employees can trade only through Schwab's employee branch, headed by the chief of Schwab's compliance department. Compliance is only negative discipline, however. To lift positive discipline, Schwab also redoubled its efforts on Vision and Core Values.

In 1992, Lindy Ashmore joined Schwab as director of Corporate Service Quality. Ashmore arrived with more than 20 years experience in financial services. She began in 1964 as an entry-level clerk in Lloyds Bank, Ltd., in Leamington, England. By 1983 she was vice president of sales and service management at a San Francisco bank. By then her primary job—and her abiding passion—was Service Quality. In the late 1980s she became vice president and director of Service Quality for Citibank in California and Nevada.

NONSTOP ENTHUSIASM

Ashmore generates nonstop enthusiasm for her work and for Service Quality. During her first six months with Schwab, she studied the company's culture while delivering work in the pipeline. Then she began developing a comprehensive design to lift Service Quality throughout the company. Early on, she recognized she could never change Schwab's fast transactional culture. So she didn't try. Instead, she looked for ways to build Service Quality into existing structures and systems.

Building on what was there meant acknowledging strengths, pointing out unusual practices that people took for granted.

These practices illustrated that Service Quality was already a Core Value, visible in every component. Schwab used the latest technology to deliver quality. Every employee went through an annual service awareness program. Every day the company randomly surveyed about 5,000 customers who made transactions that day. The survey asked about the account executive's courtesy, ability to answer questions, speed of response.

Ashmore's task was to raise the level of implementation in every structure and system. Her design is practical for any company with strong values that wants to move to the next level in every component. In fact, the whole design is a series of higher and higher levels. There is the assumption, however, that the company already strongly supports its values.

Ashmore built her first platform on a common phrase in the Schwab culture. One of Chuck Schwab's long-standing corporate goals is "to become the premier provider of service in the brokerage business." Ashmore converted that phrase into a Service Quality Vision. Working with senior executives, she identified six strategies for Schwab to reach this goal. For example, the company must provide services "that deliver the highest value for the price paid." It had to stay focused "on keeping it simple for the customer to do business with us." Schwab President David S. Pottruck personally added an emphasis on "measuring performance against our customer's standards."

KEY STRATEGIES FOR A KEY VALUE

Ashmore next cascaded the strategies into standards. The problem with many values processes, Ashmore says, is that leaders don't define what they want. "It's like saying we want everyone to meet us *there* and then not saying where there is. That can be dangerous in a company where people are bright, energetic and creative. We'll all go in different directions." The strategies point the direction to go. The standards confirm you are getting there.

Ashmore next created a roadmap for change (Figure 6.2). On the horizontal axis she listed the six strategies. The vertical

Figure 6.2
Premier Provider of Service "Roadmap"

	BREAKTHROUGH SERVICE LEADERSHIP	ENGENDERING CUSTOMER LOYALTY	INTEGRATIVE SERVICE MEASUREMENT	CONTINUOUS PROCESS IMPROVEMENT	CUSTOMER DRIVEN INTERNAL CULTURE	REVOLUTIONARY PRODUCTS AND SERVICES
Primitive	No support	Customer complaints not monitored	No measures exist	Fire fighting	No training, no recognition programs	Basic product line
Interested	Senior management buy-in speeches	Customer feedback requested	Some measures exist but little accountability Compensation tied to measures in some areas	Focus on fast, effective problem resolution "Recovery" strategy in place	Service awareness training in place Corporate service recognition program	Products matched to competition
Committed	Formal service quality vision communicated	Customers expectations defined	Initial set of service standards and measures. MIS and action planning	Focus on problem elimination	Service skills training - problem prevention - problem resolution	Innovative products developed based on customer needs
Accelerating	VP Action Plans and "Roadmap" drive service improvements in each functional area	Customers/suppliers included in planning process	Benchmark measures and full accountability Compensation tied to measures in all areas	Focus on "do it right the first time"	Service leadership training in place	Innovative products fully integrated with delivery system capabilities, meeting/exceeding customer needs and expectations
Premier Provider	Customer focused thinking incorporated into all planning, products, promotions	Customers needs anticipated	Company standards reflect dedication to Zero Defects	Focus on Zero Defects in all key systems/processes	Advanced service quality training fully implemented into culture	The Schwab brand image denotes innovative, high value products

Charles Schwab & Co., Inc.

80

axis identified six levels of corporate response to each of the strategies. The vertical axis began with Primitive—virtually no support for the strategy. It then moved through Interested, Committed, and Accelerating. The final level was Chuck Schwab's target—Premier Provider. In each box on the roadmap Ashmore created standards for each strategy at each level.

The process changed the way Schwab looked at Service Quality. Says Shelly Bays, a senior vice president who worked with Ashmore on the project: "As a company, we were doing many individual things right but we didn't have a thorough and comprehensive Service Quality system." There was an immediate positive response. How did they sell the new design? Says Ashmore, "It sold itself." In keeping with Schwab's strongly decentralized culture, Ashmore next passed on the roadmap to any operating unit that wanted to pursue it on its own.

By 1993, 20 units had prepared Action Plans to move ahead at least one level in their weakest strategy. The system was practical and energizing. It created realistic goals. Simply move forward one level in your weakest column. And then another level and then another. The design also stressed balance. There was no point in moving from committed to accelerating in one column while mired at the primitive level in another. Lift your weakest strategy to the next level and continuous improvement was sure to follow.

Today Ashmore says Service Quality is even more deeply embedded in Schwab operations. The company's recently revised Vision Statement identifies ten overriding goals. The top two—providing spectacular service and developing and empowering people—flow directly from Service Quality initiatives. Operationally, the two goals merge in a heightened emphasis on training. For example, the company now offers training on customer service skills to all back-office as well as field employees.

With her conceptual design completed, Ashmore personally entered the Service Quality trenches. In creating her next assignment, she sought a project with a clear impact on the bottom line. Reinforcing a major theme of this book, she insists: "The reason so many service initiatives don't last is that they don't impact the bottom line."

SPECIALIST TROUBLESHOOTERS

Three years ago, Ashmore launched a pilot group with a single, profit-linked mission: Recapture customer loyalty after a problem has occurred. The pilot evolved into a team of 22 specialist troubleshooters called The Chairman's Division. Representing Chuck Schwab, the division responds to complaints that managers didn't resolve at the first point of contact. Complaints come from customer surveys, phone calls, letters, the chairman's hotline. Today the team handles 700 to 800 complaints a month. Their standard is a full response to every customer within four days. Following techniques developed in her roadmap, Ashmore's team regularly completes jobs within two days.

Such improvements come from Ashmore's contagious commitment to Service Quality and her systematic approach to improvement. Her division recently carried out a 90-day improvement program that doubled productivity while reducing response time by 80 percent. The team examined every practice, policy, or obstacle hindering them from recapturing customer loyalty. It pushed back on directives from anywhere, including even Schwab's strict compliance department.

THE FOUNDER'S EXAMPLE

The biggest breakthrough came when Ashmore's team overturned a policy requiring a written answer as a first step in handling any complaint. Everyone assumed this was a regulatory requirement. It was only a time-honored company policy. With the policy revised, a member of Ashmore's team telephones a dissatisfied customer the first day the complaint arrives. Result: the department now resolves 40 percent of its complaints the day they arrive. For achievements like this, the Chairman's Division won Schwab's coveted Living Legend Award in 1995.

Chuck Schwab was once the entire values program himself. Today he leaves details to others. Appearing in television and print ads, Schwab remains the visible embodiment of his company's aspirations. In 20 years, he built a business that changed his name into a household word in financial services. Equally important, he instilled his values into his young enterprise. Beyond that, he has sponsored the evolving strategies to embed those values within every component of his company.

CHAPTER 7

ADDING VALUE TO SYSTEMS

People often change external behavior without altering who they are. However, elevate your inner values and you change your personality. The same is true for companies. Culture is an outer expression of values. Introduce or elevate values in the systems through which you work, and the corporate personality expands. A change in culture—or external behavior—is sure to follow.

Integrated strategic planning creates comprehensive strategies for growth. Those strategies support growth by building capacity in every component. However, strategies cannot work in isolation within components. The components themselves never work in isolation. They are linked by a network of activities, systems, and processes. Moving from strategy to Complete Act requires alignment. The next step in integrated planning involves bringing key systems and processes in line with Strategic Objectives and Values.

To create results, strategies must move through the company's systems and processes. (Figure 7.1) This is routine practice with Strategic Objectives. When a company seeks to increase sales in a new region, it instinctively redirects its distribution system. However, planners often overlook this step in pursuing Strategic Values. They want to elevate Respect for Each Other or Quality. Yet they forget to realign systems

Figure 7.1
Integrating Values and Mission in Strategic Planning

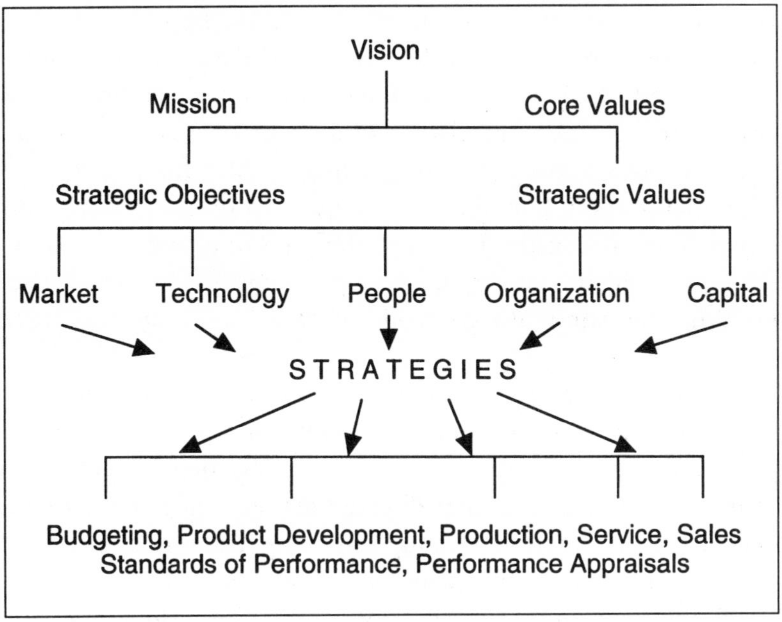

with their new ambition. Without changes in the evaluation and compensation systems, the new values are empty promises.

Individual actions are cells of achievement. Weave those actions together and you create a system. An accounting system combines bookkeeping and other financial activities into useful information. A purchasing system brings order to random buying decisions. Combine systems and you have a process.

An effective production process goes far beyond just making a product. It coordinates systems for bidding, estimating, design, purchasing, and manufacturing. At a more comprehensive level it weaves in customer service, quality control, cost accounting, invoicing, and collection. The wider this coordination, the more complete and valuable the process.

Comprehensive processes convert human effort into systemic energy. Information isn't readily available when it stays within one system or component. Take invoicing out of the production process, for example. The invoicing clerk is soon rushing around the shop floor looking for figures and dates. The floor team leaders no longer have the information on the completed job. They must stop to look it up. Meanwhile, shipping can't get the order out without an invoice. Accounting mutters about sloppiness of records on the floor. The floor complains about "people who want us to do their work." Put invoicing back in the loop, and the picture changes. Accounting and manufacturing begin operating on the same data, within the same process. You increase efficiency and lower stress.

Today managers see many reasons to recreate processes. Downsizing removed middle managers who personally coordinated systems. Computer networking lets departments share the same information. Self-directed teams want faster access to common information. Beating the competition demands faster reaction times than antiquated processes can provide.

Process redesigners usually concentrate on raising efficiency. They remove duplicate steps. They streamline the flow of paper and materials. They close gaps where systems interact. They unify the presentation and distribution of information. These are laudable goals. They will lift efficiency, reduce costs, and lower stress.

Still, most process redesign overlooks opportunities equal to these benefits combined. In process redesign you take all systems apart. You then redesign their key steps. With a little more time and thought, you can introduce at least one Core or Strategic Value into each step. Elevate values in one step, and you recharge that step. Elevate values within every step, and you energize the whole process.

GET THE SYSTEM IN THE ROOM

Nothing beats the force of focused human energy. Values-driven processes will unleash that power. There are many effective models of process redesign. Any of them will benefit by introducing values early and throughout.

Consultant John Polland of San Jose, California, honed the major elements of his system during 27 years in process quality and process engineering with IBM. In 1987, Polland left IBM to form his own company, Integral Group Communications, Inc. From our first meeting, we both saw the potential in introducing values into his already effective methodology.

Polland's approach streamlines the usual lengthy studies and analysis. In Polland's system, teams working together from eight days to two weeks completely reengineer their work flow. Polland's experience has confirmed the importance of having the system in the room. That means gathering offsite all of the people responsible for the various systems in a process. His groups range from 20 people to 40 or 50.

After we introduce a values component into his process, the design looks like this:

- Get the group to identify problems in the current systems and process. Don't settle for symptoms. Ensure the group defines root causes.
- Ask the group to create a Vision for the process. How would they like the process to work? How will each Core Value be visible within this Vision? What Strategic Values would help the most in overcoming problems? If a value is Customer Service, how will we reflect service in our revised process? If Respect for Each Other is a value, how will we treat people within the process?
- Next, the group develops and completely documents the actions required to move to the desired vision and values.

These lively sessions produce sets of charts describing Problems and Opportunities. We hang these charts on opposite walls, with the group in the middle. Their task is to build a human bridge from the present problems to future opportunities.

COMMON ISSUES

Change processes often call for participants to begin mapping the present systems at this point. This creates a long and physically laborious effort. It is more enjoyable and effective to rely on mental rather than physical energy. The existing systems are always available in the heads of the people in the room. Their early discussions surfaced problems. Common issues are accountability, delegation, duplication, and waste. They have also defined their aspiration for something better. It is time to design the future. They begin modeling the process not as it is, but as it should be.

The team naturally breaks into subteams working on individual systems. In creating the new process, people aim for more than efficiency. They simultaneously set values standards at every critical juncture. They assure they have embedded values in the redesign from the start.

On the final day of the exercise, the team presents its findings to senior management. The results of the retreat include a reengineered process, an action plan for converting from the present process, plus an analysis of the skills required for the new process.

This design sharply compresses the time normally devoted to such efforts. It has seven requirements for success:

- **Leadership support.** The redesign team makes a significant commitment in time and energy. In return, management must declare its openness to change. This is not a carte blanche commitment. Management will review the team recommendations. However, management should make clear from the start its willingness to adopt all reasonable suggestions.
- **Systems in the room.** The people who know the process must be in the room *and must stay in the room*. We discourage nonparticipating managers from dropping in. Equally, we discourage participating Associates from dropping out to attend to office emergencies. Both disrupt an effort that is time and team sensitive.

- **A framework for change.** Why is this change worth the effort? Does the need to reengineer arise from customer complaints? A change in Mission? A competitive threat? An upheaval in the environment? Management and the reengineering team should agree on the context in which change must occur.
- **Empowered people.** Management should empower the team to suggest any changes except those that are illegal, immoral or contradict the values. They should explain any other limitations in advance.
- **Concentrated effort.** The team will meet for a minimum of eight consecutive days. For a complex process, two weeks is the norm. Team members should understand this commitment from the beginning. There will be no opportunity to go to the office. Whoever handles a team member's work during the holidays will handle it during the retreat. Many sessions will run late into the evening.
- **A detailed plan for implementation.** Without an Action Plan, the retreat is only mental exercise. Converting to a new process while keeping the business running is a demanding task. You can count on the enthusiasm of participants who have created the new process. However, back at the office on Monday others are sure to say: "Congratulations. How will we get there?" The Action Plan, with defined tasks, deadlines, and responsibilities, will answer that question. The Action Plan should call for significant moves forward within the first two weeks after the retreat.
- **Skilled facilitators.** The systems are in the room. The knowledge is in the room. As the team becomes engrossed, facilitators must be on hand to keep the process on track. The facilitators' job is to manage the process to meet the schedule. The facilitators ensure the completeness of the process. In a values-centered process, the facilitators assure the new design elevates all the company's values.

Another more complex redesign effort requires tighter direction from the top. Some companies want to reconfigure not one process but their whole method of operation. In such ambitious efforts, a strong grounding in values enhances enthusiasm and prospects for success.

The more comprehensive the effort, the greater will be the focus on all five components and the systems linking them. American Express IDS Financial Services, Inc., has a 100-year-old values-driven personality. Over the past decade this Minneapolis, Minnesota, company has been consciously renewing its values. Its most recent efforts illustrate how to use values as a basis for overhauling every key process in the business.

FOUR LEGACIES

Harvey Golub, today chair and CEO of American Express, started the values renewal effort at IDS in the early 1980s. Golub's commitment grew out of his years as a management consultant and senior executive at McKinsey & Company, Inc. Working in dozens of companies, he saw firsthand the impact of values on performance. In 1984, American Express hired Golub as CEO of its IDS Financial Services subsidiary.

As a consultant, Golub had recommended the $730 million IDS purchase. Many on Wall Street said American Express had paid too much. Golub proved them wrong. In 1992, IDS earned $297 million on revenues of $2.9 billion. That represented a doubling of revenue and a fivefold increase in earnings during Golub's years on the job. American Express promoted Golub to vice chairman based on his IDS performance. He became chairman in early 1993.

For Golub, values such as Customer Service are pointless until they are criteria for decisions. To be effective, they must have clear definitions—or in a century-old firm, renewed definitions. He delegated that task to an IDS team selected from different levels of the company. The team worked for nine months. They recommended five values. Golub approved their recommendation after dropping one value he considered illogical. He then showed his commitment by stopping behaviors that were not congruent with the values.[1]

EVERYDAY WORKHORSES

The IDS values were four everyday workhorses of corporate progress: Client (i.e., Superior Service), Excellence, treating individuals with Fairness and Dignity, and Teamwork. Commitment to Golub meant improving performance. "We had to understand what service was," he said. "What are the elements of good service? Then we determined how we were going to measure them." Once the measurement system was in place, Golub read every quality service report. He assembled his senior team for three-hour meetings to discuss how to improve lagging indicators.

In the early 1990s, IDS launched a major effort to realign every aspect of the IDS sales and delivery process. They named the project IDS 1994 to honor the company's centennial, the year the project would end. On the surface, it resembled other reengineering projects now popular in American business. Even more noteworthy, however, is how IDS built the program around Mission and Core Values.

Also noteworthy was IDS's willingness to tamper with a formula that had produced a decade of success. Why take such a risk? First, values like IDS's Excellence inevitably define a transitory notion of success. Second, competitors, mirroring IDS's success, had begun imitating its core strategy. The idea of offering in-house funds through financial planners was spreading throughout the financial services industry. To keep ahead, IDS began restructuring on the run.

People involved in IDS 1994 set out to create a remodeled company. Their standard was to make the new company so effective that it could put the existing IDS out of business. As Jeffrey E. Stiefler, Golub's successor as IDS president and CEO, noted at the time: "The issue is how we can keep from being arrogant and complacent and keep ourselves fresh. We're trying to institutionalize a level of dissatisfaction. . . ."[2]

That level of dissatisfaction focused first on IDS's biggest problem. Research showed most IDS clients related to their own financial planner, not to the impersonal business in Minneapolis. The problem was that turnover among IDS financial planners exceeded 30 percent in the first year.

Retention rates improve once planners get through the first years. IDS estimates that retention among five-year veterans exceeds 80 percent. Improving customer satisfaction and profitability required keeping more planners longer. The key to keeping planners was making more of them successful earlier. IDS started by sending a team to its offices across the country.

No Single Lever

The team found there wasn't a single lever to increase planner retention. Recruitment was hasty. Training was a problem. New planners had to fend for themselves. Managers were responsible for training and support of recruits, yet the company paid them primarily on their own production.

Says Claire Kolmodin, who heads IDS's Quality Department: "It wasn't simply going in and changing one or two aspects but rather taking a look at the whole . . . way we operated as an organization." To take a comprehensive look, IDS adopted a method called Organizational System Design, or OSD. The method depends heavily on in-house volunteers. According to Kolmodin, "It's easier to take people who know the work and train them how to do the analysis."

A steering committee representing several levels of office and field employees set four interrelated goals. The IDS 1994 team would measure its success against improvements in client satisfaction, planner retention, financial profitability, and reputation in the industry. Each goal had a set of expected results. The committee then asked for volunteers willing to devote up to 60 percent of their time for at least a year.

Departments sending volunteers agreed not to ask for additional staff.

MORE THAN 1,000 RECOMMENDATIONS

Interest was high. Several hundred people applied for about 30 places on the team. Once selected, team members received a special training course on OSD practices. Next they set out to study the IDS environment. What were competitors doing? What did clients want? How is the regulatory environment changing? Building on the IDS values of Fairness and Dignity, the team analyzed employee expectations and problems. The team used surveys, interviews, and focus groups to understand what people inside wanted from the revised system.

By the end of 1992, the volunteers had analyzed the existing IDS system in depth. They began designing a new system that would support each of the goals. They sifted through more than 1,000 specific recommendations. The steering committee gave tentative approval in early 1993. Testing began in two regions with the aim of bringing the model on line throughout the United States in time for the 1994 centennial.

The revised approach develops the People component by increasing training for new planners. It matches them with more experienced mentors. The company revamped its traditional structure. The new model encourages teams of planners with different strengths. It realigns back-office assignments with planners' needs. It makes more effective use of recently available technology.

IDS sees this round of changes as only a beginning. Its Mission, Core Values, and strategy are now firmly in place. This permits the company to update its sales and delivery process routinely without changing the basics of its business.

Kolmodin says the whole redesign "stemmed from our commitment to our Mission and Core Values." The values, she adds, have been used to "drive systemic changes" incorporated in the new model. Examples:

- **Integrity and Putting Clients First.** The new model strengthens the Market component by providing clients with a quarterly comparison of investment performance by product. Before, IDS statements showed only a quarterly result without comparison.
- **Teamwork.** Under the revised compensation system, planners can develop a group practice. The previous system discouraged splitting commissions. Now groups can develop a practice with specialists in fields such as estate settlement or retirement planning.
- **Fairness and Respect.** The team went beyond speed, accuracy, and efficiency as criteria for improving work flows. The design also seeks to "consider what people want out of this work."

Systems develop over time in organizations. The people who depend on them seldom think through their full implications. Over time, says Kolmodin, "that leads to very, very mixed messages about what's the intended outcome. The messages can be very inconsistent. They can work at odds with one another." For IDS 1994, the test of any proposed systemic change went beyond whether the change does the job faster or better. The test also asked whether the change reinforced Mission and Core Values.

It will take several years to gauge the impact of the new model. Competitive advantage will grow if planner retention improves. However, the top producers pose a delicate problem. They thrived under the old system. The new model focuses more on teams. If top performers' commissions start slipping, some may leave, taking long-time clients with them.

Along the way, IDS changed its name to American Express Financial Advisors, Inc., solidifying Minneapolis's position within American Express. Whatever the final results of IDS 1994, the company has shown how to carry values down deep into every process.

How well values affect processes is a sure signal about the

strength of qualitative management. The budgeting system is a common testing ground. Most advanced companies have been preparing budgets for decades. Their system is established, well defined, and very influential. Yet many companies' Strategic Values appear nowhere in their budgets.

Where is the income expected from values? At 3M, one of the established values is Innovation. To support that value, 3M expects budgets to show that one quarter of annual sales come from products introduced in the last five years. In most company budgets, however, where are the costs for values training? For revamping systems to upgrade values? Even in many values-driven companies the budget system rolls on, oblivious to the values.

In a truly values-driven organization, the financial people don't concentrate exclusively on Strategic Objectives as guidelines for budgets. They ask also about Strategic Values. Where are those values reflected in this year's budget? Values should influence and energize every process. How do our values shape our recruiting? Our training processes? The quality of our production? The responsiveness of our Customer Service system?

Most values programs that do not achieve results fail for one of two reasons. Many focus too heavily on changing surface behavior. They never really enhance the components that add capacity to the corporate personality. Others are unable to bring higher values into processes that control daily operations. They have too little impact on the company's habitual modes of action and reaction.

Established processes resist change more stubbornly than most people. Habitual actions often take on a life of their own. Piecemeal efforts are of limited value. Yet qualitative management clearly holds the promise of creating processes that respond to challenge in new ways. Seeing the process whole and then infusing every step with Strategic Values opens the path to new opportunities for growth and profit.

CHAPTER 8

FROM CONCEPT
TO INDIVIDUAL ACT

When values impact individual performance, they become engines for growth. Toro Company struggled for years to get its values embedded in performance appraisals. What was the right balance between valuing people and getting the job done? Then the company developed a simple—but radical—technique to resolve this dilemma.

To launch integrated strategic planning, a team projects an overarching Vision of the future. They identify the company's Mission and Core Values. From this foundation, they survey the current environment. They isolate the Strategic Objectives and Strategic Values they will use to create success during the next planning cycle.

The team then measures the strength of each of the five components. How will each component support or retard the Strategic Objectives and Strategic Values? Specific strategies for improvement emerge. The team links the strategies in Operating Plans. The Operating Plans target processes that are out of alignment with Strategic Objectives and Values.

With this comprehensive approach, strategic planning is always dynamic. As an integrated vehicle for continuous improvement, it remains focused on two central questions: (1) How has our environment changed? (2) Considering our core principles, how will we convert those changes into opportunities?

At each step quantitative and qualitative must at least be in balance. In a more advanced stage they merge, creating a higher synthesis. The aim at each level is a comprehensive and unified whole. The final step centers at the level of individual acts, jobs, and performance, the subject of this chapter.

Individual departments often focus heavily on either the quantitative or qualitative. It would be foolish to separate the Mission of the accounting department from the quantitative ledger. It would be equally foolhardy to pry a heavy qualitative emphasis away from human resources.

However, every individual job encompasses both ledgers in that a specific amount of work leads to specific results (quantitative), and the contribution of any job depends on *how* the job holder carries out the work (qualitative). The greater the integration, the more fully that job contributes to both Strategic Objectives and Strategic Values.

Unfortunately, many managers fail to seek unity. They see only conflicting priorities: "Do you want me to get out the order or pay attention to those fine words on the poster?" Every values process is subject to that question. Every values-driven leader knows the answer: "I want you to do both." Unfortunately, this answer buries the problem. It substitutes the leader's will for team members' commitment. It's a sure bet the question will arise again—if not tomorrow, then the next day. Eventually, the leader will tire or the team members will go along resentfully. Either way, values lose their power. They become pawns on a chessboard of manipulation.

A VALUING CULTURE

The team leader's will is crucial in any values process. It should not be dissipated on a string of small issues but should focus on strengthening an integrated approach that makes such questions irrelevant. In the scenario we have described, the leader may have no choice except to say, "Get the order out. We'll talk about values later." Then the leader should bring her will to bear on the follow-up discussion. "Why did we have to choose between shipping the order and our values?" That's the question the team must answer. "Were our plans unrealistic? Did a process let us down? Are we missing skills?"

Conflicts between performance and values slowly give way to a more constructive balance in a "valuing organization." That's how Lynde Sorensen describes the ideal culture she and others have been working toward for more than a decade at The Toro Company. Sorensen is director of organizational development and communications at the 80-year-old Bloomington, Minnesota, firm. The unrelenting need for performance is an easy sell at Toro. Many employees still bear scars from the company's near demise in the early 1980s.

In the 1970s, Wall Street considered Toro a perfect concept stock. It sold snowblowers in winter and lawn mowers in summer. Sales climbed from $130 million in 1976 to $360 million four years later. Earnings grew an average of 68 percent annually. When sales reached $400 million, there was talk of a $1 billion company. Nature—physical or human—has a way of flattening such hubris. During two consecutive snowless winters, snowblower sales skidded from $130 million in 1980 to $6 million in 1982.

Considering that year a fluke, the company raised its production target the next year. The company's cash disappeared into a mound of immovable inventory. Losses piled up, totaling almost $30 million over 10 straight losing quarters. Meanwhile, complaints about mower quality drove buyers and dealers to other brands.

"THERE WASN'T ANYONE ELSE"

As the crisis deepened, Toro's chairman, president, and nine vice presidents left. The board selected as president Ken Melrose, then executive vice president and a 10-year Toro veteran. There wasn't time to risk an outsider. "They almost selected me by default," Melrose says. "There wasn't anyone else."

The toughest decision, Melrose later recalled, was to release half the employees. He then had bad news for the remaining 2,000 people. Despite fewer resources, he needed greater productivity. That meant financial sacrifices. He suspended executive incentive compensation. He imposed salary freezes and mandatory furlough days for office employees. Factory workers suffered through wage freezes or reductions. Melrose kept the doors open by negotiating $140 million in credit lines.

Once you make the tough decisions, crisis management is easy, Melrose says. "I almost didn't need to show up. The people were all doing what they needed to do." Strategy was only "better blocking and tackling." Toro needed better quality products. It had to manage its balance sheet. Even after the layoffs, staffing was too high. Melrose had to get out of an expensive office lease and combine facilities. "We needed to face what everyone in American industry was facing in the 1980s."

Melrose's cool demeanor built confidence on the board, in the community, and within the company. Meanwhile, however, "the whole idea of style, culture, empowering, and serving the organization remained on the tip of my tongue." By the 1990s such words were part of the vocabulary of business. A decade earlier, when Toro looked into the abyss, the business climate was different.

Business books, magazine articles, and executives talked constantly of the competitive threat from Japan. "Lean and mean" was the answer, never mind the question. Widespread understanding of the importance of culture and values was still in the future. Even the quality movement barely had a foothold in America. In that climate, Melrose believes, "everyone would have said we don't have time for that stuff. We have to survive." A prudent man, Melrose kept his thoughts to himself.

"WE SAW AMAZING THINGS"

Melrose's calm grew from deep inner confidence. His idea of a relaxing holiday is white-water rafting on a dangerous river. He is well educated. He graduated from Princeton and MIT and worked on a doctorate at the University of Chicago. Open-minded, he explored offbeat paths to personal development. In 1976, he volunteered for a six-month pilot program sponsored by the Menninger Clinic in Topeka, Kansas. Among other skills, the program taught him how to control supposedly un-controllable bodily functions. He learned to master parts of his nervous system, blood pressure, body temperature, and brain waves. "We saw amazing things. It was mind over matter."

The experience was an epiphany. It left him convinced that everyone has deep untapped potential. "We all can rise to the occasion and be better than we normally think we are." In the early 1980s, the proof was all around him at Toro. Fearing for their jobs, people sustained higher levels of productivity. Mel-rose wanted to keep this unleashed energy even after the fear passed. The payoff, he believed, would be immense. "We would be a better team. We would get more individual effort from people. People would then develop more self-worth. They would have a stronger sense of contribution." He reasoned, "One of my roles as CEO is to help make that happen."

By 1983, the survivors began to breathe easier. Toro had sold the snowblower inventory at near liquidation prices. The dealer network was recovering. Debt was manageable. The company was modestly in the black. It was time, Melrose thought, "to decide what kind of company we wanted to be as well as the kind we didn't want to be." As the crisis ebbed, he waited for a chance to offer his then-unconventional ideas. Opportunity came between the covers of a book.

In Search of Excellence galvanized Melrose. The 1982 book by consultants Tom Peters and Robert Waterman sold in the mil-lions.[1] Peters became an instant star on the lecture circuit. Throughout the nation, excited executives flocked to hear his message of hope and renewal. Peters and Waterman advanced ideas that Melrose had been waiting for. They argued there was nothing unique about Japanese management. Their case studies described American companies serving customers, empowering employees, pursuing quality. What the Japanese were doing, they insisted, some American companies were already doing. And they were doing it as well or better. Peters and Waterman proposed that what these companies could do, any company could do by following the eight attributes that led to excellence.

Melrose remembers the book as a catalyst. Calling together 80 managers, he distributed 68 pages of his own typewritten notes on the book. At another meeting, he asked which of the eight principles would most help Toro. His executive teams selected three—bias for action, productivity through people, and staying close to the customer.

Lynde Sorensen remembers Melrose's enthusiasm. "He set out to evangelize the values he believed would help Toro serve its customers and employees." Melrose formed a Pride in Excellence action team composed of employees who embraced his vision. He charged the team with finding ways to drive the three Peters and Waterman attributes throughout the company. Melrose selected Lynde Sorensen as coleader of the new team. Sorensen had joined Toro 12 years earlier, working in accounting. When Melrose selected her, she was director of systems development in the MIS department.

BALANCING RESULTS AND BEHAVIOR

The Pride in Excellence team slowly transformed the three Peters and Waterman attributes into Toro values. They worked to translate the values into specific behaviors. They were pioneers, and they found few ready-made answers to their questions. Personal and company values systems became jumbled. More than once, team members wondered how they could talk about this stuff at work and still be taken seriously.

From the start, they concentrated on ways to get the values down to the level of individual jobs. This was relatively easy when talking about values such as Service or Quality. However, Toro wanted to adopt Peters and Waterman's productivity through people attribute as well. That led to values such as Respect and Trust. Their final statement even uses the word "compassion."

While there was initial enthusiasm, there was also skepticism. Team members could immediately identify individuals who ran over people and still got good results. There were even individuals who lived the values but had poor results. Inspired by Melrose's commitment, the team stayed with it. After 14 months they published their first statement of values and beliefs.

At such moments, reactions in any company are predictable. People will immediately express enthusiasm. Then they will focus on cases where other people ignore the values. "So, what are you going to do about that?" Or more specifically, "What are you going to do about him? Or her?" Success in the old system often grows out of poor values. There is the star saleswoman who uses sarcasm to make back-office people respond faster. There is the plant supervisor who meets deadlines by instilling fear.

Management faces an awkward problem. The rules have been abruptly changed. Two months ago the sarcastic saleswoman and the disagreeable supervisor were covert heroes. "Hard to get along with, sure, but look at their results! Hey, it's a lean and mean world out there. There's bound to be some tension." Management seldom publicly acknowledges this view. When challenged, the response is predictably: "Yes, that behavior is really too much. We must do something." Of course, nothing ever changes. Not while the results keep coming. Employees are always realists about management's intentions. In time, they accept this hypocrisy as "the way we do business around here."

WHY CYNICISM INCREASES

When management announces a change, a new vision, commitment to more humanistic values, employees won't forgo the opportunity to point out shortcomings. This reaction often surprises managers. They expected praise and enthusiasm. Ironically, the new people-centered values initially cast a protective net over those who have been flaunting them most. In fairness, management must give people a chance to change. That's not a response that soothes victims of the former hero. Expect employee cynicism to grow if that response becomes an excuse to avoid the problem indefinitely.

Lynde Sorensen puts the issue succinctly: "OK, here is how we believe we should operate as a company. Now, if people aren't acting this way, what happens?" After more than a decade of wrestling with the issue, Sorensen has developed balanced wisdom. She uses a common example to illustrate her philosophy. Cruising down the highway, you hear your child say, "How come you are going 65 when the sign says 55?" Later, when that child is behind the wheel and you challenge his high-speed driving, you are certain to hear, "Well, you didn't drive 55." "If you are going to ask people to live by values," says Sorensen, "expect those people to hold you accountable."

With hindsight, Sorensen thinks the Toro effort initially talked too much about valuing people and not enough about performance. That slowed the pace of making values fully operational in every job. This is a common distortion. A company has been concentrating exclusively on the bottom line. Now it wants to highlight another dimension. Unconsciously, management often positions that dimension as an alternative rather than a support for performance. From the launch, leaders should link valuing people with valuing performance. "When you are in an unhealthy financial position, the only way to improve morale is to become profitable," Sorensen says wryly.

At Toro, the tension between values and results escalated as leaders tried to make the new values more operational. Melrose and the Pride in Excellence team kept up pressure. All the while, the old management system focused solely on the numbers. The fault line was compensation. Toro rewarded exclusively for making the numbers, Sorensen recalls. "The questions at review time never were: 'How are your people growing? Do they want to stay at Toro? Do they have pride in what they do? How motivated are they?' "

"THIS ISN'T GOING TO WORK"

Challenges to the values surfaced regularly. "We had established new expectations," says Sorensen. "People came forward saying 'I'm verbally abused in meetings. No one gives me recognition. Yet, I must work these horrendous hours. It's like nobody cares or understands.' " First there was a hum, Sorensen remembers. "Then the hum became a buzz, and the buzz became an outcry." More and more complaints went directly to Melrose or to the Pride in Excellence team. The team kept struggling with the central problem: "This isn't going to work if what we're saying isn't in fact happening." At Toro, as in many companies, it was a defining moment.

Carried to the individual work level, values always transform organizations. They force realignment of performance standards at a more comprehensive level. They elevate quantitative versus qualitative discussions from an "either/or" to a simple "and." It takes courage and an innovative spirit.

The lever was already in place at Toro. In the company's leadership program, managers rated themselves on a leadership questionnaire. Then they were confidentially rated on the same questionnaire by their supervisor, coworkers, and staff. When the results were used in training, only the individual and the trainer saw them. Even so, the results were harsh medicine for some managers.

Searching for a way to narrow the gap at the individual job level, Toro seized on this technique. What if everybody at management level got 360-degree feedback? What if that feedback influenced annual compensation? Then rewards could flow not only from what you achieved, but from how you achieved it.

A BOLD IDEA

It was a bold idea, and not an easy sell. They started slowly to mute resistance. Setting an example, Melrose asked his direct reports to review him. The officer and director levels followed. "We didn't get into anything really complicated or laborious," Sorensen says. "But we did say: 'You must go out and survey.' " Then individuals had to review their survey results with their immediate supervisors. Human resources provided facilitators for discussions between managers and supervisors when needed.

Melrose declared the first year "a free run." That meant the exercise would not affect compensation. Even so, Sorensen says, "many people said, 'You've got to be kidding. I'm here to get results.' " There were a few attempts to manipulate the results. In the second year the format and reviews became more rigorous. "Leadership Objectives" is the Toro term for what now has become annual 360-degree evaluations to ensure alignment with the Toro statement of people values (see Figure 8.1).

These words slowly began to shape behavior. By the second year, specific leadership objectives flowed from the reviews with supervisors. Success with these objectives could impact up to 25 percent of the annual review. The balance was still pegged to traditional operational objectives. Managers discussed their leadership objectives with their teams. Quarterly anonymous updates from the teams helped keep managers on track. The reports shocked many people. Many senior people had never had this kind of feedback. "The higher you are in organization," Sorensen notes, "the more out of touch you can become." Many managers insisted the effort could not last.

By the third year, some key managers acknowledged they needed help. These were people who had been with the company a long time, hard workers who knew how to get results, and had risen in a system that for years rewarded them only for quantitative results. "They began to get serious," says Sorensen, "about how well they inspired and motivated other people to do what needed to get done."

Figure 8.1

Our People Count

The Toro Company's greatest asset is its employees. Therefore we:

- Care about and support each other as individuals.
- Communicate openly, honestly and supportively.
- Build trust and display integrity in our actions as well as our words.
- Do what's right rather than what is merely convenient.
- Demonstrate compassion and respect for each other.
- Work for and care about the team's success.
- Provide every opportunity for professional growth and enrichment.

We will accept nothing less from ourselves or from our coworkers.

Their transformation inspired Sorensen. "I've seen individuals who were at the brink of extinction in this environment turn around and become our most avid supporters." She believes many of those "hard-core managers" carried a new perspective into their personal lives. They learned to listen better. They also better understand "the value of engaging in a relationship with someone who cares about you as a person."

Today, all of Toro's leadership and supervisory training programs focus on expected behavior of people and performance values. Toro's self-education never ends. The company launched a major quality initiative in 1990 as another way to marry quantitative results and people values in every job. Melrose takes his senior management team at least once a year to a Toro factory, where they work on the production line with other Toro employees.

For a decade, the company has based individual compensation on both quantitative results and performance on values. For eight of those ten years, Toro has recorded strong financial growth in tough economic and competitive environments. Meanwhile, the extension of qualitative evaluations has continued. Recently, Toro established specific, values-related behavioral expectations for all officer/salaried employees.

Both Melrose and Sorensen talk of Toro's culture change as a work in progress. However, the issues at Toro have moved to a new level. The question is no longer how to balance values and results in individual jobs. It is now how to integrate them perfectly. Every name badge at Toro has the company philosophy written on the back. The statement smoothly combines Ken Melrose's philosophy of individual human potential with honest marketplace reality. It is a blueprint for challenges that will never end.

PART III

SIX STEPS TO A VALUES-DRIVEN COMPANY

The Six Steps

- Commit
- Communicate
- Educate
- Set standards
- Align structure and systems
- Recognize performance

CHAPTER 9

SIX BUILDING BLOCKS TO A VALUES-DRIVEN COMPANY

"All happy families resemble one another," said the Russian writer Tolstoy. Like happy families, values-driven companies resemble one another in important ways. All have discovered the process of qualitative improvement. All follow a well-defined implementation path. All commit at the top, communicate, educate, set standards, align structure and systems. All recognize performance.

Values are a commonplace miracle, fully visible, partially seen. These simple operating qualities, vigorously pursued, release 10,000 elevated acts every day. Their power is available to anyone, yet only a few see its full potential.

For those who understand only partially, implementation resembles rote learning. People imitate, with personal flourishes, the actions of earlier leaders. Even this semiconscious awareness makes a contribution. The effort to maintain existing quality standards sustains many businesses today.

However, the richest rewards go to those who strike out in new directions. The potential is endless. Who can provide too much Customer Satisfaction? Where are the limits of Quality? When is creating "A Great Place to Work" a completed task?

One core value, rigorously pursued, cascades into a half-dozen more. A commitment to Customer Delight creates a dedication to Speed, Accuracy, Courtesy, Reliability, Integrity, Responsiveness, Safety, or Punctuality. At values-centered companies people are working on six derivatives of every value on the wall.

For the company president, department leader, or solo contributor, values open a path to productivity. At a deeper level, the reward is personal mastery. Choosing the values path fully complements numbers-driven management. At a higher synthesis, quantitative and qualitative merge into a single method. This comprehensive vision elevates the spirit while centering mind and hands on individual acts.

Disney World cast members behave with courtesy to hot and cranky guests. An American Steel & Wire process leader asks his team for their ideas even when the deadline nears. A 3M salesperson drives an extra 40 miles to help a customer. An Intel Corporation manager takes a risk on an associate's idea when failure means a cost overrun. As we shall see in the following chapters, these individual acts occur by design. It is more than good luck that the cast member, process leader, salesperson, or manager expresses the right values at the right time. Each act is a conscious reflection of a learned attitude. That attitude defines "the way we work around here."

AIM FOR COMPLETE ACTS

Any company can generate the same enthusiasm shown by the companies in our examples. Any effective values process energizes individual acts. Fully developed values lift individual acts to new levels. Individual acts become Complete Acts, embodying all the company's values.

A manufacturing company commits to three values—Safety, Speed, and Respect for People. To generate Complete Acts, the values must support one another. Every effort to improve Speed considers Safety and vice versa. To elevate Respect, managers must consult employees about

112

Speed and Safety. The three values move the company toward empowerment, a high form of Respect. At the highest level, every action on the shop floor or in the office reflects every value.

Although this sounds idealistic, we see it every day. Notice the next time a Federal Express driver comes to your office. Pay special attention when your package isn't ready. You will see the driver skillfully balance three FedEx values—Speed, Friendliness, and Service. We were running late when a FedEx driver called for our package. The driver waited patiently while we tried to complete the work. We finally had to tell him we couldn't make it today. He was so concerned that we ended up reassuring him that the package could go out next day. However, we noticed that he left our office *on time.*

I found my favorite example of values-driven Complete Acts at AT&T Universal Card. Imagine working in the delinquent accounts department of a credit-card company that publicly commits to Customer Delight. The banner in the department tells the whole story: "Make 'em happy, but make 'em pay." It must work. Surveys show that delinquent cardholders are likely to recommend the AT&T card to their friends.

Companies discussed in this book are very different. Whereas 3M and GE are more than 100 years old, American Steel & Wire started just a decade ago. Northwestern Mutual and IDS work in financial services. Disney is in entertainment, Intel in manufacturing. All have different values, yet in implementation they are more alike than different. All support their values with six well-defined steps. They use different words for these steps. They introduce them in different order. They assign them different priorities. They sustain them through different techniques. The steps have reached different levels of evolution in different companies. However, in each company you find versions of the same six steps. This chapter summarizes the six. Chapters 10 through 15 discuss each in more detail.

SIX STEPS TOWARD VALUES-DRIVEN LEADERSHIP

1. Commit to values at the top
2. Communicate values
3. Educate for values
4. Set standards for values
5. Align structure and systems with values
6. Recognize performance on values

STEP ONE: COMMIT TO VALUES

Commitment starts with a belief that values matter. Commitment explicitly links values with long-term health and success. Commitment means reinforcing that link frequently. Commitment is acting in contradiction to short-term logic to protect a value. Early on, as president of IDS, Harvey Golub dropped a profitable product. The decision was simple, he says. The product was a bad deal for customers. At American Steel & Wire, Tom N. Tyrrell stuck with his no-layoff policy when he had ample excuses not to. Both leaders based their decisions on clearly articulated values.

The toughest values decisions are about defining success. Do you promote or discipline individuals who produce big results in the numbers and fall short on values? Some top salespeople believe one of their perks is verbally abusing support staff. What about the star executive whose language borders on sexual harassment? Or the plant manager who saved the fourth-quarter results by shipping 50 percent over budget? The problem was he cut corners on work rules to do it. Such people force choices that bring sleepless nights. At the end of the night, committed leaders know there is no real choice. They know that every promotion or firing sends a values message. Whatever the announcement says, people read into it a clear values statement.

Commitment at the top begins wherever the values-centered leader is. Values can take hold anywhere. They can energize individual acts in any department or division. Wherever values appear, that's where commitment must begin. The leader who launches the values must commit to the other five steps.

You are not really committed until you define your values. It's never enough to say your value is Customer Delight. You must answer *what* delights your customer. Definitions put abstract values to work. For decades, 3M had well-established values in place. Yet CEO L. D. "Desi" DeSimone launched a redefinition process. Harvey Golub made values definition an early priority at both IDS and American Express.

Doesn't everyone understand words like Customer Service? Or Quality? Or Respect for Each Other? Why take the time to wordsmith the obvious? Thirty years ago, big corporations hired people from a homogenous pool. Hiring practices favored white male college graduates from certain universities. From this pool, recruiters searched for people who matched the company profile. For five years the company indoctrinated the young junior executive on "the way we work around here." It sized up his skills and potential. The young executive weighed the fit between his aspirations and the company's culture. Either party could call it quits at any time. After five years, there was a presumed commitment on both sides for life.

Today American society has opened far wider. People join organizations from a larger pool. They bring different values and attitudes to the job. They will jump companies quickly when they don't feel at home. Mergers and acquisitions create culture clashes rooted in different values. Older executives often forget that values are no longer implicit. Definition, once an interesting option, is now a requirement.

STEP TWO: COMMUNICATE VALUES

Even committed leaders lose patience with values communication. "How many times do we have to say it? The customer comes first! The customer comes first! The customer comes first!" Frustration quickly ends communication for the flavor-of-the-month fad. For true values, every day presents another opportunity to communicate.

New York Yankee center fielder Joe DiMaggio played to his highest possible level every day. For Joe, there was no distinction between the World Series or the second half of a meaningless doubleheader. Why? "Because there might be somebody out there who never saw me play before." For the values-driven leader there is *always* "somebody out there" who never fully heard the message before.

On the shop floor, the values-centered leader gathers his team to discuss the week's quality record. Mary Kay Ash reinforces company values at a three-day sales meeting *Fortune* called "part convention, part *Hello Dolly!*" Jack Welch stands alone "in the pit" at GE's Crotonville training center answering questions from middle-level managers. His words and demeanor illustrate Speed, Simplicity, and Self-Confidence. Microsoft's Bill Gates and Rosenbluth Travel's Hal Rosenbluth answer e-mail inquiries from any associate. Many leaders use video speeches to spread the word. Getting the values message out is what counts. Technique and technology are only means to that end.

STEP THREE: EDUCATE FOR VALUES

All companies reveal their values during the recruitment process, but for values-driven companies, it's a conscious step. At Disney and ServiceMaster, videos explain the values to potential recruits. Orientation programs carry the message in more detail. This early education makes recruits enthusiastic about the company culture. It also defines expected behavior. American Steel & Wire thinks these lessons are important enough to invite spouses.

Education in values never stops. ServiceMaster wraps values into its technical training. GE management courses teach the skills of Speed, Simplicity, and Self-Confidence. Intel offers team and individual appraisals in Risk Taking and other values.

Executing any value requires training in the smallest skills. One large moving company trains its drivers how to knock on a door.

On any moving day we all are anxious. We want to see the moving van in the driveway but we are not ready to begin loading. We answer frequent knocks at the door. Neighbors come to say goodbye. Children dart out for last-minute errands. People deliver or pick up items. Stress is always high. Knowing this, this company teaches its drivers how to knock on a door. When the door opens, the customer sees the driver standing erect. At chest height, the driver holds a clipboard with the company's logo clearly visible. The driver says a friendly hello and identifies himself. He then glances down his neatly pressed uniform to his polished shoes. The customer's eyes instinctively follow the driver's. The customer takes in the company's logo, the clean appearance of the uniform, the polished shoes. The simple act of knocking on a door conveys values like Reliability, Promptness, and, above all, Professionalism.

Workers need the right skills to express any value. A commitment to Customer Service requires a service rep to speak Spanish to a Hispanic customer. Reliability is an empty promise unless technicians have the necessary skills.

Most leaders endorse training for physical values like Safety or organizational values like Quality. However, many resist training for psychological values. "How can you teach people Trust or Respect for Others?" As Intel shows with Risk Taking, you can design a curriculum to support any value. Find role models for the behavior you want. Determine what these leaders do differently. Determine how they do it. Then train for what you have learned.

STEP FOUR: SET STANDARDS FOR VALUES

Even bright executives fall into flawed reasoning about standards for values. The distorted logic goes like this:

Proposition 1: The fastest way to drain enthusiasm for values is to write rules or standards.

Proposition 2: Because we have no standards, we don't know what effect values have on our numbers.

Guess what gets cut out in this company when there is a perceived crunch between values and the numbers?

Some managers don't like the word "standards." For many, it's too manufacturing oriented. For others, it's obsolete. Nomenclature doesn't really matter. Call them goals, measurements, targets. The important issue is whether you can answer two basic questions: What quantified results do you expect from values–centered acts? What results are you getting?

Isn't that applying a quantitative measurement to values? Certainly. If you can measure it, you can pay people for it. If you can pay people for it, you can get their attention. Whenever you hear values criticized as too "soft," this measurement step is missing.

Effective measurement links Complete Acts into integrated systems. AT&T Universal Card *daily* collects and analyzes more than 100 measurements for Customer Delight. The numbers form the basis for daily companywide and departmental indices. When the global numbers exceed target, everyone gets a bonus for the day. The bonus pays off only on total company indices, promoting cooperation among departments. The company constantly worries its measurement system might miss something important. To make doubly sure, customer service calls 5,000 people a month for follow–up interviews.

AT&T Universal Card tracks another value, Associate Delight, with similar dedication. An annual survey measures associates' perceptions about all values. Each month the company calls 150 of them at home for a confidential appraisal.

STEP FIVE: ALIGN STRUCTURE AND SYSTEMS WITH VALUES

At American Steel & Wire, Tom Tyrrell created innovative structures and systems to support values. It's more difficult to overhaul a long-established organization. Yet every time values prompt a realignment of structure and systems, managers get a bonus. Careful values reviews uncover overlapping responsibilities, duplication of efforts, bureaucratic bottlenecks. Every re-examined activity presents an opportunity to upgrade values. Can we introduce more Customer Focus here? Can we elevate Quality there? Can we redesign this sequence to promote more Empowerment?

Customers and employees will have new needs every day. Periodically, the company must review its values definitions of those needs and wants. Whenever there is a gap between expectation and performance, definitions must change. When definitions change, structure and systems must change with them. With values at its center, the living organization renews its structures and systems continuously.

STEP SIX: RECOGNIZE PERFORMANCE ON VALUES

The six steps draw their strength from different sources. Definition, standards, structure, and systems widen people's understanding of performance. These are largely mental processes, logical, deliberate, clear in their impact. Commitment, communication, and education release both mental and emotional responses. Learning new skills is primarily mental; accepting their value comes from the emotions.

Valerie Oberle at Disney University looks for transforming moments during Disney courses. She hopes to see mental acceptance grow into emotional enthusiasm. Such moments often occur when people put on a costume and mingle with the crowd. Oberle particularly remembers

119

one senior executive hired from another company. He began walking the property dressed as Tigger, the friend of Winnie-the-Pooh. As he strolled through the crowd waving, a young boy rushed up to him. "Oh, Tigger, Tigger, Tigger! It's me! It's me!" The executive melted as the youngster jumped up and down in joy.

In Disney jargon, he was sprinkled with "pixie dust." He had left the classroom with a mental understanding of a quality Disney experience. He returned with his mental concepts deepened by emotional knowledge.

Of all the steps, recognition draws its strength most purely from the emotions. Emotional resonance gives recognition its power to influence behavior. All human beings respond to sincere attention. Dale Carnegie made millions teaching people that simple truth.

True, some people distrust emotion. Some individuals say, "Forget the recognition, just give me $50 instead." They miss the point. The role of awards is not only to honor recipients, but to encourage others. Cash payments have their place but are more useful in recognizing quantitative achievements.

Recognition generates so much enthusiasm, some give it too much weight.

The CEO announces the new values definitions. She assigns a team to create awards expressing the values. So far, OK. However, sometimes the values effort stops there. No standards, no training, no realignment of structure and systems. Just a verbal expression of commitment at the top and extensive recognition at the bottom. Recognition cannot carry this load alone. Eventually, awards will ring hollow even to recipients.

How much recognition is too much? When was the last time you had too much sincere appreciation? Leaders like the late Sam Walton of Wal-Mart Stores, Inc., and Mary Kay Ash of

Mary Kay Corporation tapped into this secret early. They used frequent recognition of forgotten people to leverage small businesses into giants.

BECOMING A VALUES-DRIVEN LEADER

Look at business as a numbers game and you limit your potential. You operate on half power. True, there are always more opportunities in the numbers.

Today, you can give workers their own numbers every day. Figures that used to galvanize the monthly managers meeting can be available daily at the workbench. Statistical Process Control already has a strong foothold in manufacturing. Even there, there are still many opportunities. And SPC has barely gotten off the ground in the service, nonprofit, and government sectors. This is only one example of the benefits still available from quantitative management.

Yet in size of opportunity, values dwarf the numbers and will do so for years. Values unleash enthusiasm throughout the organization. They open doors for productivity, profitability, and growth. The six-step process offers a practical design for success and deeper meaning at work. Committed, the leader puts in place the six steps. The following chapters show how each step strengthens and expands the whole.

Values, the ever-receding challenge, always call forth greater effort. Greater effort requires steps that are higher, wider, stronger. With each strengthened step, the leader grows in knowledge and will. Colleagues look for reasons behind the leader's expanding mastery. However, the search leads to the obvious. Personal mastery grows from dedication to a commonplace miracle called values.

CHAPTER 10

IMPLEMENTING STEP ONE: COMMITMENT

The values you choose are immaterial, says American Express Chair Harvey Golub. Widespread acceptance and execution determine success. At Northwestern Mutual Life Insurance, doing "the right thing" is a habit. Values-driven execution is routine. Commitment links generations. On retirement, the Northwestern Mutual chair challenges successors to "keep the faith." This is the first of six chapters on implementing values.

The only reliable predictor of success with values is commitment at the top. At the top can mean the leader of a company, a division, or even a department. At any level, commitment must be visible and sincere.

Beyond an initial commitment, sustaining a value takes years of effort. Will that effort diffuse a company's focus? Will it distract attention from survival goals like sales, profits, and shareholder value? Any leader can only direct people's energies toward a few goals. With so many priorities, what drives experienced leaders to commit to values?

At the deepest level, assigning priorities is irrelevant. Leaders commit to values from the deepest wellspring of their personality.

Paul O'Neill is the first outsider to run the Aluminum Company of America. When O'Neill arrived at Alcoa's

122

Pittsburgh headquarters in 1987, he had already identified his priorities. High on that list was the value of Safety. Why focus on Safety in a company that already had the best safety record in its industry? To be injury free is something everyone wants. For O'Neill, that made safety "a good place to drive a stake into the ground."[1] Before the end of his first day, O'Neill had announced he wanted a goal of zero accidents.

In 1987 Alcoa had a lost workday rate of 1.87 per 200,000 work hours. (The U.S. manufacturing average was about 4.2.) By 1994 Alcoa had dropped its rate to .72, a 60 percent improvement. The goal remains zero. For O'Neill, there is an unmistakable link between the value of Safety and financial results. As he told The New York Society of Security Analysts, "if you can improve safety performance, your likelihood of being able to improve other things is much more substantial . . ." His emotional commitment came out in the same speech: ". . . if you can't deliver people safely home after their shift, your position as a leader ought to be in question."[2]

Marion Wade and Paul O'Neill committed from a belief about what is right. Others commit from a conviction that elevating values improves performance. Few are more coolly rational about a commitment to values than Harvey Golub, chairman and CEO of American Express.

The remarkable fivefold increase in profits at IDS under Harvey Golub was driven by an intense commitment to four values. For Golub, the test of values is impact on individual acts. Go to any organization and ask what their values are. You'll get an answer like Customer Service, or Quality, or Excellence. "That's immaterial," says Golub. "What's material is whether there is acceptance of those values, agreement about the implications of those values, and then execution."

HARNESSING ELECTRIC POWER AND MEDICINE

Two decades before Golub arrived at IDS, Earl E. Bakken committed to the values that shaped Medtronic, Inc., another of Minneapolis's fastest growing companies. In the best entrepreneurial tradition, Bakken and brother-in-law Palmer Hermundsie had opened their company in a garage. They had discovered a niche market—repairing medical electronic equipment for hospitals and research laboratories. Their sales in the first month totaled $8. Today the company averages $142 million a month.

Bakken discovered his niche hanging around the University of Minnesota teaching hospital. Although enrolled in the University School of Engineering, he couldn't stay away from the hospital. The idea of harnessing electrical power and medicine had fascinated him since he was 10. His defining moment occurred while watching the famous Boris Karloff *Frankenstein* movie. While others cowered in terror, Bakken watched awestruck as Dr. Frankenstein used electricity to reanimate a creature of assembled body parts. The movie shaped Bakken's life, permanently melding electricity and medicine in his imagination.

Doctors at University Hospital soon learned the young man asking all the questions was a graduate engineering student. Before long they were asking him questions. They needed advice on repairing their high-tech machines of the day, electric cardiographs. One request led to another, and in April 1949 Bakken quit school to go into business. His brother-in-law quit his job at a lumber yard to join him in the new firm with the futuristic name Medtronic, Inc. They created the name to symbolize the blending of medicine and electronics.

By the mid-1950s Medtronic was selling as well as servicing cardiographs. On service calls, Bakken became friendly with the young doctors pioneering new heart surgery procedures at the University of Minnesota. One day he found the doctors devastated by a setback. A young patient had died after surgery when the machine controlling his heartbeat stopped during a power failure. The most advanced medical technology had been undone by electrical failure. The doctors asked Bakken to design a battery power source for the machine. From this innovation, he patented the first wearable external pacemaker in 1957. In 1959, Medtronic helped develop the first implantable pacemakers.

Medtronic's pacemaker sales were soon roaring, leaving every other company component in disarray. "We were really up against it," Bakken recalls. "Every day, we were getting deeper and deeper in debt." His insurance agent called to congratulate him on his sales. He added that Medtronic's annual liability premium would now be $30,000 a year rather than $300. Bakken's bank was ready to foreclose. An investment corporation promised cash, but with strings. The corporation must have two seats on the Medtronic board. Another bank would provide a loan under the same conditions. Reluctantly, Bakken agreed. He said later the advice of the outsiders was even more important than their money.

They made him choose whether he wanted to be president or chief engineer. When he chose president, they insisted he write down what he wanted to achieve with his company. Focusing on every word, he created the six business principles of Medtronic's Mission that guide the company today. The Mission is a mixture of quantitative ("to make a fair profit on current operations") and qualitative ("the greatest possible reliability and quality in our products").

Medtronic today is the world's leading producer of pacing technology. It is also a developer and manufacturer of many other types of therapeutic medical devices, including heart valves and angioplasty catheters. Its sales top $1.7 billion. Its 10,600 employees serve medical communities in 120 countries. Everything has changed except the mission. It still appears in the annual report as Bakken wrote it 35 years ago. The only difference is that now Medtronic must translate it into seven languages.

PRESERVING VALUES

Golub renewed IDS's values. Bakken created Medtronic's mission. For others, commitment translates into preserving a legacy. Northwestern Mutual Life Insurance Company defined its values in 1888. The Milwaukee company's credo, adopted that year, gives explicit guidance. "The ambition of the Northwestern has been less to be large than to be safe; its aim is to rank first in benefits to policyholders rather than first in size." The statement also established the company's Vision: "preeminently the policyholders' company."

When Donald J. Schuenke became CEO of Northwestern Mutual in 1983, the insurance industry was in turmoil. "The world as we knew it was coming unglued," Schuenke recalls. The decade opened with inflation running at 13.5 percent. The prime rate topped out at 21 percent. Home mortgage rates exceeded 15 percent. Consumers were separating protection from investment. In record numbers they cashed in or borrowed against insurance policies to buy cheaper term policies and higher-yielding investments.

At Northwestern Mutual, policy loans reached 30 percent of the company's portfolio. In one day the company sold $300 million of common stock to meet expected demand for policy loans. "Whole life seemed as outdated as the leisure suit," says Schuenke, "and the career agent seemed as threatened as the snail darter or the spotted owl."

In response, many insurance companies cut their agent forces. They abandoned mature products. "Some," says Schuenke, "wandered into that dark forest called financial services." Bolstered by its credo and its traditions, Northwestern Mutual stood firm. For Schuenke, the key issue was simply making sure Northwestern could keep its promises. Universal Life policies, a seductive mixture of protection and high yields, were the rage of the industry. One publication called them "the hottest new product in decades." Another proclaimed them "the white knight of the insurance industry." To the consternation of many agents, Schuenke refused to offer Universal Life policies. While they would attract new sales, they were not a sound risk for policyholders.

"WE DID THE RIGHT THING"

Unburdened by extravagant promises, Northwestern could stay out of the high-risk, junk-bond market. Secure in its identity as an insurance company, it refused to scuttle its career agency system. While sticking primarily with life insurance, the company arranged for its agents to offer equity products, pension plans, and group life and health policies.

The result? In the past 10 years, the company's new business has more than doubled. Its insurance in force nearly tripled to $363 billion. Assets rose to more than $51 billion, up from $21 billion in 1985. The company holds the coveted AAA rating from all major rating agencies. It has led *Fortune*'s list of most admired insurance companies for 13 straight years. In contrast, Schuenke notes, some insurance companies "have laid off more people than we employ."

In 1994, Don Schuenke retired after more than 30 years at Northwestern Mutual. In his final appearance before the company's Association of Agents, he reflected on the lessons of his years as CEO:

> We must have done something right in the last 10 years, and what we did was simplicity itself. We did the right thing. . . . We took traditions passed down from leaders long gone and gave them new life.
>
> We maintained our integrity. Since its foundations, this company has been built on a bedrock of commitment to values. We didn't lose sight of that during the shifts and turns of the Eighties. Our values sustained us then . . . as they do now.

DIFFERENCES IN STYLE

Northwestern Mutual, ServiceMaster, Medtronic and IDS are all consciously values centered. They talk about their values. They make consistent efforts to align values with operations. Despite their common commitment, they differ in the style and emphasis of values implementation. One can't imagine Bill Pollard leading a company without values such as honoring God and developing people. At both American Express and IDS, Harvey Golub pushed for values that put clients and customers first. Don Schuenke so identified with the Northwestern credo that many saw him as its human embodiment. Medtronic's present CEO and president, Bill George, continues Earl Bakken's legacy by ensuring the mission is the driving force behind the company's strategy.

Harvey Golub displayed his commitment by launching a systematic review to align mission, values, and everyday practice. He pushed for rigorous measurement systems and standards. Pollard encourages alignment with values at ServiceMaster, yet he relies heavily on energizing people through personal visibility and persuasion. His phone line is always open to employees who spot a discrepancy between words and deeds on values. Schuenke reinforced the Northwestern values in large matters and small. He reflected his commitment by refusing to offer Universal Life and in the short personal notes he wrote to staff members. George set ambitious standards to improve Medtronic's already near perfect quality.

Earl Bakken, now in his 70s, lives in semiretirement. He still travels occasionally to meet with groups of Medtronic employees. At every meeting he tells why and how he wrote Medtronic's mission and distributes special medallions showing a recumbent figure rising and striding away in good health. Above the figure is the company slogan—Toward Full Life. Every employee receives a medallion as a reminder of the company's purpose.

Each approach is different. Which is right? Realistically, the answer must be that all of them are. Each approach works effectively in its environment. None would be as effective in the other environments. What matters most, however, goes beyond technique or approach. The common principle is *visible commitment at the top*. Each leader pays visible attention to defining, re-defining, and teaching the company values.

When commitment is strong, values lessons pass without interruption from one generation to the next. The example of his predecessors gave Schuenke strength in a troubled time. Another values-driven company, 3M, has passed down a value of Innovation for decades, continually renewing its creative spirit by listening to customers and employees. That tradition began with William L. McKnight, who joined the company in 1907 and retired as chairman in 1966. To this day, 3Mers talk of "Mr. McKnight" as the company's spiritual founder.

John T. Myser retired recently as vice president of 3M's commercial and consumer markets group. In his early days with the company, Myser met McKnight briefly. Throughout his career, he quoted McKnight's principles in speeches and talks with employees. He referred to the principles in making decisions. He hung one of McKnight's most quoted statements in his office:

Those men and women to whom we delegate authority and responsibility, if they are good people, are going to want to do their jobs in their own way. These are characteristics we want, and people should be encouraged as long as their way conforms to our general pattern of operations.

Myser showed his commitment in a highly visible way. One day every month he moved his office to one of his laboratories, plants, or sales offices. He cleared his calendar for the day, inviting anyone to come talk about any issue. On another day every month he made sales calls with one of his local sales representatives. Thirty years from now, another generation of 3M leaders will be putting their own spin on lessons they learned as young executives from John Myser.

In communicating commitment, definitions are as important as the values they describe. Values are guiding stars, but their definitions must evolve over time. Definitions that merely reflect society's general expectations become stale. They lose power to attract customers and inspire employees.

In the 1890s Sears, Roebuck & Company defined Customer Service as "Satisfaction Guaranteed or Your Money Back." That value definition started a sales revolution. In two decades Sears grew from a Midwestern catalog store to the world's largest retailer. Over time, that definition lost relevance. Copying Sears, other companies offered money-back guarantees. Once the guarantee was commonplace, customers looked for other definitions of Customer Service. They wanted speed, convenience, variety, price, easy access to follow-up service. When competitors redefined Customer Service, Sears lost the retailing crown.

HOW TO MAINTAIN A DYNAMIC CULTURE

Keeping the values message contemporary is a priority at 3M. By late 1991, when L.D. DeSimone took over as 3M's CEO, the company's values were already clear in principle and practice. 3M had formally defined the values in 1980 in a statement called Goals and Objectives. Still, after 12 years, the new chairman decided it was time to take another look. DeSimone established a committee to review the statement.

Human resources vice president Richard Lidstad, a 37-year 3M veteran, served on the committee. He expected the task would involve only fine-tuning. The committee took soundings at various levels and worked through three drafts. The third version easily cleared the company's executive conference, a quarterly session of the top 130 3M executives. The committee then sent what it thought was the final version to DeSimone.

To Lidstad's surprise, DeSimone revised the document, giving it a different structure. "Probably nobody is more important to corporate values than the CEO," says Lidstad, "so I liked his engagement in this process."

DeSimone presented the revised values statement at the next management conference. Lidstad was in the audience and later reflected on his feelings:

> I remember thinking "That's a good document. I'm proud of that work." I also can remember paying attention and not sensing a lot of reaction. . . . But as I thought about it, that's probably the right reaction. What we did was capture the reality. And, I think people were saying, "Yes, that's 3M all right."

The 3M process illustrates why definition discussions are so important. In the early meetings, Lidstad found "80 percent agreement" about the values on a committee composed of 3M veterans. However, the other 20 percent was significant. Lengthy discussions led to a more contemporary focus on the environment and diversity. The values embedded long ago by William McKnight are even stronger for those changes.

CALLING ON DEEPER RESOURCES

Even after more than a decade of retelling, the story of Johnson & Johnson's Tylenol crisis remains the most compelling example of the power of redefining values. General Robert Wood Johnson wrote the original J&J Credo in 1943, summing up the company's responsibilities to customers, employees, the community, and shareholders. Unusual in its day, or even in ours, the Credo says the company's *first* responsibility is to its customers.

By the 1970s, J&J Chairman James Burke felt the Credo had become more an honored artifact than a living code. In 1975, he decided to challenge the document, a process that took four years. First, 28 executives from J&J debated Burke's challenge— leave the Credo alone, change it, or get rid of it. While no one wanted to get rid of it, everyone wanted changes. Managers continued the challenge process in their own companies. Even today, managers go through a similar process. (For a discussion of this phenomenon, see Chapter 18.)

In 1982, seven people died in Chicago of cyanide poisoning after taking a J&J product, Extra-Strength Tylenol Capsules. The case is still not solved. Johnson & Johnson immediately re-called all 31 million Tylenol bottles at a cost of $100 million. A few weeks later, the company decided to relaunch the product in triple-sealed, tamper-proof packages. Contrary to experts' predictions, the product regained 90 percent of its market share within a year. Today, Tylenol remains by far the market leader.

Jim Burke, retired as J&J chairman, says the challenge process shaped J&J's response. After the poisoning, J&J people made hundreds of critical decisions on the run. The driving force be-hind those decisions was "the Credo, which had become a liv-ing document for all of us through the challenge process." The right decision and the practical decision were identical. "We re-ally had no alternative than to do what we did."

Commitment is the first building block of the values-driven company. With it, everything is possible; without it, nothing.

CHAPTER 11

IMPLEMENTING STEP TWO:
COMMUNICATE!
COMMUNICATE! COMMUNICATE!

Leaders communicate values best by example and definition. Medtronic CEO Bill George redefines near-perfect quality by asking for a tenfold improvement. Written values definitions speed communication throughout a company. Values start to live when every unit writes definitions for itself. At Levi Strauss they aim for definitions from every employee.

Leaders communicate values by example, by definition, and through consistent reinforcement.

Nothing substitutes for visible example. If Punctuality is the value, the leader must be on time. At Disney, Showmanship is one of four values. Every senior executive will pick up a candy wrapper from the ground. Even the newest cast member knows that a discarded candy wrapper is "poor Show." Senior Medtronic executives stand next to physicians in operating theaters, watching their products during heart surgery. Don Schuenke's constancy during the tumultuous 1980s inspired imitation throughout Northwestern Mutual.

For the values-driven leader there is little margin for error. At times we all tend to dismiss our faults as lovable idiosyncracies, but the values-driven leader cannot suffer this delusion. A value-linked deficiency is more than an idiosyncracy; it is an explicit threat to the whole process. This doesn't mean values-driven leaders always must be perfect. It means they always must be conscious of the example they set.

The leader also communicates through definition. Effective definition begins with a question. What do these values mean to us now? Words such as "Customer Service" or "Diversity" describe a general route. They gain strength from specificity. Management's definitions are useful, but the best definitions involve everyone. Management defines values for the company or unit. Then individual subunits define the values for themselves. Don't values derive strength from a common definition? Consistency has its place. However, nothing substitutes for challenging every unit, every individual, to define the values for themselves.

AN UNCONVENTIONAL RETREAT

At Levi Strauss, values redefinition began at an unconventional retreat. For this San Francisco company, the challenge was to reinterpret its heritage in contemporary themes. Levi Strauss & Company is the world's largest manufacturer of branded apparel. Its trademark ranks with The Coca-Cola Company, Disney, and McDonald's in a small group that enjoys worldwide recognition.

Lists of socially responsible companies always include Levi Strauss. In 1995, it ranked first in the apparel field on *Fortune's* most-admired list. At the time of the 1985 retreat, the 135-year-old company had been back in private hands for just a year. The Haas family, descendants of the original founder Levi Strauss, had taken the company public in 1969. In 1984, the family repurchased the company in a leveraged buyout. For CEO Robert D. Haas, great-great-grandnephew of the founder, the LBO was a fresh beginning. Free of quarterly reports to Wall Street, he adopted a leadership style more in keeping with company traditions.

A year after the buyout, a group of ethnic minorities and women managers asked Haas for a private meeting. The managers complained of invisible barriers blocking their careers. In response, Haas organized the retreat. Ten senior managers, all white men, each sat with a woman or minority manager from their work group. The senior managers believed they were doing a good job of addressing discrimination issues. The company was an acknowledged leader in hiring minorities. Females were moving up, although slowly.

Indignant rebuttals from people in their own groups caught the senior managers off guard. People cited examples of discrimination. They noted that attitudes were more important than hiring numbers. After two and one-half days, the meeting ended with general agreement that Levi Strauss still had a long journey to true Diversity.

Between 1985 and 1988, 16 more sessions paired senior managers with women and minorities. The discussions dug deeper into discrimination and hidden attitudes. In 1987, Diversity was included in the company's Aspiration Statement.

INCREASING QUALITY TENFOLD

Communication by definition often means reinterpreting existing values. The entrepreneur is the first link in a chain of values leadership. Eventually that chain must cross generations. William George, a former Honeywell executive, joined Medtronic as CEO in 1989. Following Earl Bakken's example, he began to observe operations and learn from the surgeons who were working with his company's products. He quickly absorbed Medtronic's commitment to Quality. "Seeing it firsthand is very different from reading a report," George says.

How far can you take Quality in a company with near-perfect reliability? George wants to test the outer limits. He has redefined Quality by challenging his company to lift its Quality performance tenfold. George exemplifies the challenges of communicating a strong value at a higher level. New definition means new targets. Some units measure defects per million. Others watch customer response time. Measurement goes down to the operator on the floor who keeps her own control charts. Human resources measures employee turnover. In every case, the numbers start from good to exceptional. In every case, the goal is a tenfold improvement.

Effective definition cascades from level to level. The cascading value gains freshness with each definition. It becomes more specific. It relates the value to the work of a specific unit.

To follow up on Bill George's Quality challenge, Walter Cuevas of Medtronic's tissue valve unit at Irvine, California, brought his team together to define new Quality requirements. Cuevas's Medtronic heart valves team evolved and defined four supporting values they call "the four Cs": Customer, Compliance, Consistency, and Creativity. Detailed action plans flow from each definition. There is an ergonomics plan under Consistency to improve the flexibility of chairs and microscopes used by workers.

Harvey Ernest read Desi DeSimone's restatement of the 3M values. Ernest is manager of sales and marketing operations at 3M's Federal Systems Department in Washington, D.C. Ernest is proud of what he calls "the 3M identity." He recalls working as a sales rep for the company in Mississippi. "I would call on customers wearing a coat and tie every day." Many days topped 100 degrees. Competitors wore short-sleeved shirts. "I wanted to project an image that said, 'We're doing business. I don't care if it's 100 degrees. I'm coming in to do business, not to play volleyball.' "

He used the 3M values statement to reinvigorate that identity within his unit. He took key words from the 3M statement. He added words that had special meaning to him. He challenged his senior people to take the words and create a values statement for their unit. A skillful rewriting produced two paragraphs of principles. Read vertically, the first letters of each line spell the unit's overarching value—Results Oriented.

Levi Strauss & Company is carrying the definition process down to the individual worker. Like many companies, Levi Strauss published its values and waited for change. Nothing happened for nearly a year. James Schroth, former manager of corporate initiatives on values and strategy, told me: "Senior management came to us in 1988, and said 'How come we're not seeing the changes?' " In response, Schroth's group developed a core curriculum to communicate the Aspiration Statement. In 1989, Schroth launched the first "Leadership Week" course. It targeted not only leaders, but all 32,000 Levi Strauss employees. "The idea here is everyone is a leader," said Schroth.

By the end of the session, participants have developed their personal statements of Vision and Core Values. "It's an invitation for people to look at what they value, what's important to them," Schroth told me. "Then they check to see whether their statement is consistent with the company's values. Usually people say, 'Yes. Those are my values up on the wall.' " By the end of 1994, nearly 7,000 Levi Strauss employees had completed the leadership course. Follow-up sessions of the core curriculum deal specifically with Diversity and Ethics.

THE LEADER'S ANNOUNCEMENT

Leaders set the tone for values communication in their first announcement. The context should be Performance, Performance, Performance. From the beginning, the leader should link values and operating results. The announcement must balance the excitement of something new with an emphasis on continuity. Properly selected values grow out of a company's history and current challenges. As Richard Lidstad felt when Desi DeSimone presented the revised 3M values, the audience should feel "That's right, that's our company." Finally, the announcement should link the values with the organization's future success. Again, the right values will flow logically into the organization's current prospects and concerns.

For many employees, the values announcement is a subtle threat: "How will my behavior measure up to that new standard?" In unveiling values, effective leaders project empathy for those feelings. Here's Robert Haas's approach:

When I talk to employees about the development of the Aspiration Statement, I describe the stark terror I felt when I took over this company, just having turned 43 years old. . . . I had no bold plan of action. I knew values were important but didn't have the two granite tablets that I could bring down from Mount Sinai to deliver to the organization. I talk about how alone I felt as a senior manager and how tough it is to be held up as a paragon to the organization.[1]

Modern technology enables any leader to engage in a values dialogue with people throughout the company. Videotapes or broadcasts by satellite can carry the leader's message. The announcement also should be available in written form. The leader can invite everyone to comment via e-mail. Since values touch an organization's core issues, a lively discussion is sure to follow.

THE LEADER'S FOLLOW-UP COMMUNICATION

After the initial announcement, leaders should reinforce values in action and speech, taking care to link high-impact decisions with values.

In the 1980s Levi Strauss & Company shifted about half its manufacturing to contract plants overseas. Like most multinationals, Levi Strauss at first paid little attention to working conditions in these plants, as the contract laborers were not on its direct payroll. In the early 1990s, however, the core curriculum got people talking about values. The hard questions wouldn't go away. To what extent did the values in the Aspiration Statement apply to workers in the company's contract plants? In early 1992, Levi Strauss adopted guidelines for hired contractors overseas, later halting production in Burma and China in response to questionable labor practices.

Often, management no sooner identifies values than a conspicuous choice challenges its good intentions. This phenomenon occurs so often, I have learned to expect it. When you resolve to lose weight, a friend is sure to ask you to dinner in a gourmet restaurant. Life always tests our new aspirations.

A NEW LANGUAGE

You know something new has caught on when it enters a company's vocabulary. Visitors are strangers until they can translate a company's initials and code words. Communication is effective when values-linked words become part of this language. Customers are "guests" at Disney. Employees are "cast members." In many values-driven companies the word "boss" is disappearing. "Team leader" is a popular replacement. Unconscious acceptance of such terms signals acceptance of values. Corporate publications need to reflect values early. Annual reports and company newspapers should pick up values themes and reinforce them regularly. Long-service ceremonies should honor people not just for their length of service but their commitment to the company's culture and values.

First impressions count in any communication. After adopting values, a company should review materials used in hiring and orientation. Both ServiceMaster and Disney show videos about their values during the hiring process. Most orientation programs concentrate on benefits and regulations. Values provide a welcome and inspirational addition. However, before going too far, ensure that middle managers who will lead these recruits also receive values training. Otherwise, enthusiastic recruits report for work only to hear: "They told you *what*? Let me explain how it really works around here."

COMMUNICATION TOOLS

The chief communicator of values is always the leader of the unit. Example is the leader's primary communication tool, followed by the stories the leader chooses to tell. We all love stories, particularly stories about a champion overcoming dangers. Most successful leaders are good storytellers. However, many leaders do not fully understand the force their stories carry.

Do their tales center on the salesperson who outsold the competition? The clerk who went to the extreme to help a customer in distress? The computer support team that brought out a complex new application ahead of schedule? Each of these stories conveys support for a different value.

Leaders habitually pick up and retell stories from within their organizations. The values-driven leader selects stories that reinforce the company's values. In the early days of any values process, leaders usually make time to talk about the values. CEO trips to spread the word are a common follow-up to initial announcements. For the alert CEO, listening is even more important than talking. If the values reflect the company's core, many people are already living them. Articulation of the values is formal recognition of what they are already doing. The leader should find these people and add their stories to his or her repertoire.

A second opportunity also involves listening. Raising consciousness of values initially highlights gaps between aspiration and performance. These gaps are opportunities to reinforce the values. Positive actions soon after publication of values reinforce the commitment of both leader and team.

Values-driven leaders use unexpected events to reinforce values. At Toro, Ken Melrose invited a group of managers to his office without explanation. The managers quickly realized he had invited all members of a team that had failed in a costly innovation. Expecting a rebuke, they found the CEO hosting a party in their honor. "We are here to celebrate a good try, an attempt to do something innovative," he told them. "It didn't work. So what? Go back to your jobs and try again." With this simple action, Melrose enabled these managers to retain their enthusiasm. More important, he created a company legend to reinforce Toro's value of Innovation.

NEW COMMUNICATION TECHNIQUES AND VALUES

Managers can deepen values communication through use of new group discussion methods. Dialogue and Open Space are two such techniques. The late nuclear physicist David Bohm is the father of Dialogue in its present form. Bohm noted the word "Dialogue" comes from the Greek words "*dia logos,*" meaning "through meaning." "Discussion," Bohm said, comes from the same roots as "percussion," suggesting a clash of ideas. Dialogue aims to give people a periodic alternative to the constant testing and battling of ideas.

Leaderless Dialogue groups operate with guidelines different from regular business meetings. Participants work to listen with open minds, to test their own assumptions, to follow the trail of an agendaless conversation. There are no goals or minutes. The group temporarily suspends its hierarchy.

Values make an excellent launch point for a Dialogue group. Begin with a values-focused, open-ended question. What do we mean by Respect for Each Other? What's holding us back in Customer Service? Why can't we get our Quality right? Dialogue groups strengthen teamwork by opening unexpected paths for group learning. Dialoguing about values adds a new and deeper level of meaning to other values communication.[2]

Open Space Technology is the creation of consultant Harrison Owen, a former Anglican priest. Owen discovered that he learned more during conference coffee breaks than during the regular programs. That led to an unorthodox question: Why not have a conference entirely of coffee breaks? Owen and those he has trained have created Open Space meetings in the hundreds, sometimes for thousands of people.

The process is amazingly simple. Before the meeting, the facilitator researches to learn a central issue weighing on the group's mind. Usually that issue is values related. A typical example: How can we raise the spirit of Customer Service in our organization? The company then invites people to attend an Open Space Technology meeting on this issue. Attendance must be voluntary. There is no agenda or leader after the first few minutes. As in Dialogue, participants ignore hierarchy.

At the start of the meeting, the facilitator asks the group for discussion topics on the central issue. Volunteers suggest topics of interest to them. They write their topic on a piece of newsprint and post it on a wall. Anyone who wants to discuss that particular subject signs up on the newsprint. Soon they have filled the wall with topics and self-selected groups. The groups quickly negotiate times for sessions, creating a schedule for the conference.

Each group brings back a written summary of its discussion. Managers distribute these comments and recommendations to all participants, often right at the conference. The managers who sponsored the conference review the record for follow-up actions.

Open Space offers a promising method to accelerate values communications. Normally, companies introduce values slowly through hierarchical levels. Open Space Technology shortcuts the normal approach. It immediately taps into the energy flowing around values at many levels. It creates almost instant plans for improvement. Best of all, it gathers volunteers in cross-functional teams around issues that most concern them. If management decides to act, these are the logical teams for follow-up.[3]

Whatever the method, effective communication is a primary building block in launching values-driven companies. Beyond the launch, communication for the values-driven company is an ever-expanding challenge. Through example, by creating heros and champions, through rewards, through recognition, and, above all, by constant reminders, values-driven leaders communicate values. At the most developed level, everyone in the company considers the values her or his personal credo. Then values communicate invisibly. When newcomers ask about them, they simply hear: "That's the way we do things around here."

CHAPTER 12

IMPLEMENTING STEP THREE: EDUCATING CHAMPIONS

Values training must be specific. Case studies must be real. Courses must be interactive. Trainers must acknowledge tensions in pursuing conflicting values. To convey reality, introduce Values Role Models. They illustrate how to make values live, in this company, at this time. Intel uses these principles in teaching an apparently unteachable value—Risk Taking.

Forty years ago, executives doubted you could train people to be managers. Some people, the argument went, were "born leaders." What use was training to them? As for the rest, some would pick up the knack and others wouldn't. Why make a science out of teaching the obvious? Fortunately, that attitude has faded.

However, suggest training for values and you're back in the 1950s. A senior training executive once told me there was no useful purpose in training for values. "We need to find role models for the values," she said. "Then we'll get people to imitate them." She was right in her enthusiasm for role models. However, she overlooked the opportunity to use role models as a template for training.

Formalized training is necessary to elevate values in any company. People need to understand the values. Even more, they need the skills to translate values into action. Announcing a set of words as "Our Values" is only a first step. Without training, any values process degenerates into a flavor of the month.

Quality and Customer Service, the two most developed values processes, introduce training early. However, the same principle applies to any value. Without training, people wander around professing the value themselves and complaining that others ignore it. They wonder why nothing significant is happening. After a few months of this, the company is ready for the next fad to solve its problems.

TEACHING RISK TAKING

I got interested in Intel when I learned they were trying to teach people to be better risk takers. If ever there was an apparently unteachable value, this was it. However, only 20 years ago managers said you couldn't teach Quality. That was the "I'll know it when I see it" era. Now we teach Quality, Customer Service, or Teamwork every day. Tomorrow we will teach values like Trust, Respect for Others, or Risk Taking with equal ease.

Intel is a no-nonsense, results-oriented company. It competes for survival in computer chips, one of the world's toughest markets. Despite some slips, it usually wins. The $11.5 billion company supplies the microprocessors in about 80 percent of all PCs sold. Results Orientation is another of its six values.

Values training survives at Intel not because it's a fad or because the human resources people think it's a good idea. There are plenty of other priorities in a company where overcommitment is a way of life. Intel holds every manager accountable for quantified goals every quarter. A zero-based budgeting system ranks the importance of every project. Values training must make the cut in such an environment.

DRIVERS BEHIND ALL SUCCESS

Laurie Price, who became a values champion at Intel, explains why:

Many companies in our industry have access to the same resources. We're not any smarter. But, there is something about us that is helping us to be more successful. And, we believe it's our culture, the way we operate, the way we do things. So, the more we can encourage this behavior . . . the more we believe we'll continue to be a success.

Price makes a telling point. Any company's success rests on the strength of its culture. At the heart of that culture are fully or partially defined values. Well-defined or not, values are drivers behind all success. Yet, in a period of rapid growth or crisis, stressed executives can easily shove values aside.

From its start in 1968, Intel dazzled the industry with one chip revolution after another. Early on, the company adopted a Customer Service value. Then came the chip market's feverish boom, followed by its bust in the early 1980s.

In 1985, Intel lost $180 million. CEO Andrew Grove had to downsize many facilities and lay off one-third of the company's workforce. He pulled the plug on the DRAM memory chip business that Intel had invented. Grove then gambled everything on the development of another Intel innovation—the microprocessor. The gamble paid off when the market exploded.

The scare encouraged serious soul-searching behind the numbers. The quantified side of the ledger identifies lost market share. It doesn't always identify root causes. A failure to focus on the customer? A drop in quality? A lack of trust in management? Whatever the cause, its roots lie in a missing or forgotten value.

To get accurate answers, information from customers is important. However, market data usually confirms only what employees already know. A first step in discovering a gap in values is accurate, confidential feedback from employees.

At Intel, a 1988 employee survey revealed problems in the understanding and implementation of Intel's original nine values. Most employees could not complete a question asking them to name the values.

TOO MANY VALUES

"We learned we had too many values," says Christine Oster, manager of human resources research and development. Senior management responded by paring the list to six:

- Risk Taking
- Quality
- Discipline
- Customer Orientation
- Results Orientation
- Great Place to Work

The six revised values formed a quarter of a four-color poster distributed to all Intel facilities. The poster linked the values to three other definitions of success—mission, objectives, and strategy. The values identified qualities that were always aspirations at Intel. With the poster, management recommitted itself to the aspiration.

Intel launched an intensive one-week management training program, one component of which stressed the importance of role modeling the values. The course rolled out by level, from seniors to supervisors. At each program, senior executives made presentations linking the values to Intel's success. The company reshaped its employee orientation program around the redefined values. By 1991, Intel was ready to survey employees again on values.

Second-round surveys focus more sharply on issues arising from performance on values. Discussions in the training courses heighten awareness. People see more clearly the discrepancies between prose and performance. Repeat surveys can probe issues more deeply. Focus groups also can help.

Second-round scores that don't show big improvements often dampen enthusiasm unnecessarily. Performance on some values inevitably lags others. If managers for years have overstressed employees while driving for better customer service, it will take time to restore balance. That doesn't mean that efforts are unsuccessful. Publicizing values renewal inevitably makes people critical of performance they used to accept as normal.

A SECOND LOOK

In the 1991 survey, the gaps between intent and performance were far clearer. Risk Taking, particularly, proved difficult to understand. Responses, says Oster, ran like this: "My managers mean well but they inadvertently punish me when I take a risk and fail. Then I feel like I shouldn't do it again."

Oster and her R&D team went beyond the numbers in the survey. They grouped and analyzed 16,000 individual comments. After that analysis, they knew what to do next.

"I get the big picture about Results Orientation," said a typical comment. "But what does it mean to be Results Oriented?" Without definition, values cannot translate into action. Intel had bypassed that step. The message came back loud and clear: What do you want us to *do*?

In response, Intel's Values Task Force identified five specific behaviors associated with each value. The Risk Taking definition identifies these behaviors:

- Embrace change
- Challenge the status quo
- Listen to all ideas and viewpoints
- Encourage and reward informed risk taking
- Learn from our successes and mistakes

Even at this level of detail, people needed more explanation. That's why the process stalls at this point in so many companies. By this time people are more aware of the apparent tension among values. At Intel, for example, how do you balance Risk Taking with Quality? Management must address such issues through communication and training.

In addition, employees need tools to look at themselves as well as others. As one manager in another company put it: "I don't mind that our people carry around a magnifying glass. However, I also want them to carry a mirror in the other hand."

Intel distributed a poster with the five behaviors for each value. Oster's group next developed a values self-assessment survey with questions relating to all values. The survey has since evolved and is now included as part of a 360-degree core-management survey used around the world.

For example, under one risk-taking behavior, "Encourage and reward informed risk taking," the assessment asks employees to rate themselves and have others rate them on how often they do the following:

- Fail to clearly define expectations and limits
- Reward only successful activities
- Communicate that failure is not tolerated
- Provide insufficient time for implementation
- Criticize employees for preapproved risks that fail
- Insist on clear ownership and accountability

Consciously elevating values begins by raising commitment, definition, and training. Somewhere near the end of this phase, management needs to send a second and deeper message of commitment.

LOOKING FOR ROLE MODELS

This is when people start looking for role models. Is there anyone around here who really is living this stuff? Role models embody the organization's best aspirations. They show that it is possible to balance the tension among values. Their example reinforces the link between the values and personal success.

For Risk Taking, Intel began with a distinct advantage: very visible role models at the top. The founders, after all, had left secure jobs at Fairchild Semiconductor to start the company. Innovation was in the company's DNA from the beginning.

148

CEO Grove's current strategy involves risk in both established and new markets. He wants to keep PC users and makers captive by continually introducing faster, cheaper chips. There's a risk, of course. Are corporate users willing to install new generations of PCs as rapidly as Grove wants to produce them? At the same time, Grove is making Intel a brand name among the consumers and home office users, a market he believes will continue to grow rapidly. Intel is investing billions in this double risk. When Grove talks about Risk Taking, he carries credibility.

Christine Oster put out word that she was looking for role models. She wanted people known for the specific behaviors identified on the redefined values. For Risk Taking, she and her staff interviewed more than 25 role models. Some effective people had trouble explaining what they did. "I don't view myself as a risk taker," one widely recognized role model told her. "I just do my job." Oster did not settle for that answer.

We all do our jobs every day. Sometimes we work at a routine level, sometimes at a higher level. People recognized as role models are working at that higher level more of the time. They behave differently. This is the key to using role models effectively. Find out what they do when they work at a higher level, then teach others how to copy their behavior.

Oster found discrete behaviors and skills among the role models. Risk Taking role models, for example, were superior planners. Oster's R&D group next developed new training kits for individuals and teams. The top priority again was Risk Taking, published first with a separate training kit of its own. A kit on the other five values and the dilemmas inherent in balancing the six values followed six months later.

The Risk-Taking kit features 10 items, including individual and team exercises, advice on specific problems, and a list of additional resources. There are also written and video interviews with the role models. The videos reinforce the central message: others are doing it, you can too.

MOVING INTO LINE OPERATIONS

In large organizations, formal values initiatives usually start at headquarters. However, they come alive only when line divisions take ownership. In the early stages, formal programs depend on the enthusiasm of the corporate staff. Line operations commonly salute the new initiative and then go back to work, waiting for a signal that this one is for real. At this stage, corporate must be consistent and insistent with its message even when few outside of headquarters are listening. In time, innovative divisions will decide to be role models for one or more of the values.

At Intel the first divisional role model appeared about a year after publication of the first values poster. In 1990 Ken Fine, an Intel vice president and one of Oster's values role models, became general manager of the semiconductor products group. Fine called the first planning meeting of the group's senior managers in Denver—a central location for a team that came from four states. Many of the senior executives were meeting for the first time. They came from different divisions with different operating styles. One group, from a unit recently purchased from RCA, had little understanding of the Intel values or culture.

To pull his team together, Fine turned to one of the six Intel values. He set a goal to make the group "a multi-site model of a Great Place to Work." Judy Mente, the group's senior human resources manager, emerged from the Denver meeting as divisional "owner" of the Great Place to Work value. Mente assembled a team of volunteers, who selected strategies to implement the Strategic Value. Among the strategies: identify and promote role models for the value.

OWNING A PROCESS

Laurie Price, a manager at the group's Princeton, N.J., facility, became "owner" of the role-model strategy. "Owner," Intel-speak for having primary responsibility, is an apt word in a values process. Before you can own a value or a value process, you must first fully understand it. Early on, Price and her team took Intel values behaviors and translated them into the work of the semiconductor group.

Your first job as an Intel "owner" is to recruit people willing to be co-owners with you. Price sent out an electronic message to 600 people asking for volunteers. There were only a handful of responses. Disappointed, she excused her colleagues by saying, "Everyone here is 120 percent committed."

Another explanation is possible. Even with senior management's endorsement, people were still waiting for signs this was a high profile effort. Price was also at another disadvantage: no one was sure at this point what role modeling the values actually meant.

Price pushed ahead, gathering volunteers as the project took shape. She contacted others working on Intel role models and training. She interested Christine Oster, gaining access to the R&D group's research. She told Ken Fine and Judy Mente she wanted to create a one-day course on the Intel values. She committed to produce a pilot within six months, though no one on the team had experience in designing training courses. Their lack of experience actually gave them a fresh outlook.

No Off-the-Shelf Modules

Values training can't use off-the-shelf modules. Courses must be very specific to the experience of the participants. Case studies must be real. The course must be interactive, tapping fully into the participants' experience and enthusiasm, not just their minds. Trainers must acknowledge the tensions in living up to conflicting values. That means avoiding step-one, step-two, step-three solutions.

At adjournment, people must understand the values and how they apply. They must see practical opportunities to elevate their own performance. For years Intel people had joked: What if Andy Grove unexpectedly asked you to name the six values? Her team, says Price, built their course around that question and two related challenges: Do you know what the values mean? How does your behavior match them?

Price shrewdly used the course as a demonstration model for the semiconductor group's new digital video interactive technology, which enables a trainer to put a whole course, including videos and overhead transparencies, on a single computer disk. Using a mouse, the trainer can easily cut back and forth across course material, following up on participants' interests.

For example, trainers used a cartoon of a circus seal balancing six balls, one for each value. When a question came up about tension among the values, the trainer, with one click, could bring up the cartoon on a screen. Humor reinforced the importance of balance.

REINFORCING BALANCE

Price's training course reinforced balance in other ways. In one exercise, one team had to argue a perfect Quality position while another took a pure Results position. They learned "they couldn't stay in one position," says Price. "They balanced values naturally because it was stupid not to." The point was "hey, look, you're already doing it!"

The course dealt with the boss who didn't support the values. Participants learned several coping strategies, including how to appeal for help at a higher level. Price trained senior managers to teach the course. "I'm not very good at some of these values," confessed one manager. "Use it," replied Price. "Show them that you know it's hard."

Attendance at the course topped Price's 80 percent target ahead of schedule. Pre- and post-testing showed far greater awareness of the values plus some significant improvements in performance. Most satisfying of all, Intel University added the course to its curriculum of offerings for all employees.

Price's team recommended that Fine's group sponsor a Role Model Advocate award. Anyone can recommend anyone else, but then the selection process is rigorous. The award goes to just three or four people a year. It recognizes outstanding balance among the six values, not just outstanding performance on one or two. Recipients can accept the award only if they agree to be outspoken advocates as well as role models for all the values.

Laurie Price was one of the first winners. She attributes this to feeling compelled to elevate her performance when she became involved with the project. "I'd be in a room and people would say, 'Oops, Laurie's here. We need to make sure we're behaving well.' "

Such, even in jest, is the power of a values champion.

CHAPTER 13

IMPLEMENTING STEP FOUR: THE ABOVE-AND-BEYOND QUALITY STANDARD

Visitors search for the secret behind "the Disney Way." The people who make it happen say there is no secret. Just a commitment to Mission and Core Values plus common sense. Disney communicates common sense through measurable standards. Then everybody is empowered to ignore the standards if that's what it takes to exceed guests' expectations.

Values define Quality. How does a business define Customer Service? Is it Speed? Courtesy? Cleanliness? How does it define quality treatment of employees? Individual development? Commitment to Diversity? Safety? Identify its values, grasp how seriously the company pursues those values, and you will know how the organization defines Quality.

Seriously pursued, values are the above-and-beyond standard for Quality. Everything an organization does to commit to values, to define them, to educate for them, must aim to empower people to go beyond the words.

Thirty-six thousand people work at Walt Disney World in Orlando, Florida. From the most senior executive to the most junior street sweeper, all have completed the two-day Disney Traditions course. All of them understand the company's exacting and detailed rules. Any of them can tell you the four values that produce a quality experience at Disney—Safety, Courtesy, Show, and Efficiency.

Disney trains everybody in the mechanics of his or her job. Skilled, experienced trainers also teach them the detailed actions that create values-driven performance. Yet the training courses, the rules, even the four values merely lay the foundation. The above-and-beyond value standard is to take whatever action you have to do to exceed the guests' expectations. The training, the regulations, the skills are merely tools. The basic Disney standard is that guests visiting The Magic Kingdom will experience only perfectly complete individual acts.

"WHAT A FUN PLACE TO WORK!"

Disney World is an ideal place to watch core values transform ten thousand very routine acts into high performance. Visitors often think it's easier for Disney. After all, Disney has Mickey, Minnie, and Donald. "What a fun place to work!" is a common comment. True, there are exciting activities every minute. There is the atmosphere of a perpetual carnival. Cast members appear genuinely enthusiastic. They are always eager to share their enjoyment. What interesting work, visitors think. Imagine earning a good paycheck while having fun.

Fun? On summer days the temperature in Orlando rises above 95 degrees. Cast members in heavy polyester costumes must amuse hot-under-the-collar customers waiting in long lines to enter attractions. Demand at soft-drink stands is non-stop for hours.

A vacation atmosphere? Disney people work hardest when others play. Christmas, for example, is one of the year's busiest days.

A good paycheck? Most cast members are hourly workers, paid at competitive wages.

Interesting work? Some 30,000 of the 36,000 cast members work at the same physically monotonous tasks necessary at any resort. They wait tables, stuff hot dogs into rolls, mop floors, clean hotel rooms, work around the clock in a humid laundry.

A Mission to Make You Happy

Despite these deterrents, everywhere at Disney you can feel the energy of a values-driven culture. That culture has one mission: to make you happy. Cast members smile at you, take the time to speak pleasantly, volunteer to help you. Ask anyone a question and you will get an answer, usually with extra information. Meeting an openly disgruntled employee is a rarity. Spotless floors and smiling faces convey an atmosphere of high morale and fierce dedication.

Maintaining this atmosphere 365 days a year is as difficult for Disney as it is for anyone else. Yet people come to Orlando from all over the world to learn the secrets behind "the Disney Way." Disney people smile at this curiosity. To experienced cast members, the Disney Way consists only of unwavering commitment to Mission and Core Values plus common sense.

Everyone from senior executives to Christmas holiday part-timers learns about the Disney Way at the company's compulsory Traditions course. Course trainers are on part-time assignment from their regular duties. Every year Disney University selects 20 to 30 people from the 300 cast members who apply for these prestigious, one-year, part-time jobs. Their enthusiasm is contagious. Their zestful stories and examples illustrate just how hard Disney works to make people happy. Their message is that the techniques are, indeed, only common sense. Rather, it's Core Values and Mission that generate the Pixie Dust, Disney slang for enthusiastic commitment.

Barbara Farfan tells a story you hear frequently at Walt Disney Company. "I actually had a career going in Birmingham, Alabama. . . . This thought kept nagging in the back of my head: you've always wanted to work for Walt Disney, why don't you just do it?" She packed and moved to Orlando without a job, determined to work for the Walt Disney Company. Like most recruits, she started at the bottom, as a hostess at Disney's MGM Studios theme park. After about a year, she transferred to bell services at the Grand Floridian Beach Resort. When I spoke with her, she was in training to work at the front desk while working part-time as a Disney University trainer.

In addition to training new hires at Disney University, Harriet Rejonis teaches educational programs on Discovery Island. Every day she picks up a new group of 10- to 15-year-old youngsters, some glad to be there, some not. Working alone, she has six hours to keep her charges safely together, administer any required medication, teach them something, and give them a good time. All the while, she is carrying around "forty-seven pounds of cameras and other gear" on a humid Florida summer day.

Like Farfan, Louie Gravance always wanted to work for Walt Disney Company. He moved to Orlando without a job in 1989. In an audition of 1,000 people, he won one of 15 jobs as an improvisational comic actor. Gravance plays a fictional, eccentric millionaire, Shelby Mayer. Shelby is in Hollywood in 1947 determined to prove that with enough money, he can make anyone a star. As Shelby, Gravance roams the property looking for candidates, improvising conversations with guests. To expand his repertoire, Gravance keeps auditioning for other roles. On his second try, he won a role as a Traditions assistant.

"THIS IS WHAT I WANT TO DO"

On the first day of the Traditions course, the trainers' goal is to explain the company's history and values. There is an important subtext, however. The trainers want to tap in on what Gravance calls the "emotional tie that people have with Disney." Traditions assistants use their own personalities, stories, and above all, their sincerity to seize the enthusiasm of the new hires. As Rejonis explains: "We have to get them to think, 'Yes, this is what I want to do.' Even if they are seasonal cast members, we want them to understand their role in the show."

Everyone has a role. For some it's Mickey Mouse or Snow White. For others it is preparing food. "They are not flipping hamburgers," adds Rejonis. "They are food hosts and hostesses and they are going to be serving their guests."

The Traditions assistants speak with authority. Preparing to teach the course, they work for two and one-half weeks at the most menial Disney jobs. They clean toilets and press shirts in a sweltering laundry. As Rejonis says: "How could we stand up in our suits, pantyhose, and heels and tell these cast members, you're going to love working in the laundry? Naaaa. I hated doing that laundry. I know how hot it is down there."

The recruits learn the language. No one wears uniforms, only costumes. Customers are always guests, with a capital G. Staff are cast members whether they work on stage or back-stage. There are no jobs, only roles. The work may be routine, but the values-driven culture makes it special. Says Rejonis: "We try to take them out of that mundane everyday persona and say, Look—you are going to be a star. You are going to be on stage." They sell the career opportunities at Disney. "We try to get them to realize that they can be a lot more than they were when they walked in that day."

In the second and third day, cast members learn the specific skills of their roles. A role at Disney means providing a quality experience for guests even if you never see a guest in person. At Intel, employees must balance equal values. At Disney, cast members learn to rank their values in strict order of impor-tance.

SAFETY, ABOVE ALL

Safety tops the list. When a guest falls, cast members break all other rules. They step out of role, interrupt another guest, do what they have to to help. The first cast member on the scene asks whether the guest wants help. If the guest refuses, the cast member must offer two more times. Cynics correctly say this procedure lowers Disney's potential liability. For an injured guest, however, the procedure conveys the caring attitude that Disney wants to project.

Everybody is a safety officer. See a splinter on a chair, call maintenance. Spot a more serious hazard such as broken pavement, stand over it until someone comes to fix it. Other work tasks, no matter how important, must wait. No senior executive or part-time summer employee takes up a role without learning such procedures.

For every job, there are specific safety skills. Everyone learns how to use a fire extinguisher. Restaurant cast members learn the Heimlich maneuver—when to use it and when not to. Supervisors provide continuous informal training in safety procedures. What would you do if that person fell? How would you handle it if the engine in your attraction stalled?

Talking with the supervisor in one of the Disney restaurants, I tested the system:

> "What would you do if a guest had a seizure or heart attack right now?"
>
> "Call 911."
>
> "The Orlando emergency service?"
>
> "No, we have our own emergency service here on the property. They can be here in minutes."
>
> "Even so, with a heart attack, minutes count. Anything else you could do?"
>
> "See those four people on the cash registers? We've trained two of them in CPR."

FOUR LEVELS OF COURTESY

Disney's second value, *Courtesy*, is becoming a lost art in our society. However, it is alive and well at Disney. In the Traditions course, Harriet Rejonis asks recruits what comes to mind when they hear the word "courtesy." "They always throw out the same words—polite, kind, friendly, helpful. I say that's a good place to start. That describes courtesy everywhere else." At Disney, there are at least four levels of courtesy.

The routine courtesy standard is cheerfully answering the same question you've already answered 20 times in the last hour. Courtesy means remembering that for this guest it's the first time. It also means kneeling to make eye contact when you answer a child's question.

At the second level, the courtesy standard is to provide helpful, accurate information.

> Gravance explains: "Someone asks me directions to the Brown Derby restaurant. I've just left the Brown Derby and there's no way they are going to get in now. I have to have other options." The options must match the profile of the people he is talking to. If they have children, he may say they will enjoy the Sci Fi restaurant or the Prime Time Diner, where there is sure to be room now.

At the third level, the courtesy standards focus on dealing with unpleasant situations. Late on a 100-degree Saturday afternoon, the sturdiest cast member feels the strain. Families who started their day at 9:00 A.M., fresh and full of enthusiasm, ready to see everything, suddenly give out. As Gravance describes it: "The crankiness meter goes up and you hear this collective whine." Any cast member is a target for complaints.

Barbara Farfan says such moments distinguish Disney courtesy from ordinary standards. In a typical place of business, "the manager might give five reasons it has to be that way. Sorry for the inconvenience, but too bad." At Disney, "I want you to know your problem is important to me." Sometimes, of course, just listening is enough. If it's not, Farfan told me she would assure a guest: "I will do everything in my power to solve your problem. If I can make you feel like . . . you are the most important person to me right now, then you are going to get a feeling of what it means to have some Disney-style courtesy."

At the highest level, courtesy standards become what Disney cast members call "aggressive friendliness." Cast members won't wait for you to ask. If you are taking a snapshot, they volunteer to use the camera so everybody can be in the picture. Farfan approaches guests to ask what they have done that day. What did they like best? Have they seen her favorite, the Muppetvision 3D? Rejonis keeps a special eye on T-shirts, baseball caps, and Mickey Mouse hats. They provide clues to common interests. "So you're a Minnesota Vikings fan?" Or, "I'm from the University of Alabama myself." She often surprises children with her cheerful "Hi, Bobby" greeting. They have momentarily forgotten their name is on the Mickey Mouse hat.

Everyone responds to sincere attention. Farfan notes that guests "will be more likely to forgive our mistakes, forgive the weather, or forgive the long lines" when they receive friendly attention.

SHOWMANSHIP ONSTAGE AND BACKSTAGE

Show or showmanship is the third Disney value. It's what people consciously remember. However, much that Disney considers show is unseen by guests. Rejonis recalls how a supervisor rebuked her when she worked in a pizza parlor. "Honey, that's not good show. When my pizzas go out, they all have to have cheese on each corner." She thought: "This is what it's all about. Whether you are onstage, dancing, performing, whether you are sweeping the streets, or working backstage making pizzas, the show is total."

Show governs the controversial personal grooming standards for which Disney is famous or infamous. No earrings or facial hair for men. One ring per hand for women. Men's haircuts above the collar. No dangling earrings and only very subtle makeup for women. Despite orientation during hiring, some male recruits show up for training with long hair. "I just couldn't get to the barber. I really tried." The solution is simple. Either they leave without a job or they take a turn in what Rejonis calls "Harriet's happy hair chair."

Even dedicated cast members sometimes grumble about this forced conformity. In Traditions courses, someone always points out that Walt wore a mustache. Gravance defends the strict standards with this example:

> You've arrived at the park with young children. The Magic Kingdom castle is glistening in the background. Standing in the foreground, with her back to you, is Snow White. You recognize her by her costume. You are all rushing to take a picture of Snow White with the kids when she turns, and . . . she's smoking a cigarette.

When I laughed, Gravance asked why. Because of the incongruity of the scene. "Exactly right," he replied. "We might not be able to explain verbally what Disney is or what our show is, but you know it when you see it. And you know it when you don't see it. Our guests are exactly the same way. They know when they see something that is Disney, and they know when they see something that is not Disney."

Show means cleanliness. Nothing spoils the fantasy faster than dirty streets, overflowing trash bins, and scruffy staff. Forty years ago, Walt Disney's new theme park in California introduced this revolutionary concept. Before Disneyland, amusement parks were dirty, often dangerous places, avoided by middle-class adults. There were no standards for dress or cleanliness and few for safety. Disney changed all that, creating a whole new entertainment industry. Today, any Disney cast member, from CEO Michael Eisner to the newest Traditions graduate, will pick up an empty cup on the ground. Show is everybody's job.

EFFICIENCY OF COST AND MOTION

Fourth on the hierarchy is *Efficiency*, a value that would lead the list in many American corporations. Efficiency begins with presenteeism, the opposite of absenteeism. The standard is you show up on time and ready to go onstage. If you are part of the three o'clock parade, you're not getting dressed at 2:59. Disney recognizes presenteeism with gift certificates, plaques, and mentions in the company paper, *Eyes and Ears.*

In pursuit of Efficiency, Disney builds only attractions that accommodate a profitable number of guests per hour. Monorail schedules promote maximum capacity. Step backstage and you will see the exact point where the expensive paint used onstage stops. Offices and staff breakrooms are spartan. Periodically, an official counter follows Gravance measuring his hourly eye contact with guests.

Specific on-the-job training emphasizes efficiency of cost and motion. Gravance plays the comic lead at the Hoop-Di-Doo Show. Forgetting his improvisational skills, he stays exactly on schedule three shows a night, each 100 minutes. At each seating, people must eat a full meal, pay their checks, and exit in time to set up for the next show. Cast members stay on schedule without a trace of what Disney calls bad show or discourtesy to guests.

On her first assignment, Barbara Farfan worked in intervals of 17 minutes and 28 seconds. In that time, she ushered 584 people, including up to eight in wheel chairs, in and out of a theater. Since many had been waiting in line for 30 or 40 minutes, she had also to manage a cheerful greeting to maintain Courtesy and Show.

To Valerie Oberle, vice president of Disney University's professional development programs, Efficiency means attention to logistics. She cites this example:

> You check in at a Disney resort. The computer isn't working. They can't find your key. It takes you 30 minutes to get up to your room. That is not a quality experience. That's not efficient. If we don't have efficient systems that back up the quality of Show, then you don't have quality Show.

163

To support Efficiency, checkout clerks use the latest equipment and learn how to move guests along promptly. However, they learn not to sacrifice higher values. As Farfan explains:

> It's a busy day and I am working on a merchandise cash register. You're still trying to decide between the 101 Dalmatians watch and the Beauty and the Beast hip pack. You are standing there, talking to your wife, going back and forth. I'm looking at my line. People are shifting their feet. My supervisor is walking down the street. I know I am just going to get it for having this line out the door. I don't turn to you and say, "This is not a rocket science. Make a decision." I just don't do that. I don't sacrifice those other three elements to get you through the line. I don't do it!

BACKSTAGE VALUES

Disney wins in the marketplace by lavishing attention on its guests. Backstage, it uses four internal values to pay attention to its cast members. The four are commitment to Training, Communication, Recognition, and a Supportive Environment. Try as it may, Disney can't fill all its roles with enthusiasts. Even for the enthusiasts, the work cannot always be its own reward. Recognizing this, Disney uses education both to teach skills and to reinspire cast members.

The Traditions course is only the first step in a training program Disney supports even when business is off. Upward mobility is a key ingredient in the Pixie Dust formula. If a housekeeper wants to advance, there's training in clerical skills at the University's learning center. Valerie Oberle is a conspicuous role model. She started as a clerk typist 23 years ago, progressed through six different careers before becoming head of Disney University's professional development programs.

Disney managers get refreshed on the values at every key transition. Disney Way I for new managers is highly experiential. Students practice taking "good show/bad show" walks on the property until good show becomes second nature. Later in a career, Disney Way II deepens this knowledge. Leadership skills training focuses on how to keep cast members' enthusiasm high.

According to Oberle, the scores on cast members' opinion surveys are among the highest in any major corporation. To keep it that way, Disney University emphasizes Communication, especially listening skills for managers. "People are proud to work here," says Oberle. "They have ideas on how to improve. They want their ideas heard."

Recognition training stresses the personal touch. Disney Way I teaches how to give effective compliments. Says Oberle: "We encourage a lot of handwritten notes," another tradition started by Walt Disney.

Oberle says providing a Supportive Environment means treating cast members like guests. Cast members studying at Disney University are her guests. "In the cafeteria, I am their guest."

> Like most guests at Disney, I filled every minute of my schedule. Oberle, also on a busy schedule, agreed to meet for our interview in a formal reception area. When she learned I had missed lunch, she immediately brought me a tray of food. Even I knew it was "bad show" to eat in that spotless reception area. Yet Oberle instinctively honored the higher value of Courtesy over Show.

BRUSHING OFF PIXIE DUST

Not everyone has such a good experience, of course. Gravance monitors Orlando talk radio where he proffers feisty challenges to those who complain about Disney's hardball competitive methods. Some in Orlando still argue that Disney got unfair zoning control over its 30,000 acres by promising and then failing to build a residential community for 20,000 people.

Many would never visit a Disney theme park in the first place, pronouncing them imitation reality. To a disgruntled guest, aggressive friendliness is only greasepaint to disguise high prices and long lines. Some employees resentfully brush off Pixie Dust, insisting it's a job, not a role. When supervisors are away, individualism can break out. Waitresses will sport an extra bracelet or dangling earrings in small acts of defiance.

Sometimes whole communities rebel. Disney's first international expansion in Tokyo was a success. Conformity-minded Japanese cast members and guests adopted the Disney Way wholesale. In Europe, however, Disney hit high, hard cultural walls. At EuroDisney, French cast members resisted grooming codes. Initial attendance was disappointing. Tourists, surrounded by well-preserved historical reality, were less than enchanted by Disney's manufactured past.

Undeterred, the company next announced plans for Disney America in Haymarket, Virginia, outside Washington. Opposition mobilized instantly. There were arguments about who was going to pay for the necessary roads. Critics also contended Disney's artificial reality would stifle appreciation of nearby historical sites.

Some of this criticism arises from the company's hardball business methods. Disney competes to win, calling on either Pixie Dust or high-powered lobbyists as necessary. Still, a lot of badmouthing of Disney is simple elitism. Disney is unabashedly middle-class, sentimental, and patriotic, making it an inviting target for intellectuals.

"WHAT A GREAT JOB THAT MUST BE"

Whatever critics say, Disney has achieved well-rounded success in implementing values. It has clearly defined values. It is committed to them at every level. It skillfully uses values role models and education to inspire and reinspire its cast members. It uses hundreds of standards to transform four values into thousands of complete individual acts every day. Then it turns around and empowers people to ignore the standards when that's what it takes to exceed the guests' expectations.

This above-and-beyond quality standard governs all others. It inspires cast members when the day is hot, the crowd cranky, and the energy level low. At such moments, Louie Gravance often sneaks a look at his fellow cast members. He marvels as cast members, some in hot polyester costumes, keep up the unrelenting effort to sustain Courtesy and Show. "Every so often at such moments," he says, "I'll hear somebody say 'what a great job that must be!' And they're right."

CHAPTER 14

IMPLEMENTING STEP FIVE: THE EMPOWERED ORGANIZATION

When is it pointless to preach Empowerment? When the structure continues to give supervisors tight control. When is Diversity an empty promise? When the recruiting system continues to focus on white males. Get serious about any value and you'll soon realign structure and systems. Cleveland's American Steel & Wire offers an intriguing look at reengineering for values.

Individual acts are the source of all profit. Income flows from the competence of the Service-Master repair people, the enthusiasm of the Disney cast members, the integrity of American Express IDS financial planners, the risk taking of Intel managers.

What of the company itself? Every company is a living organization. It is a structure organized for work. It is a web of systems moving information and coordinating actions. A company's structure and systems can be in good health, bad health, or a mixture of both.

One aim of any values process is a healthy company capable of carrying unusual pressure. Well-supported values invigorate structure and systems everywhere. Conversely, a lack of alignment among values, structure, and systems creates a palpable strain.

The CEO announces a values initiative. Employees respond with enthusiasm. Human resources people produce training modules on the new values. Plaques and posters appear everywhere. Yet six months later, employees grumble, "Nothing has changed." Exasperated, management searches for another fad. Postmortems miss a key point. Structure and systems never changed. The value was Empowerment, but supervisors retained tight control. The value was Diversity, but the pool of promotable people remained the same. The value was Customer First, but the compensation system rewarded only sales and profit.

Reengineering is a popular technique today. Yet companies that reengineer solely to cut costs will reap few lasting benefits. The big successes will be those who reengineer to reduce costs *and* elevate values. These reengineered processes will reenergize people. They will lift the efficiency and completeness of ten thousand individual acts.

American Steel & Wire, a division of Birmingham Steel Corporation, regularly reengineers its structures and systems based on two values—Customer Satisfaction and Employee Empowerment. Tom Tyrrell, a former AS&W CEO who now serves as vice chairman and chief administrative officer of Birmingham Steel, launched the AS&W process in 1986. Tyrrell speaks of this effort with rapid intensity. His logical presentation, even his use of visual aides suggests a professor or a consultant. Tyrrell, however, has done exactly what he talks about. When he warns of a pitfall, it is a place where he has stumbled. When he advocates patience, he has learned its importance. When he talks of Empowerment, he has built a structure and systems to create it.

A Lost Opportunity

Born in Chicago in 1945, the oldest of six children, Tyrrell grew up working. As a child he sold soft drinks to construction workers. During his high school and college years he loaded boxcars, sold shoes, painted pallets, worked on the production lines at a can company. Such jobs left him with a deep respect for the average worker's ideas.

"I would sit next to guys in a locker room in one of these industrial plants. I would see pictures of their wives in their lockers. Occasionally, they would have tears in their eyes about the way they were treated." When Tyrrell remembers the emotions that swept over him in those locker rooms, he speaks as if the incidents occurred yesterday: "That's unfair! That's really unfair!"

Even worse was the lost opportunity. The guys in the locker rooms knew far more about the equipment than their managers did. "And I would think, why did they make the decisions . . . when these guys know all about it?"

Tyrrell worked 20 years at Bethlehem Steel and a New Jersey rod and wire manufacturer. In 1986, he got his chance to create the company he wanted to work for. Cincinnati investors chose Tyrrell as CEO in the leveraged purchase of three Ohio U.S. Steel plants. The flagship plant of the new American Steel & Wire was Cleveland's Cuyahoga Heights works, closed two years earlier after a bitter labor dispute.

Tyrrell publicly committed himself to the press, potential customers, and workers. American Steel & Wire would be a different kind of steel company. A bracing challenge followed immediately.

A Six-Month Strike

Some original lenders pulled out, forcing Tyrrell to raise $30 million. He found the money days before the expiration of the company's purchase option. U.S. Steel, AS&W's sole steel supplier, went on strike. Like many in the industry, Tyrrell expected a two- to three-month strike. Instead, the union was out for six months, the longest strike in the industry's history. Even after searching in Europe, American Steel & Wire couldn't find enough steel.

AS&W returned $25 million in orders rather than make delivery promises it couldn't keep. Tyrrell held to a no-layoff policy despite first-year losses of $9 million. In the final month of

170

its first year, the company turned its first profit. Tyrrell had committed to profit sharing. He persuaded his board to distribute the entire profit to employees. In his first year he astonished customers and employees alike. He had kept his word.

Problems continued. When the strike ended, the economy was declining. Sales fell in the automotive industry, the company's prime customer. In 1990, the Cincinnati investors insisted on a large dividend. To pay, the company took on heavy debt, reducing profit sharing and financial flexibility. The United Steelworkers moved to organize the company. A unionized plant would have ended job flexibility, a key element in Tyrrell's plan to avoid layoffs.

Tyrrell had set out to create a different kind of company. He wanted a climate closer to that of Silicon Valley than that of a traditional steel mill. Yet external circumstances kept driving him toward a company based on principles he hated. He stuck with his principles. He asked for workers' trust, even though the debt and recession had reduced profit sharing. The workers turned back the union by 184 to 40. Local investors bought out the Cincinnati group. The new board quickly aligned behind Tyrrell's goals. The recession ended, and earnings turned up.

BLURRING TRADITIONAL LINES

Through it all, Tyrrell kept building structures and systems to match his value of Empowerment. He blurred traditional lines between management and workers. Everyone wears the same color hardhat. Parking spaces go to the people who arrive earliest. The sales reps have company cars, the CEO doesn't. The CEO's pay is ten times that of the lowest-level worker, well below industry ratios.

To Tyrrell, this is the common-sense aspect of Empowerment. Trust begins with setting an example. He dismisses executives who tell people to work harder from an expensive car or club. "That's like telling your kids not to smoke with a cigarette in your mouth. It just doesn't work." Trust means management takes the first steps. No one punches a time clock. Parking is inside the factory gates. Most plants have an external parking lot to reduce pilfering.

Tyrrell modeled his empowerment-centered design on Maslow's hierarchy of needs. Like Maslow, Tyrrell insists higher needs motivate only after you satisfy basic wants. (See Figure 14.1.) Recognition programs ring hollow when there is no job security.

Many companies talk about empowerment. At progressive companies, empowerment is now part of supervisory training. However, few can match Tyrrell's level of achievement. Figure 14.1 shows the elements in Tyrrell's hierarchy of empowerment needs. At every level, AS&W now has specific structures and systems to support empowerment. Examples:

Job Security	"As long as we're here, we'll have a no-lay-off policy," says Tyrrell. That means running lean. There's overtime when business booms, less when business slows. It means you have to produce. People still get fired for poor performance. What if lack of business threatened the company's existence? Then everyone gets a pay cut.
Pay Program	All hourly workers went on salary in 1989. The next year absenteeism dropped from 1.2 to 0.8 percent. Salaries are about 90 percent of market. Profit sharing of up to 25 percent of base pay keeps pay high in good years and reduces costs in poor.
Benefits	The CEO's benefits are almost the same as the workers. Vacations are equal. Everyone has access to a 401(K) plan.
Training	AS&W pays workers to learn new skills. Once qualified, workers always receive pay for the skill whether called on to use it or not.

The company trains everyone in statistical process control. A problem-solving course prepares people to work on about 30 special teams operating at any time. Supervisors, called process managers, get nine days' leadership training. Topics include situational leadership, coaching and counseling, interviewing, listening, and facilitation skills.

Development Virtually all promotion is from within. Annual evaluations focus on development opportunities in addition to performance. Employees with identified weaknesses get quick access to external training and development classes.

At first the self-directed work teams faltered. People lacked experience or skill or were just uneasy about the unknown. Even enthusiasm at the top was not enough. Tyrrell next provided specific training. Kellie Bendik, former manager of corporate team facilitation, trained 400 employees in individual and team decision making. Her work was sometimes tough going. Not everyone welcomes empowerment. However, Bendik believes AS&W has passed "a critical mass" in team development.

Communication Communicating values begins with a three-day, 24-hour orientation for new employees. Spouses attend the first day. The course includes question-and-answer sessions with senior executives and a visit to two customers' plants. Every month there are open forums on issues such as Quality and progress on empowerment.

Openness is the watchword. I worried

my tape recorder was not picking up Tyrrell's soft, fast style of speaking. When I asked to shut his office door, he agreed but looked uncomfortable. "I hate closed doors," he said.

Involvement

Teams of workers handle the recruitment process. Anyone with a grievance can appeal to an Employee Council of specially trained workers. Even in cases of firing, the council overturns management decisions about a third of the time.

Customer Value Teams can investigate any situation involving quality or customer complaints. Concerns Committees at each plant work to improve policies and procedures. A team of workers designs the company's safety procedures.

Measurement

There are specific Quality goals for the company and each unit. Variances are a hot topic at the monthly staff meetings. Tyrrell acknowledges frustration in creating a system of employee evaluations fully supporting empowerment. However, AS&W teams keep working on it. "Every 18 months we redesign it," he says.

Recognition

Recognition reinforces the team concept. Two years ago, AS&W replaced Employee of the Month and Employee of the Year awards with team awards. The company's annual Appreciation Dinner Dance honors employees with perfect attendance. AS&W treats five-year award winners to a four-day cruise in the Bahamas. Winners and their spouses all go together. When I visited, attendance for the previous six months stood at 99.8 percent.

Figure 14.1
AS&W's Hierarchy of Empowerment Needs

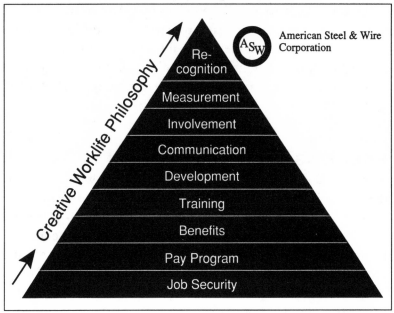

If this sounds like a workers' utopia, it isn't. "This is a steel plant," says Tyrrell. "It's cold in the winter. It's hot in the summer. It's dirty. It's physical. It's not an easy environment. People don't wear togas and olive branches and skip through the plant singing, 'How Wonderful Life Is.' . . . They look at this in the perspective of what else they could do with their lives. And this is pretty good. The reason is they know people care about them. They have a voice."

American Steel & Wire is a work in progress. Its acquisition by Birmingham Steel makes the empowerment goals "harder" to achieve, Tyrrell admits. Birmingham, more of a commodity producer, has a style different from that of more specialty-steel-oriented AS&W. Many questions are unanswered. Debt continues to limit flexibility. AS&W's workers are the children of the men who sat with Tyrrell in the locker rooms of his youth. For steelworkers, suspicion of management remains a family legacy.

After only a few missteps, trust would evaporate. The United Steelworkers are certainly waiting for an opening.

AS&W wants to be the number-one American wire and rod manufacturer. They want to produce a quality product equal to that of the Japanese, a goal that eludes them. They set Ford Quality 1 as a template for their quality process. Yet neither AS&W nor any company in its sector has qualified for Q1 status at Ford.

FRENETIC INTENSITY

Also worrisome is the frenetic intensity of the whole effort. Is there a limit to the empowerment people want or need? If so, AS&W may be coming close. There are some 350 places on teams at a company with only 530 employees. Someone still has to make the wire and rods while the teams are busy solving problems. Some teams meet on company time, many of them don't. Tyrrell contends enthusiastic people will always find time to create a new kind of workplace.

So far, the evidence supports his optimism. Walter Robertson, Tyrrell's handpicked successor as AS&W president, strongly supports the company's empowerment goals. Volunteers sign up quickly for open spots on teams. Day by day, teams strengthen the structures and systems to support empowerment. The key to quality, Tyrrell insists, rests within these self-directed teams.

Tyrrell makes it sound simple. Give workers the right systems, structures, and skills. Then empower them to make continual improvements. Their improvements will serve the customers better, improve quality, lower costs. Success will encourage more empowerment of everyone.

American Steel & Wire's experience reinforces an ironic lesson for any company setting out to empower workers. Creating freedom requires strengthening structure and systems. Kellie Bendik, the former AS&W facilitator, now an independent consultant, uses an example familiar to any American:

The Founding Fathers got together and envisioned a nation like no other before. Their mission was to create a democracy with freedom for all. The Constitution defined their structure, the Bill of Rights their values. Charters of national, state, and local government defined structure in more detail. Processes and systems support structure and values. Prominent examples include the legal system and the rules of due process. For national empowerment to work, we must be sure our structures, processes, and systems stay aligned with our common mission and values.

THINKING ANEW

For country or company, adjusting structure and systems to match Mission and Core Values requires thinking anew. Structure and system are forms, temporary containers to shape dynamic ideas. The assembly line is a highly efficient form for delivering products at a low cost. Its longevity, even today, attests to its utility. Over time, the form atrophied. In companies competing with low-wage countries, managers had to increase productivity. That meant making better use of the brains of American workers. That led to questions about the cost and efficiency of after-the-fact quality systems. These questions triggered the redefinition of our Quality and Empowerment values.

Values-driven leadership sees structure and systems as temporary conveniences. From the moment of creation, every structure or system begins to decay. People make small, practical exceptions when they make use of the new structure. Parallel systems, set up to solve long-forgotten crises, duplicate work. External circumstances change, making a structure obsolete or a system too bureaucratic.

To the values-driven leader, structure and systems are always means, never ends. Raising aspiration for any value always suggests realignments of structure and systems. When aspirations rise constantly, realignment is constant. Constant realignment need not be radical. Once in place and supported by structure and systems, elevating values promotes a steady-as-she-goes mentality.

American Steel & Wire is years away from steady as she goes. The company still displays the exposed structure and systems of a living organization in the making. If Tom Tyrrell's dream becomes a reality, today's visible structure and systems will fade into the background. Conscious design will become unconscious culture. A generation from now, visitors may search in vain for the secrets behind American Steel & Wire's dynamic culture. When they do, they will likely meet baffled expressions. "Why, that's just the way we work around here."

CHAPTER 15

IMPLEMENTING STEP SIX: RECOGNIZING SUCCESS WHEN YOU SEE IT

Can you get too much recognition? CEO Hal Rosenbluth doesn't think so. He reversed the usual business values and put his employees ahead of his customers. Heresy? Maybe, but 7,500 percent growth in 15 years suggests he's on to something. Of course, you can't eat recognition. Nothing really takes hold until values impact the pay packet.

Straight-talking Jim Baughman, former manager of corporate management development at General Electric, hits the mark on putting values to work. "A values statement isn't worth the paper it's printed on unless you use it in two ways," he says. "It has to drive your appraisal process, and it has to drive your development process."

At GE, 50 percent of an annual review focuses on what Baughman calls "the catechism that's in the values statement." Toro links 25 percent of incentive compensation to performance on values. At Levi Strauss & Company, it's one-third of all compensation, with some units weighing the values component even higher. In addition to blocking raises, low values ratings constitute a career killer at Levi Strauss. Says CEO Robert Haas, ". . . a low rating on aspirational management means improvement is necessary no matter how many pants they got out the door. Promotion is not in the future unless you improve."[1]

From the start, employees attending Levi Strauss's Leadership

Weeks raised pay and performance issues. They noted that the company's compensation system didn't align with its Aspiration Statement. In response, the company created a task force of 100 employees from all functional areas. The group worked for months realigning compensation and evaluation practices with the aspirations. Management reviewed and endorsed its recommendations. The board approved the revisions in November 1991. The revised system added a category concerning performance on aspirations to evaluations for salaried employees. It established achievement of "aspirational expectations" as one of two criteria for annual and long-term incentive pay.

Levi Strauss's Aspiration Statement mentions "Recognition—both financial and psychic." Psychic is the mental lift we feel when someone appreciates our work. Psychic recognition, like Shakespeare's mercy, "blesses him that gives and him that takes." Psychic recognition conveys commitment. It reinforces the reality and the image of sincerity. It inspires imitation. For the recipient, psychic recognition renews enthusiasm. It strengthens identification with the company. It sparks determination to do even better.

A USEFUL LEVER MISAPPLIED

Why is so useful a lever so commonly overlooked? Why is it so often misapplied?

Psychic recognition runs afoul of deeply embedded attitudes such as: "We pay them to do a good job. Why should we make a fuss when they do it?" To be sure, pay is the most immediate form of recognition when linked to individual performance. In most workplaces, however, this connection was lost long ago. Parity, not performance, is the common basis for pay scales.

A related attitude focuses on unintended results: "Give them recognition and they will expect more money." It depends on what you recognize. A trip to the Bahamas for the star salesperson is recognition, not a substitute for commissions. American Steel & Wire's cruise for employees with five-year perfect attendance is recognition for above-normal productivity. Neither recognition will likely spark demands for more pay, but both acknowledge something beyond the basic terms of employment.

"People around here don't go for that stuff. It embarrasses them." This common barrier can reflect a modest, hardworking culture. The solution is simple: recognize teams rather than individuals. You unleash the power of recognition without violating cultural norms.

For a final example, there is this type of objection: "The superstars already get too much attention. How about the people who get the work done every day?" Levi Strauss's Aspiration Statement addresses that one quite clearly. It calls for recognition for "all who create and innovate and also those who continually support the day-to-day business requirements."

Values recognition in most experienced companies comes in five varieties, each with a distinct purpose:

- **Widespread spontaneous recognition.** The purpose here is continuous recognition for continuous improvement. Companies distribute to all associates certificates representing different Core Values. An associate who sees outstanding performance on any value can recognize it on the spot by presenting a values certificate. Typically, recipients hang certificates at or near their work stations. Some companies add a special recognition for those who collect a specified number or variety of spontaneous recognitions.

- **Above-and-beyond awards.** Although signifying a higher level of achievement, these awards are still based on a single values-driven incident. Their purpose is to inspire imitation of the exceptional. At AT&T Universal Card, an associate received such an award for helping a customer find an ill spouse. The husband, who suffered from Alzheimer's disease, disappeared, taking with him his AT&T Universal Card. The associate sent out a notice alerting retailers.

181

When the missing husband used the card, police returned him home.

- **The CEO's award.** For most companies this is the Academy Award. It recognizes consistent performance on all values. Committees review nominations at several levels. People from throughout the company attend the presentation. Runners-up are also recognized. Company publications and brochures feature the winners' stories.

- **Team recognition.** At Medtronic, Earl Bakken created one of the most heartwarming team-recognition programs in corporate America. Medtronic invites patients who wear its devices to attend its annual holiday program. Often the guests bring their physicians. To an enthralled and sometimes teary-eyed audience, people describe how their lives have improved. Thanks to tight quality standards, which include precise tracking of products from manufacturing to patient registration, Medtronic is able to recognize the teams who created a specific patient's device. At Medtronic, Quality and Reliability values wear a human face.

- **Departmental awards.** The philosophy here is recognition begins at home. These awards empower departmental leaders to recognize values contributions within their units. Corporate should encourage but not control such awards. AT&T Universal Card doesn't even know the number of departmental values awards that its leaders give out.

A CORNERSTONE OF LEADERSHIP

Large organizations must institutionalize recognition. However, nothing substitutes for the leader as chief values advocate. CEO Douglas J. Herst of Peerless Lighting Corporation keeps up the drumbeat of values recognition through the year. Recognition of values is a cornerstone of Herst's leadership style at the San Francisco-area lighting company founded by his grandfather in the 1890s.

Most values-driven companies concentrate on three or four

values. Herst actively promotes ten. Every quarter, Herst gives out special pins to employees as recognition for high performance on different values. Working with an artist, Herst created the value icon for each pin. Some Peerless employees have collected as many as seven pins. Originally, Herst handed out the awards annually. He switched to quarterly in 1993. His specialty is keeping everybody continually focused on values.

Doug Herst recalls the drawing that started his pursuit of values. In 1986, at a management seminar, the instructor asked participants to write their own obituaries. The exercise startled Herst. At the time, he had been CEO for five years. The instructor's question forced him to think for the first time about what he wanted for his company. Herst studied art as an undergraduate, and he thinks in pictures. On the plane home, he drew pictures of a child's seesaw. On one side, he drew icons for innovation and growth/profitability. Balanced on the other, he sketched a building with a heart, symbolizing a Great Place to Work. Looking at the picture, Herst redefined his job as CEO. He saw his main task as sustaining equilibrium between growth/profitability and Great Place to Work.

Back in the office, he shared his concept with his senior people. When their reaction was tepid, Herst temporarily retreated. Nearly a year later he tried again. By that time, simmering personnel animosities had broken into a full boil.

RECOGNIZE "PRECIOUS PEOPLE"

Herst made a list of every value that could help Peerless maintain equilibrium on the seesaw. He then narrowed the list, eventually settling on ten values. To create definitions, he researched in books and articles. He talked with people he respected. He was then ready to take on his doubting managers. He recalls telling them there were two ways to deal with the escalating personnel problems. "We can create firm rules like the army, or we can create values." He invited them to help him build the environment he wanted. "Rules don't work," he told them. "What works is the recognition of one another as precious people, not only as employees but as individuals who need the opportunity to flourish, grow, and develop."

Through intellect and intuition, Herst arrived at the heart of recognition. It is not the pin or the plaque or the name in the paper. They are outward symbols. The force behind recognition is personal attention to "precious people." There are few greater powers in life. The politician who remembers your name. The teacher who knows you can do better. The leader who trusts your intellect. The parent who believes in your destiny. The team leader who says "well done."

Each act of personal attention releases a stream of human energy. Everybody needs that energy replenished. I've sat with executives who are among the most successful people in America while they confided their frustration with a board that didn't appreciate their work. Financially they are well rewarded, yet they still crave the elixir of personal recognition. Idealists complain we should not be like this. We should take satisfaction from our work alone. We should outgrow this childish hunger for attention. The idealists are right. Meanwhile, realists accept us as we are and put our hunger for attention to positive use.

A PEOPLE FIRST COMPANY

Imagine the power of a company continually refueled by recognition of its employees. A global travel agency provides clues to how such a paragon might behave. Hal F. Rosenbluth led his company to a revenue growth of 7,500 percent (to $1.5 billion) in 15 years by deliberately moving beyond purely market-driven leadership. Rosenbluth reversed the traditional Market-first wisdom to make People his lead component. With Diane McFerrin Peters, his director of new ventures, Rosenbluth describes his unorthodox approach in a book with a title that reveals his philosophy: *The Customer Comes Second and Other Secrets of Exceptional Service.*[2]

In 1892, Hal's great-grandfather, Marcus, established Rosenbluth as a small steamship office in Philadelphia. People deposited a few dollars at a time with Marcus until their accounts totaled $50—enough to bring a relative to America. The $50 paid for transatlantic passage to New York and a train seat to Philadelphia. According to Hal, Marcus had a wider vision than the travel business. He was really in family immigration, helping whole clans reassemble in America. Hal Rosenbluth credits Marcus with the Customer Service value that the company honors to this day.

After immigration slowed, Rosenbluth Travel turned mainly toward vacation business. Strong customer focus produced growth and success. When Hal Rosenbluth joined the company in 1974, it was the largest travel agency in Philadelphia. Hal began as a gofer, running errands and stamping brochures. Early on he sensed something missing in Rosenbluth's customer-first, customer-first, customer-first philosophy:

> Everyone felt pushed to do heroic deeds for the client . . . Booking agents competed. Vacation consultants fought over who got to sit at the desk nearest the entrance. People played up to the receptionist who directed calls. There was a lot of politics, a lot of scorekeeping, and a lot of stress.[3]

Rosenbluth was seeing market-driven leadership in late bloom. The company was generating about $25 million in annual bookings. It was hard to argue with success. Yet, he says, "I just didn't like the way people treated each other. Our star performers could get away with murder, and did. Teamwork was nonexistent." Rosenbluth worried the staff would pass along their stress to the customer. "It was not a terribly pleasant place to work."[4]

By 1978, Rosenbluth walked into a low-profile, start-up unit handling the company's business travel. The atmosphere was electric. These agents worked together. When one person was talking simultaneously with a client and an airline, someone jumped in to help. The work was demanding, the teamwork contagious. Rosenbluth picked up a phone and started working. He stayed all day and came back the next. After a few days, "I demoted myself from vice president to reservations agent and went into corporate travel full time."[5]

SEEING OPPORTUNITY IN DISASTER

Rosenbluth walked into corporate travel as everything was spinning out of control. Deregulation spawned new airlines, new routes, dozens of new fares every day. Where many travel companies saw disaster, Rosenbluth and his corporate travel team saw opportunity. Today, business travel accounts for 90 percent of the company's operations.

Rosenbluth soon realized he was in the information business rather than the travel business. Business travelers had little time to sort through the many new routes, prices, and schedules, so Rosenbluth purchased the technology to do it for them. It also guaranteed they would pay the lowest fare between any two points.

Many executives would have concentrated on developing Market and Technology components to exploit this unfolding opportunity. Rosenbluth saw a deeper truth. He consciously worked to keep his People component not merely even with, but actually ahead of Market and Technology. "Companies must put their people first," he says. "Yes, even before their customers. There. Now I've said it. I know it's controversial. It makes most people nervous just to hear it, but it works."[6]

Perpetual training is a secret weapon at Rosenbluth. While the company has excellent skills training, what really drives enthusiasm is the emphasis on recognizing associates as full human beings, not just employees. For example, associates can participate in *Leader in Learning* seminars. Associates from offices across the country volunteer to present these sessions, dealing with topics ranging from listening skills and stress management to enhancing the reservations process and international faring structures. Rosenbluth estimates his company invests thousands of hours every year on this training alone.

Recognition programs reinforce Rosenbluth's values. The salmon, a fish that swims against the tide, is the company mascot. When a customer writes in to compliment an associate, the associate gets a copy of the letter bearing a salmon sticker. Associates use salmon notecards to express thanks and appreciation. The highest honor in the company is the salmon pin, reserved for associates who exceed even Rosenbluth's expectations. August is Associate Appreciation Month. Something special happens every day. The month ends with leaders at every level sending a personal note of thanks to each of their associates.

WIDENING THE APPRAISAL SYSTEM

No matter how intense, psychic recognition alone is never enough. Performance on values must also be recognized in evaluations and rewarded in compensation. The appraisal system widens its focus when you introduce values, says Jim Baughman, the former GE executive, now managing director of J. P. Morgan Company. If you construct a chart with performance on values on one axis and performance on numbers on the other, evaluations will fall into four quadrants (Figure 15.1). You will have people who are:

1. Missing their numbers and not living up to the values,
2. Making their numbers but not living up to the values,
3. Missing their numbers but living up to the values,
4. Making their numbers and living up to the values.

The first is a "no-brainer," according to Baughman. "They are hopeless," he says. Each of the other three represents a different challenge. Many people consider the fourth group a no-brainer

Figure 15.1
Values/Performance Decision Grid

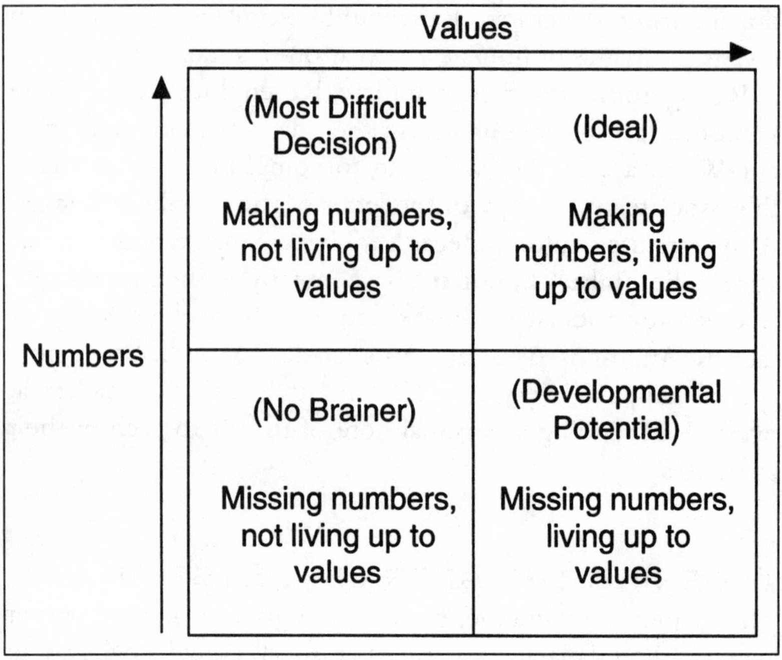

Numbers ↑	Values →	
	(Most Difficult Decision) Making numbers, not living up to values	(Ideal) Making numbers, living up to values
	(No Brainer) Missing numbers, not living up to values	(Developmental Potential) Missing numbers, living up to values

as well. Baughman disputes that. "Even the best and brightest need mentoring, coaching, training, and sometimes a job rotation. You can't take them for granted. If you do, you're making a mistake."

For most companies, the second group is the toughest challenge. Baughman outlines a typical interview in what he calls these poignant cases:

You go to a person of 40 or 50 and say, "Look, you've always delivered but you've got to lighten up. . . . And they say, "You're crazy. I'm a fullback. You made me a fullback. Every time you wanted a fullback, you called my play. I got where I am by being a fullback. . . . And it's going to be very hard for me to work through these issues that you want me to change."

In some cases, Baughman adds, the only answer is "You're right. It's not going to work. Here's a fair way for you to go to another company or go into retirement." You try to work with the others "the best you know how, with coaching, with mentoring, with training." However, the failure rate is high. "You're not going to change a lot of them late in the game."

The third group, people with good performance on values who are missing their numbers, have a much higher success rate. At GE Baughman and his team tried to help them use their values strength to lift their performance on the numbers.

Baughman cautions against too literal an interpretation of the four-quadrant paradigm. In balancing values and performance, all of us spend time in each quadrant. "On any given day, you're in one or the other." The four-quadrant paradigm has another limitation. It implies that achieving proper balance is strictly an individual problem. The deeper issue is team effectiveness. Someone who always wins but ignores values may report to someone who has all the values but has trouble winning. You end up with a lose-lose pair. At GE, getting the balance right became increasingly a team, not just an individual, process.

Recognition, rewards, and development together form the final element in the six-step process to create a values-driven company. Appropriately, this step ends where values begin—with the individual act. The entire effort has one all-embracing goal: to lift individual performance. One cycle properly ends with recognizing and rewarding achievement while laying the foundation for further growth through individual and team pursuit of values.

PART IV

VALUES IN ACTION: APPLICATIONS

- Entrepreneurial values
- Turnaround values
- Global values
- 33 questions
- Leading with values

CHAPTER 16

AT THE CREATION: ENTREPRENEURIAL VALUES

Nowhere are values and personal aspiration more closely linked than in entrepreneurial companies. Consciously or unconsciously, the entrepreneur is the values communication program. Using instinct or reason, wise entrepreneurs pick values that propel their companies to higher levels of performance.

Entrepreneurs implant values into the genetic codes of their companies. Eleuthère du Pont came to America in 1800 as a refugee from revolutionary France and founded E. I. du Pont de Nemours in 1802. He brought a technology for making better gunpowder. Of longer significance, he brought a belief in the worth of every human being. In 200 years, his company evolved from a gunpowder factory near Wilmington, Delaware, to the most admired chemical company in the United States. In part, that admiration grows from the company's enduring commitment to its founder's value of safety.

Founder du Pont created safety traditions from the start. His workers stood behind thick walls when handling gunpowder at its most dangerous stage. He or his general manager personally operated new mills before they opened for employees. Today, Du Pont's safety record remains the wonder of its industry. Its workdays–lost rate (related to accidents) is about forty times better than the U.S. average for all industries and ten times better than the average for U.S. chemical companies. This commitment permeates the company. When I gave an offsite seminar for Du Pont managers, the first item on the agenda was the hotel's safety procedures.

Successful entrepreneurs establish values by example. Willard Marriott, Sr., opened a small restaurant in Washington, D.C., in 1927. His principles were simply stated: "Take care of your people and they will take care of your customers." Marriott personally visited workers when they were sick. He lent them money during troubled times. Today, the $8.4 billion Marriott International, Inc., has a highly sophisticated human resources Department of more than 400 people. One of them once told me: "Everything we do today is an extension of what Willard Marriott, Sr., started."

Founders of new businesses should consciously try to instill values early. Any new business is survival driven. Adding a market-driven value elevates perspective and performance. Simultaneously committing to a people value releases energy for expansion. The entrepreneur should think through her vision of the company. She should then analyze her present situation in light of that vision. Which values would help close the gap between vision and reality? For a physical value, she might choose Speed, Cleanliness, or Safety. Which organizational value would help her most? Teamwork? Discipline? Systematic Functioning? For a psychological value, she might choose Respect for Each Other or Trust.

Never again will Core Values and personal aspiration be so closely intertwined. It is a moment laden with potential for personal and corporate growth. The entrepreneur should feel her values as a palpable extension of herself. She should experience the surge of energy that flows from commitment. She should bring her people together for formal or informal sessions to discuss and define values.

At the beginning, the entrepreneur *is* the values communication program. In a small start-up, everyone looks to the owner for guidance on behavior. As every owner has discovered, not all good behavior is imitated. To have any chance of success, however, the owner must make a conscious effort. You can't inculcate devotion to customers while complaining about their demands. The value of Respect won't take hold while the owner relies on shouting as her main discipline tool.

Even aligning personal behavior and values is not enough. "They see me in here late every day ensuring the work gets out. Yet they go at five o'clock sharp even if there are customer calls waiting." So complains many an entrepreneurial CEO. What's missing? Even with a half-dozen employees, the owner/entrepreneur must begin thinking about standards. Owners usually insist that employees handle customer requests promptly. To the owner, promptly means *now*. To one employee, it means by the end of the day. To another, as soon as I can get to it. In an entrepreneurial enterprise, standards may be few. However, they must be specific on those operations immediately touched by values.

In the small company, training is mostly on the job. The values-driven owner is above all a trainer and coach. Usually, the owner has the best command of all technical aspects of the business. Many small companies stumble in answering a critical issue: How willing is the owner to grow personally? Many small business owners don't understand the question. They think training and development is for everyone else. After all, they have arrived. It is the others who still must struggle to succeed. For the entrepreneurial company to keep growing, the owner must grow too. Growing means institutionalizing your values at a higher and higher level.

Organization is always in flux in the small entrepreneurial company. Teams gather and disband around the owner's priorities. This gives the small firm a flexibility admired by many big companies. However, the values-driven entrepreneur must create structures and systems to deliver her values. If the owner wants to foster individual initiative, she should be careful to reduce managerial layers. From the beginning, she should pay special attention to salary and bonus. What message does the owner pass out with the bonus checks? If Teamwork is the value, where is the Teamwork incentive?

ENTREPRENEURIAL CONSISTENCY

Consistency is not a value frequently associated with entrepreneurs. However, William Popp, founder and owner of Popp Telcom Inc., has built his company on the value of consistent Systematic Functioning. Telephones fascinated Popp from childhood. "I couldn't figure out how you could be talking to Grandma when she wasn't there. As soon as I learned how to operate a screwdriver, I started taking telephones apart." In 1971, Popp landed a part-time job installing and servicing phones to earn money for college. The company so liked his work that they offered him a full-time job. Soon he was designing phone systems. By the late 1970s, he was selling custom-designed phone systems for business.

Like many entrepreneurs, Popp saw opportunity in telephone deregulation. In 1982, he quit his job to set up Popp Telcom, Inc. The company buys long distance time from AT&T, MCI, and Sprint at bulk rates. It then retails the time to small- to mid-sized businesses at discount rates.

To purchase equipment and hire staff, Popp raised $85,000. He tapped relatives and friends. He tried bankers, but couldn't get a hearing. "They were too busy laughing," he says, acknowledging they had reason to laugh. He was 27 years old with no college degree. He had never run a company. He had no security. The industry was brand new. And he was taking on AT&T's long distance service. So far, however, he has had the last laugh. Today, Popp Telcom serves nearly 10,000 business customers in 12 states. It employs more than 140 people. Revenues in 1994 topped $35 million. Popp has repurchased all the stock from the initial investors, all of whom made a handsome profit.

Popp put an exceptional stamp of consistency on his business. He personally wrote every page of the policies and procedures that govern all aspects of his business. There are separate books for the Golden Valley (Minnesota) headquarters staff, the salespeople, and the regional offices. He divided the regional office books into ones for large offices and ones for small to make expansion easier.

These large administrative manuals are out of favor in big companies. They are a specific target in Jack Welch's campaign to increase Speed and Simplicity at GE. Entrepreneurs with big-company experience also eschew administrative manuals. The heavy books are a symbol of why they fled corporate life. Popp, who never worked for a big company, has rediscovered the raw power at the other end of this values spectrum. Welch wants more innovation, less consistency. Popp uses consistency to speed decision making in his expanding company.

The risk for Popp Telcom is that the manuals, each running three to four hundred pages, will gather dust and become obsolete. Popp has created structures and systems to prevent this. During his thrice-weekly teleconferences with his six regional managers, two items are always on the agenda. The team reviews any event that suggests need for a review of policy or procedure. There is also a systematic review of several pages of the policy book. By consistently following up, they review every policy and procedure at least once every two years. For all new employees, there is a two-week course closely tied to what Popp calls simply "the books."

Consistency, says Popp, relieves pressure and lowers stress. "We can train new people easier, faster, more consistently. We don't have to use our memories. . . . Write it down. It's easier to share. Use your memory for what happens inconsistently." This is the energetic voice of a leader committed to a value. Leadership to Popp means being first in every morning and last out every evening. It also means "being totally consistent with policies and procedures."

SUCCESS IN A COMMODITY BUSINESS

Popp built success in a niche within an unusual technological market. Values also differentiate a new company in markets that are almost a commodity. In 1980, Denise Marie Fugo and Ralph DiOrio opened Sammy's, a trendy restaurant in the Flats section of Cleveland, Ohio. The Flats was then a 10-mile stretch of abandoned warehouses and factories winding around the Cuyahoga River. Sammy's was a pioneer in an area that is now a thriving entertainment district, attracting more than three million visitors a year.

Fugo and DiOrio, a husband-and-wife business team, put up all their savings as a down payment to buy the three-story building where Sammy's is housed today. Friends and relatives chipped in another $30,000. A local bank came up with a $25,000 building improvement loan. DiOrio's uncle built the restaurant railings. Fugo's parents refinished the chairs. Still, the owners couldn't raise enough for a fully equipped kitchen. So Sammy's operated for 10 months as a nightclub-bar. A relative prepared the food for the seafood raw bar on borrowed equipment. It was, says Fugo, "your typical small entrepreneurial start." Except for something extra. These partners opened their doors with a deep commitment to four ambitious values.

Fugo and DiOrio were high school sweethearts. Even as teenagers, their idea of a big evening was dining out. In both their Italian–Slovak families the kitchen was the center of family life. The idea of opening a restaurant was always there, something they would do someday. Fugo worked at Burger King and Chinese restaurants to pay college expenses. She earned an MBA in Chicago and worked there as a Goldman Sachs stockbroker. DiOrio, with an undergraduate degree in business, went to work as a technical sales rep. At home, his love of food blossomed into a flair for gourmet cooking.

On visits to Cleveland, the city called them back. Where friends and relatives saw urban decline, they saw opportunity. Somehow, Fugo says, "it looked better than we remembered it as kids." They returned in 1979 determined to open a restaurant with $40,000 from the sale of their Chicago house. They called their company City Life to show they wanted to create a cornerstone for renewal.

198

They committed to four challenging values. Says Fugo: "We wanted World Class Food, World Class Service, World Class Ambiance and World Class Management." Other entrepreneurs might have aimed for the first two. However, by combining all four, they concocted a comprehensive recipe for success. They grasped intuitively that success meant balancing all five components. World Class Food and Ambiance set standards for their Technology or Product. World Class Service described their aspiration for their Market and for their People. World Class Management required consistent development of their Organization and Capital.

A VALUE AT EVERY LEVEL

Looked at another way, they selected a value at every level. At the physical level, they aimed for World-Class Food. Organizationally, their goals targeted World Class Service and Management. At the psychological level, they strived for a World-Class Ambiance. By inference, World-Class Service also required meeting the higher psychological needs of their staff.

They committed to follow the implications of each of these values. World Class Food requires the highest standards. They make fresh foods from scratch. The menu is contemporary American with a mix of world cuisines. When what they needed wasn't available, they developed it. They couldn't find exotic herbs locally, for example. Fugo called local hothouses until she persuaded one farmer to take a chance on herbs. Today, her herb farmer has 600 accounts, including Sammy's.

World Class Service requires measurement. Sammy's surveys 10 percent of reservations by phone the next day. Fugo, her husband, and their chef read every report. Any dissatisfied customer gets a call from Fugo. The effort, she says, "keeps everybody focused on how do I please the customer, rather than how do I please my manager."

World Class Service also requires a World Class staff. Sammy's application forms test spelling and math skills. "The

199

idea that dishwashers don't have to read is ridiculous," she says. "They use chemicals. We've got computer systems everywhere." Sammy's tests all floor staff every year on questions customers are likely to ask. What is the largest freighter that comes down the river? What is the best-selling cognac? How many champagnes are on the wine list? Servers learn the food process so they can understand what Fugo calls "the poetry and presentation" behind every dish. They have to know what's in each sauce to advise customers with allergies or who are on diets.

World Class Management means understanding what restaurateurs call "the economics of the plate." If a torte consists of 26 slices, there's no profit in slice one. The profit is in slice 26. It's a tough concept to sell. "Your staff believes that you're making money with every scoop of soup," says Fugo. World Class Management means setting up procedures to overcome the bane of the industry—theft. Fugo visited large companies to learn how to create a modern purchase order and receiving procedure. She put her father in charge of receiving. Her dad "counts every lemon," she says proudly. He weighs everything coming in the door on a special scale. That includes meat, vegetables, and even stationery.

DiOrio runs the day-by-day operations, particularly purchasing. He has specifications for everything. "My favorite," says Fugo, "is 'a tomato must be red.'" An advisory board of senior Cleveland business people reviews major management decisions with the owners. Every year the board and two owners go on a retreat to discuss the future of the business.

ENSURING WORLD CLASS AMBIANCE

To ensure World Class Ambiance, Fugo personally coordinates most of the interior decorating. "I want it to feel like your living room," she says. Designs on the plates pick up the theme of the bridges visible from Sammy's spectacular view of the river. Sammy's has become a favorite spot for international visitors.

Fugo brought in a trainer to teach her frontline staff the differences between Japanese and U.S. dining norms. On another occasion, the staff learned that only the maître d' should approach German guests, not the server. "We're a little restaurant, 130 seats, in the Flats of Cleveland," says Fugo. "Yet World Class Ambiance requires all this knowledge." The standard behind the Ambiance value is that "people who travel extensively must feel comfortable here."

High performance on demanding values attracts attention in any arena. *Nation's Restaurant News* named Sammy's to its Fine Dining Hall of Fame in 1987. It was the first restaurant in Cleveland and only the second in Ohio to receive the honor. The judges noted the restaurant's role in the development of the Flats and the rejuvenation of Cleveland. Fugo was Chivas Regal Entrepreneur of the Year in 1988. In 1992, City Life won a business leadership award from *Restaurant Business* magazine.

Fugo and DiOrio don't want another destination restaurant, but people keep knocking on their door with interesting offers. Their catering business has grown fourfold since 1988. They manage the Keynote restaurant for Cleveland's Severance Hall concert house and five other locations. City Life's annual sales now top $5 million.

The owners of Popp Telcom and City Life intuitively grasped values that would make their business successful. They didn't talk about a values process or the five components. Yet they created a process that can be repeated by any entrepreneur. Bill Popp applied his value of Consistency to every component of his business, using his procedure books to get the job done. Fugo and DiOrio, filled with high aspiration, selected values that required exceptional performance in every component. After that, as Popp likes to say, "it was just common sense."

Thousands of other entrepreneurs rush into business unarmed with values that could improve their odds of success.

Through hard work and gritty determination, many of these survival-driven companies do manage to succeed. However, they will never understand how much more success and satisfaction was available from the commonplace miracle all around them.

CHAPTER 17

ON THE BRINK:
TURNAROUND VALUES

When the company's going under, who has time for values? Only the daring—and farsighted. The values-driven formula for a rapid turnaround: Tap into values that created initial success. Examine collapsing components for clues about new values to add. 3Com published its revised values in the same packet that announced its biggest layoff.

$\mathbb{T}$urning around troubled companies is a science and an art. The science is a set of numbers-based techniques. The art lies in reviving values that made the company successful in the past. Short-term results flow from application of the science. Enduring success grows from effective use of both science and art.

Turnaround is becoming a formal discipline. The Turnaround Management Association, established in 1987, already boasts 1,600 members. At conferences and in publications, members exchange effective techniques. They talk about how to stop cash-flow hemorrhages. They trade tips on rebuilding collapsed markets. Leading business schools now offer courses on turnaround management. Consulting companies have specialists in reviving dying organizations.

Investment bankers and venture capitalists are also players. In pulling together family businesses into mega-retail chains, they surface plenty of turnaround opportunities. The financiers bring in urgently needed capital. However, their fast turnaround techniques are the real bedrock of their business.

The turnaround specialist is above all a simplifier. It's easy for operating managers to forget the basics. They rationalize away signals from an unforgiving market. They ignore deteriorating cash flow. They permit the skills of their organizations to wither. Lack of attention brings trouble. Sustained lack of attention escalates trouble into crisis. Too weighty a crisis creates paralysis. Enter the turnaround specialist.

A NATURAL TALENT FOR CRISIS

Twenty years ago, turnaround specialists were known as troubleshooters. Every big company had some. They were managers with a supposed "natural talent" for working through a crisis. Bored on maintenance assignments, their specialty was jumping into troubled situations. Like today's turnaround specialists, they were quick studies, able to analyze situations and propose solutions in a few days. They would stay long enough to put their solutions in place and move on. Today, in downsized Corporate America, their role has been largely filled by outside consultants.

Unfortunately, too few troubleshooters are around to help build the discipline of turnaround. Instead, today's model is the consultant, the CPA, the venture capitalist. Their skills are formidable, but their concentration is heavily on the quantitative. Effective turnarounds require solid building blocks on both sides of the ledger. Wall Street and the business press always applaud the quantitative. Stocks will rise on news of staff cutbacks, cancellation of expensive dud products, and the sharpening of market focus. These are important moves to reduce costs and restore confidence. Alone, however, they will not guarantee long-term revival. For that, the turnaround specialist must renew the power of the company's values in every component.

In any situation warranting a turnaround, the five components are seriously awry. Attention goes immediately to capital, specifically to cash. By the time the turnaround specialist takes charge, cash is usually the priority problem. I once asked a top European troubleshooter what he did first. "Get my hands on the cash flow," was his instant reply.

Lack of cash is a problem and symptom. Like hospital emergency teams, turnaround specialists must keep the unconscious patient breathing. They must also find out what's wrong. In near-death cases, all the components may be reeling. Perhaps the *market* has migrated elsewhere. The company's *people* may be dispirited and unproductive. Its *technology* may be obsolete. Its bureaucratic *organization* may strangle all initiative. Its *capital* strength may be buckling under a heavy debt load.

Troubleshooters lacked the sophisticated tools of today's turnaround specialists. However, they knew how and where to look. Like skillful mechanics, the best of them had a clear mental picture of how a healthy company functions. They contrasted what they found with that picture and determined what it would take to close the gaps in weak or collapsed components. Then they did it.

WHEN MORALE MATTERED

Troubleshooters were seldom consultants or financiers. Most of them had worked for the company a long time. They understood the company's values and had internalized them. Their actions were shaped by those values as much as by the demands of the immediate crisis. Troubleshooters worked in an era before downsizing was an automatic reaction to every setback. In most cases, their revival depended on the existing workforce. Morale mattered.

One troubleshooter I knew worked for a highly successful company. Immediate cash flow was seldom his problem. His job specialty was turning around unsuccessful subsidiaries. He would show up on Monday after the local manager had been fired on Friday. "What's the first thing you do on that Monday?" I once asked him. "Paint the place," he replied. "It lifts morale and tells people better times are coming."

"Always?" I asked.

"Always. By the time the local manager is replaced, the physical plant has always deteriorated."

Such small touches flow from the art rather than the science of successful turnarounds. Even in the midst of crisis, what values does the turnaround manager espouse? How do those values link with the qualities that carried the company to its former success? How visibly does the turnaround specialist demonstrate commitment to those values?

In time, values will emerge more fully in the quantitative discipline of turnaround management. For the moment, however, they are most often visible when the turnaround specialist is someone with a deep commitment to the company. Often that person is a newly appointed CEO who faces a crisis from day one. The revival at 3Com Corporation, against high odds, illustrates how a committed leader creates a turnaround by combining logical quantitative decisions with deeply felt values.

FROM NEAR EXTINCTION TO REVIVAL

3Com moved from success to success to near extinction to stunning revival. This Santa Clara, California, company was one of Silicon Valley's early showcases. Its networking technology Ethernet revolutionized the way personal computers communicate and share information. After a decade of success, the company made a near fatal move into the broader computer business. "Few companies," noted the *San Francisco Chronicle*, "have gone through such travails as 3Com Corporation and lived to tell of them."[1]

Debra Engel, 3Com's vice president of corporate services, says the company had a "desire to be great" from the beginning. Many of the original entrepreneurs had worked at

Hewlett-Packard Company and brought HP's commitment to values with them. They created a high-performance climate. The company's personality was characterized by technological strength, trust, integrity, and concern for staff. From its founding in 1979 until 1987, 3Com grew to be a $110 million company. "We had the right technology and were in a new field," says Engel. "It was a great place to be."

Then came a string of blunders that 3Com people discuss with exceptional candor. The first was a merger with Bridge Communications, Inc., in September 1987. On paper it was a nearly perfect union. 3Com's products facilitated networking within an office. Bridge's specialty was wide area networks, linking computers in different sites. The deal even added management depth. Bridge founder William Carrico was to succeed 3Com CEO William Krause, who was to become chairman for a few years and then bow out.

It seemed a textbook-perfect merger. However, no one had checked for values. While 3Com "was very participative, very consensus oriented, Bridge was much more autocratic," recalls Engel. Since the two companies were only a few miles apart, it made sense to combine offices after the merger. From the beginning, "there were massive conflicts at the behavioral level," continues Engel. Managers argued "over what appeared to be very simple things like whether you were going to have offices with walls or no offices." Doors became an issue. Compensation and perquisite philosophies differed.

Conflict spilled over to the executive level. There was perceived sweet accord at the conceptual level when executives met to combine operations. When the agenda shifted to the everyday details, things fell apart. Nerves began to fray. CEO Bill Krause angrily stomped out of a joint meeting at one point. Strong issues emerged around which executives would manage which surviving units. "It was difficult to have a conversation," says Engel. "The foundation wasn't there. The basic principles weren't agreed upon."

"How Could There Be a Problem?"

These were not strangers brought together by some Wall Street wizardry. The companies had done business together for years. The executives knew and liked one another. There were social ties beyond the business. "We were almost intimate," says Engel. "So it was like, how could there be a problem?"

Looking back, Engel says the merger negotiations moved too quickly. Even basic discussions like how to combine sales organizations got scant attention. The negotiators were action-oriented entrepreneurs. Their success grew from technological virtuosity. They understood the direction their markets were moving. They saw their technologies fit together. They brought complementary market strengths. Unlike many mergers, there would be few staff redundancies. It seemed a no-brainer, a winning deal for everyone. "So, it was the market's out there. We get along. We'll be better together than apart."

"Then," Engel adds, "came Monday morning."

By Spring 1988 the split was obvious to everyone. People were well mannered, according to Engel, but the underlying atmosphere was hostile. When the two groups came together, "participation would just drop. It was very perfunctory. People withheld information." The two staffs stayed apart, "speculating about who would win and what would happen next." The mounting problems became "a win-lose type of game."

Krause and Carrico reached stalemate. They brought in an organizational psychologist to help them work through the issues. The one saving point, says Engel, was they both wanted the company to win. Shortly thereafter, Carrico decided to leave, together with Bridge cofounder Judith Estrin. Carrico told Engel that he had not realized how strongly the 3Com culture was embedded. He understood he would have to embrace that culture to lead it. Trying to change it might destroy the company. Since his own style had been highly successful, he did not want to change. The only logical solution was to leave. Robert Metcalfe, the inventor of Ethernet and founder of the company, told the *San Francisco*

Chronicle: "The 10 things you can do wrong in an acquisition we did."[2]

TROUBLES BARELY STARTED

Troubles had barely started. Business orders, which had remained strong throughout the leadership crisis, now began to falter. 3Com had invested heavily in a technology joint venture with software giant Microsoft Corporation. Distracted by the project and its internal upheavals, 3Com had neglected the field it knew best—networking hardware. In 1989, Microsoft abandoned the joint venture and 3Com's earnings began to fall. On a single day in June 1990 its shares fell by 28 percent. 3Com stock that had been selling for close to $20 a share eventually dropped to $5.

Krause recognized that drastic action was necessary. With his usual candor, he later admitted, "I didn't have the emotional courage to do what needed to be done."[3] He determined his final contribution would be to put in place a successor who would carry out the necessary radical surgery. For practical purposes, he handed the daily operations of the company over to three senior executives. "The hope was," remembers Engel, "that this foursome would work effectively enough that we could buy some time to see who would emerge as the next president of the company."

The triumvirate, known on the grapevine as "the three amigos," worked reasonably well together. There was little relief from the tension in the company. Business continued to decline. Polarization got worse. "I thought it was a disaster," Engel says simply. She remembers "the company was torn apart because many were placing bets" on who would be the next president. Even so, she admires the four leaders, especially Krause. They kept things steady by consistently holding the interest of the company above their own ambitions and desires.

The cycle of bad luck continued. In the fall of 1990, the

board attempted to bring in an industry leader as CEO. After the attempt failed, the board no longer had time to search further outside. Given the multifaceted crisis, Engel says, they had to look inside and "take their best shot." Surprising many, they passed over Robert Metcalfe, the inventor of Ethernet. Instead they chose Eric Benhamou, one of the three amigos and a founder of Bridge Communications. Benhamou had been running 3Com's software products division. Metcalfe left the company.

"COULD HE GET IT DONE?"

Benhamou was 35 at the time he became CEO in September 1990. He was born in Algeria and raised in France where his parents immigrated. He had come to Palo Alto, California, to attend graduate engineering school at Stanford University. He joined Bridge as vice president of engineering shortly after graduation. Engel remembers thinking he had little of the charisma of Krause, Metcalfe, or Carrico. He had impressed the board because it was "obvious that he knew what had to be done." Yet the question was, "Could he get it done?" Benhamou was soft-spoken and never eager to impose his ideas on others. However, Engel believed him implicitly when he told her, "I didn't take this job lightly. I will do whatever I have to do to be successful."

Benhamou has an unusual personal asset that still amazes Engel. She believes he acquires skills as quickly as other people acquire knowledge. If, after reading a book or having a conversation with an expert, "he decides the content is of value, he can just take it on. He can demonstrate those skills. He can just do it."

Benhamou's first months as CEO gave him ample opportunity to demonstrate his rapid learning skills. To pull 3Com back from the brink, he had to realign the company's products. He had to bring costs quickly in line with income. Difficult as these were, they were standard turnaround management moves.

From the beginning he also placed heavy emphasis on reviving 3Com's qualitative ledger. That meant strengthening the company's wounded personality.

"We had lost three years," Benhamou said later, "but three and one-half or four years would have been fatal."[4] In January 1991, 3Com announced plans to abandon computer hardware and network operating software. It would concentrate exclusively on networking hardware used to link computers in multiple locations. The move meant a layoff of 235 workers, about 12 percent of 3Com's workforce. The company took a $45 million charge against earnings. Even in retreat, Benhamou emphasized the company's future as "a global data networking company."

Benhamou insisted the layoff be handled with integrity, one of 3Com's values from the beginning. Most layoffs occur on Friday, leaving the victims and survivors without support for the weekend. 3Com reversed the process. On Friday, January 4, 3Com briefed supervisors who would have to tell people they were fired on Monday. The company provided training and counseling sessions for those supervisors over the weekend. After supervisors told staff members they were fired on Monday, counselors were immediately available. Training courses on lowering stress and preparing to get a new job began on Tuesday. An outplacement center opened following the training sessions.

PAYING ATTENTION TO SURVIVORS

Unlike most downsizing companies, 3Com paid as much attention to survivors as it did to those who lost their jobs. On January 8, the company published a two-month calendar of support activities for all employees. There were courses and events every workday. Special seminars focused on dealing with the transition for staff and for managers. Other trainers offered tips on stress management and managing change personally.

Managers' brown-bag lunches featured lectures on specific transition skills. A Moving Ahead as a Group seminar was available for individual work groups. Engel's human resources teams scheduled drop-ins every day. At these sessions, HR people talked with whoever showed up. There was no agenda. Grief was not only acknowledged, it was institutionalized. The company encouraged going-away parties for employees who lost their jobs and celebrations as they found new employment.

The first day there was an information packet explaining the changes for every employee. In addition to the schedule of events, the packet contained specific advice for "taking care of yourself." Benhamou's cover letter spoke of his "consternation" over the decision. He asked employees to bring any issue to his attention via e-mail. He invited them "to feel free to stop and chat with me in the halls and the cafeteria."

Also included in the packet: a newly updated statement of 3Com's seven core values. Publishing the statement at such a moment was a high risk. Callowness in implementing the downsizing would make the statement seem a product of fools or hypocrites. After a botched merger, a collapsed deal with Microsoft, an upheaval over succession, and now a layoff, management had precious little credibility to waste. The statement would certainly sprinkle salt on open wounds. In bold capital letters, it talked about people as **OUR MAJOR ASSET**. It stressed the need to Value the Individual.

The conventional wisdom was certainly to "save those happy thoughts for a happier day after we get through this." Instead, Benhamou challenged himself and his team to be judged by those values during the worst crisis most of them had faced. Topping the list of seven values was "Act with Honesty and Integrity." The definition gave explicit guidance, almost as if written for such a crisis. "Be honest in all our dealings. Tell the truth. Make clear commitments among ourselves and with our customers and partners. Meet those commitments. Communicate openly."

A TEST OF FIRE

Seldom have corporate values been put through such a test of fire so quickly and so dramatically. The risk paid off. "I've never had such positive impact from such a negative event," Engel says. Even years later, the effort continues to pay off. In the computer business there is always risk of another layoff. However, says Engel, there is now an underlying confidence in how such a crisis would be handled. Management works hard to avoid that eventuality. Careful management of headcount and outsourcing of work keep permanent staff below capacity. When small redundancies do occur, the company offers affected employees either severance or a temporary job while they look inside and outside. How long does a temporary job last? The limit has never been tested, Engel says.

The seven values had been developed at the top levels of the company. In the months after the layoffs, Benhamou took 3Com's revised strategy and values to groups within the company. In revising the values, senior management had focused on a key question: "What in the old culture is inhibiting us from being successful?" Three themes emerged. The company needed greater urgency. As a technological leader, it had not paid enough attention to the customer. Finally, given the turbulence of its market, it needed better understanding of competition. Those issues translated into three of the seven values:

- **Walk Constantly in the Shoes of Our Customers.** Always decide and act with the customer as our major focus. Listen to our customers; act on what is heard. Continually improve our quality to meet customer expectations.
- **Be a Tough Competitor.** Know our competitors. Keep them present in our mind in every action we take. Outthink them; outmaneuver them. Improve on their ideas, products, and processes. Beat them to market.
- **Act with Urgency.** Focus on what needs to happen now. Own the issue. Make decisions that need to be made. Fight

the "big company syndrome." Keep long-term strategic goals in mind.

Benhamou kicked off each session by highlighting how the 1990s were different from the 1980s. He emphasized the need for speed and competitiveness—new themes to a company that competed largely on technology in the 1980s. He began to change standards, processes, and structures to match the new values.

Under a new time-based competitiveness program, teams elevated the value of Urgency in major processes. New product introduction cycles fell from 16 months to less than a year. A newly created central marketing organization gathers in-depth information on customers. A new strategic accounts system coordinates customer relations. Formal tracking and benchmarking against competitors began in earnest. To link all employees with the market, stock options continued to be the main bonus system, and a profit-sharing program was revitalized. Neither employees nor shareholders had reason to complain. The stock rose from a low of around 5 at the time of the layoff to nearly 100 (after a two-for-one split) four years later. In the years since the turnaround, 3Com has gone from revenues of $400 million a year to $400 million a quarter.

ESSENTIALLY A SIMPLIFIER

3Com stands for Computer Communication Compatibility, a phrase coined by Robert Metcalfe in 1979. Benhamou's strategic vision is to extend that concept into the emerging world of global data networking. Like all turnaround leaders, Benhamou is essentially a simplifier. He wants to make building and managing data networks easier anywhere in the world. Today, 3Com is a global company with about 4,500 employees and 71 offices in 30 countries. Now only 50 percent of 3Com's manufacturing, R&D, sales, and services resources are in Santa Clara. Benhamou says the company must compensate for this physical dispersion with forces that bring the company together, most notably "a common set of values." Values, he says, act as a primary "binding agent" around the world.

A substantial portion of 3Com's growth is fueled by the nine companies it acquired between 1992 and late 1995. After the Bridge Communications experience, 3Com pays scrupulous attention to the qualitative side of any proposed acquisition. Comparing values is the "very first thing" assessed, says Benhamou. "I know if this doesn't fit, the rest is irrelevant, even if the financial models look great." High-tech companies are moving so fast, he explains, that 3Com is not really acquiring a technology at all. "The most important thing we are buying is the goodwill of the people" who will keep the technology state of the art.

A TIME FOR REINVENTING

In late 1995, Benhamou launched a reassessment of the company's values. When a company is on the way up, as 3Com is now, "is the best time to start reinventing" the future, he says. The result will be replacement "of the old dream with a new dream for ourselves. . . . And it should be something more than just being bigger and making more profits."

3Com plays in a fast league. The global marketplace glitters with promised riches, yet technological change can make that promise obsolete overnight. "We know," says Benhamou, "all it would take is a delayed product cycle for the company to be in difficulty." By the time you read this, 3Com could be in trouble again. If that happens, Benhamou's accomplishments may look less impressive. All except one achievement, however. With courage and commitment, he has brilliantly combined values and the numbers in a highly successful turnaround. No matter what happens to 3Com now, Eric Benhamou has successfully foreshadowed the future of turnaround management.

CHAPTER 18

CROSSING THE FRONTIER: GLOBAL VALUES

Values are seldom culture specific, but their behavioral expressions usually are. H. B. Fuller and Johnson & Johnson implement values globally, yet they're careful to respect local differences. This is a necessary skill today, when being the low-cost producer is no longer enough. The only sure path to global success is being qualitatively number one.

Outpacing global competitors requires superior performance on both the quantitative and qualitative ledgers. This becomes more apparent every day as low-cost producers challenge Western supremacy in the global marketplace.

For the values-driven company, the global market is the ultimate test. It's hard work defining consistent customer service standards in New York, Des Moines, and Los Angeles. You add cultural and language barriers when you extend that effort to São Paulo, Paris, and Hong Kong. Choose a psychological value such as Trust or Respect, and the required effort expands rapidly.

So do the benefits. Global market analysts traditionally focus on being the low-cost producer. Yet cost is the beginning, not the end, in competing globally. Japan was a low-cost producer in the 1950s and 1960s. It became a serious global competitor through its Quality in the 1970s. It solidified competitive advantage in the 1980s by adding superior Service and Responsiveness. South Korea followed a similar path.

Today, low-wage/low-cost exporting countries are striving to follow suit. All are rediscovering the same obvious truth: Low price is always important, but it is never enough. The single exception is pure commodity businesses. For everyone else, continuing relationships built on enduring values build competitive advantage.

Winners in the international arena always understood this. Three centuries ago, the Dutch sent their mercantile fleets roaming the world in search of markets and suppliers. From the beginning, Dutch captains understood that building mutually beneficial relationships was more intelligent than getting the best deal on this trip. True to this tradition, the Dutch have worked diligently to set up productive partnerships throughout the world.

Global competition has two playing fields—home and abroad. Many managers pay little attention to competition "out there." Then one day that competition suddenly takes market share "right here."

Harold Corner is founder of C&J Industries, a Meadville, Pennsylvania, mold-making business. For years, Corner lived securely with a myth shared by many American businesspeople. He neither feared nor had much interest in foreign competition. How could foreigners compete for his business? For generations, industrial mold making required close distance between supplier and customer. How else could you handle revisions and corrections on molds in progress?

Then Corner's customers spotted an opportunity in the global marketplace. Why not buy molds at far lower cost overseas and then send them to local suppliers for final modifications? By the time Corner woke up, the Japanese were offering lower-priced, custom-made molds delivered to his customers. Worse, the molds were arriving in the United States in half the time he was quoting to supply next door.

To fight back, Corner identified the Strategic Values critical to the survival of his business. He focused on Productivity, Speed, and Standardization. Over the next two and one-half years, he revamped his product line, production technology, operating systems, and employee training in line with these values. Along the way, he cut delivery time from 32 to 16 weeks. He lowered his costs to below those of his Japanese competitors. By the end of three years, he had tripled his revenues.

The second, more widely recognized playing field for global values is abroad. Many companies discover the pitfalls of expansion when they open their second restaurant, office, or factory in another city or state. Competing internationally in countries with different regulations, standards, customer expectations, and language multiplies the challenge at least tenfold. Going global requires organizing globally.

Anthony Andersen is chair of the 107-year-old multinational H. B. Fuller Company. He says his company has a "Minnesota mindset," meaning progressive business practices are in its genes. Tony Andersen is famous in Minnesota—and, increasingly, around the world—for his friendly homespun style. He says he is not "your typical *Fortune* 500 CEO." True, but in the last quarter century he has guided Fuller from annual sales of $60 million to over $1 billion.

Despite Andersen's just-one-of-the-folks style, Fuller is a sophisticated, hard-driving multinational. It operates manufacturing plants in 32 countries. Non-U.S. operations provide slightly less than half of revenues and a like amount of profits. The company has been on the *Fortune* 500 industrial list for over a decade, moving up every year to its present rank of 368.

Fuller makes and sells industrial adhesives, sealants, and coatings. There is a good chance Fuller-made glue holds this book together. In addition, Fuller manufactures paint in Latin America, waxes in Europe, and sanitation chemicals and powder coatings in the United States.

THE SHAREHOLDERS COME THIRD

Wall Street knows Fuller as the company that puts shareholders third but treats them better than most. Its Mission statement clearly prioritizes four constituencies: customers, employees, stockholders, and communities where it operates. However, shareholders seldom complain. Over the past 10 years, the company has returned almost 20 percent annually to its investors.

Andersen took over as president from his father in 1971. Fuller was already a U.S. leader in safety practices. In its budding international business, it adhered to local regulations. At the time, that seemed progressive enough. Then a disaster halfway around the globe dramatically expanded Andersen's and Fuller's safety commitment.

In 1984, in Bhopal, India, more than 2,000 people died in an industrial accident at a Union Carbide plant. Press and government scathingly compared local safety standards there with more stringent U.S. requirements. Critics contended Carbide might have averted disaster by enforcing its domestic safety policies. At a minimum, tighter safety rules would have reduced the death toll. Carbide eventually agreed to pay $470 million in claims.

The unfolding story engrossed Andersen. He followed news of the accident for months. Fuller was in a different business, but it did deal with toxic materials. Its policy of enforcing local laws and regulations meant different standards at home and abroad. "What if it had been us?" Andersen kept asking. Many senior U.S. executives and boards asked the same question. Safety standards in many manufacturing multinationals did get more rigorous. That wasn't enough for Andersen. He wanted to live up to Fuller's commitment to Safety everywhere by establishing consistency with the value of concern for employees. He went to his board with a bold proposal: As quickly as possible, Fuller would have the same safety standards in its U.S. and foreign operations.

A year later, when the scope of the task was clear, he asked

219

the board for an even more sweeping commitment: A board resolution giving *automatic approval* of capital expenditures to correct safety and environmental problems anywhere. "We will discuss how to do it," said Andersen. "We will no longer discuss whether to do it."

When Andersen requested this policy, he lacked the prestige he enjoys today. He had been president for only 10 years. The company had sales of less than $450 million. Yet he asked for carte blanche endorsement for a safety and environmental program that was sure to be expensive. He wanted the board to send "a clarion call throughout the company." When the board endorsed his request, the message resonated everywhere. It instilled pride that continues today. Visible commitment to a stretch target generated uncommon energy.

AN EVER-ADVANCING TARGET

Fuller needed that energy. Andersen had defined Safety by an ever-advancing measurement—the U.S. standard. That meant the company had to play catch-up around the world. The challenge was formidable in the Third World, where regulations were nonexistent or years behind the United States. Fuller had to create a global monitoring system. It had to extend its domestic safety improvement program around the world.

Fuller also had to live up to other commitments and values. It had to keep customers happy. It wanted to remain among the top employers in pay and benefits. It had to generate cash to pay for the new safety and environmental program. It also required cash to finance its global expansion and provide its usual high return to shareholders. Finally, it had committed to give 5 percent of pretax profits to the communities where it operated.

Any major values effort requires a new structure to support it. At Fuller, the new structure consisted of two permanent committees. The first, chaired by Andersen, brings together senior people in an oversight role. The second, an operating group, consists of managers from every region worldwide and staff people from St. Paul.

Joe Pellish, an enthusiastic former in-house lawyer, heads WEHS, the Worldwide Environment, Health and Safety Committee. WEHS tracks health, safety, and environmental issues in 105 locations. It ensures, for example, that each Fuller facility updates its annual emergency plan, covering everything from fires to tornadoes. WEHS requires complete safety inspections at every location every month. It audits health, safety, and environmental standards on a three-year schedule.

In the United States, OSHA requires U.S. companies to have updated Material Safety Data Sheets (MSDS) with instructions for handling hazardous materials produced by the company. Fuller provides MSDSs in the language of every country where its products are sold. Pellish estimates the company distributes more than 110,000 copies of the material safety sheets annually.

SHORT-TERM SOLUTIONS

Initially, WEHS settled for short-term solutions while addressing underlying problems. A survey revealed a serious lack of fire-alarm equipment in some locations. Acting quickly, WEHS required every facility to have an audible warning device within 90 days. Then it undertook a three-year plan to install the right equipment in every facility. Some managers asked to extend the three-year deadline. Other deadlines were more pressing, they explained. The oversight committee turned them down flat.

It's not all audits or requirements. WEHS answers nearly 2,000 customer questions a year about safety issues relating to Fuller products. It coordinates and monitors the company's extensive safety and environmental training programs. Fuller teaches fire prevention and how to handle hazardous materials. It offers courses on first aid and CPR. Now that all standards are at least equal to those of the United States, WEHS is pushing into new areas. Joe Pellish insisted that I try out one of the new secretary's chairs bought under WEHS's office ergonomics program.

Fuller spends an estimated $4 million annually on the safety program, not counting the capital costs. How much of that money comes back in savings? Fuller doesn't track numbers like that. It does know accidents per 200,000 hours of production in Latin America are now at two, compared with eight near the start of the program. Joe Pellish remembers another number very well. He went to Costa Rica to present the first award in Latin America for one million hours without an accident.

PERSUASION AND COMMUNICATION

Fuller has installed strict universal standards to support its value. The Fuller example proves the global applicability of basic corporate values. They are not culture specific. With enough management support, even standards can be universal.

Another admired multinational relies on persuasion and communication rather than standards to keep its values consistent around the world. *Business Week* calls Johnson & Johnson "a big company that works."

Decentralization is a key strength behind that accolade, says the magazine: "... presidents of [J&J's] 166 separately chartered companies are not just encouraged to act independently— they're expected to. . . . they decide who will work for them, what products they will produce, and which customers they will sell to."[1]

A commitment to decentralization is half of J&J's success formula. The other half, a 50-year-old values statement, is the glue that holds J&J together internationally. J&J has a manufacturing or direct sales presence in some 60 countries. It operates, through distributors or other sales channels, in another 150. Its sales top $15 billion, with 51 percent coming from international markets.

Commitment to what we call empowerment today is a tradition at J&J. In the 1930s, Chairman Robert Wood Johnson,

son of a J&J founder, encouraged independent decisions at J&J units. Sixty years' experience, says *Business Week*, makes J&J "a model of how to make decentralization work."

Johnson left another important tradition at J&J—the Credo. He personally wrote the document in 1943 as he was taking the company public. Chapter 10 described how James Burke, a later chairman, rejuvenated the Credo in 1975. Burke left a tradition of his own—the Credo challenge. Every J&J president, managing director, and general manager participates. Decentralization unleashes energy throughout J&J. The challenge channels that energy into common commitment.

James D. DeVito, vice president of educational research and services, is responsible for Credo challenges. Every challenge mixes Americans with senior managers from many countries. Johnson, a patriotic American, wrote the Credo primarily for an American audience. How do non-Americans respond? Every challenge must deal with that issue. J&J has been "very deliberate in our efforts to make this a universal document," says DeVito.

UNDERWHELMING IN DESIGN

Credo challenges are simple meetings, "underwhelming" in design, says DeVito. Any international company trying to unite people around Core Values could easily adapt the J&J design. Challenges take 24 hours. Participants assemble at 5:00 P.M. J&J chairman Ralph Larsen begins by challenging the group: How is J&J performing against its statement?

Larsen "speaks personally and passionately about his own belief system as it relates to the Credo," says DeVito. Larsen bases his remarks on experience, observation, and the J&J Credo Survey. Every two years, J&J invites its 82,000 employees to respond on this anonymous survey. The survey asks standard human resource questions plus specific questions about performance on the Credo.

After dinner, the thirty participants break into three smaller groups for discussion. There are usually four issues on the agenda. The group debates the *relevance* of the Credo. Is it a competitive advantage or disadvantage? They discuss *performance* on the Credo. How effective are they in communicating the Credo to lower levels? *Change* is the third issue. Does operating reality require changes in the Credo? Today, heated discussions center on the Credo's statement that J&J employees "must have a sense of security in their jobs." Is this unrealistic in an era of downsizing? Finally, there are specific issues raised by the chairman.

Differences in cultural and national perspectives quickly emerge. Discussing communities, the Credo says: "We must encourage civic improvements and better health and education . . . protecting the environment and natural resources." Europeans often view such tasks as a governmental responsibility. The Credo says compensation "must be fair and adequate." When carried to specifics, that guideline often sparks controversy during discussions.

ALL SENIOR MANAGERS MUST ATTEND

"We tell people they need to be open," says DeVito. "They need to speak their minds. It's okay for them to debate. It's legitimate for them to argue. In the process, people get in touch with their own values. They examine whether their value system is compatible with the values portrayed in the document."

At 2:30 P.M. the following day, Larsen returns to hear their reports. He asks questions. He gives his own views. DeVito and his team keep careful records of discussions. They catalog suggestions. When patterns appear, J&J's senior management reviews the issue. Credo challenges prompted a worldwide review of extra compensation practices.

At the close of the session, each participant gets a Credo challenge meeting kit. The package provides everything necessary to conduct a Credo challenge back at their unit. J&J requires all senior managers to attend at least one challenge during their careers. In keeping with decentralization, it doesn't follow up on who runs sessions at home. Based on anecdotal evidence, DeVito believes the percentage who follow up is high. After a Credo challenge, a Japanese company reviewed its policies on promoting females. A Hong Kong company refused a lucrative contract from a customer involved in pirating the trademark of a U.S. company.

The Credo's emphasis on "clean, orderly and safe" working conditions has prompted action plans around the world. The Credo calls for "development and advancement for those qualified." That can be a problem in countries where the companies are struggling to create net income, says DeVito. In such cases, discussions focus on on-the-job training. Matching limited resources with Credo requirements is always a hot topic.

That's why DeVito believes commitment to "a sense of security" for employees should remain in the document. While J&J has not gone through major companywide layoffs, it has sold, consolidated, or closed companies as markets shift. That prompts discussion at Credo challenges. Are we living up to this statement? Will we do so in the future? "The document enables us to have those conversations," says DeVito. "It legitimizes those conversations. It doesn't mean that we come up with easy answers or answers everyone agrees with. However, it allows the conversation to take place." DeVito argues that without the "sense of security" phrase, "we wouldn't have these conversations."

DeVito believes the psychic contract between company and workers is evolving. A "sense of security" may soon mean being at the "top of your craft." The company's obligation would then shift to helping employees improve their skills rather than guaranteeing jobs. Credo challenges keep the dialogue open about such issues at J&J.

DeVito organizes four or five challenges every year. The Credo forces people to think beyond self-interest, he says. If career advancement is the only driver, "you have an environment that's contentious, tricky, self-centered, and difficult to survive

225

in." In contrast, a values-driven environment "pulls people beyond immediate self-interest." When that happens, "working in a large organization can indeed be fulfilling."

INVISIBLE PROCESS

At Johnson & Johnson, the values-driven culture has become "the way we work around here." After 50 years, identification with the values requires only periodic reinforcement. Process, so important in creating a values-driven company, has become almost invisible. Jim DeVito sounds puzzled when I ask for reinforcement methods other than the challenges. "We don't have a recognition program, a Credo-of-the-year person. We don't have a Credo office. We don't have a Credo ombudsman. Our belief is simply that all employees own this document. We want everybody to exercise Credo leadership."

In global business, values are *the* competitive advantage. Compete on price? Forget it. Compete on quality? In the global arena you are up against the best of each nation's best. If quality isn't a given today, it will be tomorrow. The tools and techniques of quantitative management are essential. However, everyone has access to them.

Global companies need fast and flexible local operations. Autonomy on the local scene is clearly part of the answer. However, managing strictly by the balance sheet has spelled disaster for many companies. The glamorous conglomerates of the 1970s ran into major problems despite their world-class numbers crunching. When the local manager has all the authority to compete, what does the company stand for? With 50 years' experience, Johnson & Johnson keeps adjusting the balance. It makes subtle shifts between centralization and decentralization. It keeps its values and the numbers in careful balance. Anyone heading for the global frontier would be wise to learn from such a tested example.

CHAPTER 19

33 COMMON QUESTIONS ABOUT VALUES

What to do when your boss doesn't "walk the talk." Any hope for values after a downsizing? How can you recruit for values? How do convinced staff people persuade line managers to take action on values? Any difference between values in for-profit and not-for-profit organizations? A potpourri of 33 common questions about elevating values.

When I help groups identify and define values, people respond with quick enthusiasm. People want to find meaning in their work. They already understand work is more than just a way to pay the rent. They know work at its best frees hidden energies. Those energies open a wellspring of self-development. People quickly grasp the connection: values-driven work releases energy, leading to self-development. The mind, searching for higher organizing principles, seizes on Core Values with a certain joy.

Then come the doubts. Can this work for me? In this job? With this boss? In this industry? At my level?

Doubts are healthy. Doubts alert us to pitfalls. Doubts are the force behind careful planning. Left unchallenged, however, doubts smother enthusiasm. Groups undertaking a values effort quickly segregate themselves by their response to common doubts. **Enthusiasts** ignore the doubts and charge ahead. **Skep-**

tics articulate the doubts, but move ahead if properly supported. **Resisters** convert doubts to negativity.

Leaders cherish enthusiasts, particularly at the start of a new venture. However, skeptics and resisters have their place. Skeptics temper the blind energy of enthusiasts with practicality. Resisters embody the opposition to new ideas within the organization. They are often among the strongest, most secure people on a team. Viewing resisters as a purely negative force is a common mistake. Their resistance may be self-serving, but so is the zeal of the enthusiasts and the caution of the skeptics.

All of us embody each of these traits. The greatest enthusiasts resist a change that is too threatening. The fiercest resisters grasp at a change that advances their personal agenda.

Values-driven leadership seldom starts with a team of enthusiasts. More often, the values-driven leader must deal with every reaction. The leader's task is to spark sufficient enthusiasm to keep going. She must use the doubts of skeptics to avoid pitfalls. She must find ways to meet and deal with the arguments of the resisters. Strength grows from acknowledging enthusiasm, skepticism, and resistance wherever she finds it, even in herself.

The task is mental and emotional. Core Values touch the emotions first. Then the mind must be convinced and stay convinced. The mind works best at analysis. It divides, sorts out, explains. Breakthrough ideas begin as intuition. Then the mind finds the path to implementation.

This section is for readers already intuitively committed to elevating values at work. It provides additional analysis to overcome doubts. In my values work, I frequently encounter these questions in one form or another. Wrestling with answers reinforces the intuition and strengthens the mind's analysis.

1. What if the boss doesn't "walk the talk"?
2. Any hope for values after a downsizing?
3. Aren't all other values a subset of Quality? How do you

fit other values programs with a Total Quality Management program?

4. We are already working on TQM, diversity programs, and three benchmarking projects. How do we coordinate these efforts and set priorities?

5. Why spend all this time defining values? Why not just do it?

6. Senior management announced our values and then took a conspicuous action contrary to the values. Why should we support the values program now?

7. Even in my values-driven company, many people come to work just for the paycheck. Isn't it hypocrisy to get people to mouth platitudes they don't believe in?

8. How do you make values work when you face a suspicious labor union?

9. Can values be effective in a civil-service atmosphere?

10. Aren't these values programs just a lot of work for consultants? If you live by the Golden Rule, isn't the rest just obvious common sense?

11. Does it take a charismatic leader to get values off the ground in a company?

12. How can you recruit for values?

13. Is it in keeping with the idea of values to test potential new hires on their personal beliefs and attitudes? Yet how can you hire for values if you don't?

14. Isn't making a profit the ultimate value for any business?

15. How do you make your financial compensation system more responsive to values without losing focus on financial results?

16. How do you reconcile conflicting values?

17. What are the highest values? Is this absolute or situational?

18. In my company people with poor values, or even no values, succeed all the time. Why?

19. If I investigated any company you cite as values driven, I would certainly find some abused and unhappy employ-

ees, ignored customers, or other failures of business values. How do you account for these discrepancies?

20. What is the best values-implementation model?

21. How do you handle a key individual in a group (not the boss) who won't buy into an effort to upgrade values?

22. What are signs a values process is working in an organization?

23. How do you identify training and development needs arising from values?

24. We staff people are convinced. How do we persuade line people to take action?

25. How can values help when external change is destroying your market?

26. We are a division with an effective values process in place. We've been working on this for five years. Now, corporate has published its four values and wants us to implement them. What are we supposed to do? Throw away five years of work?

27. What's the best approach when two companies with strong values merge?

28. Is there a difference between values in a for-profit and those in a not-for-profit organization?

29. How do values differ from social responsibility and business ethics?

30. Where I work, you don't get promoted because you have the right values. You get promoted because you have the right results. What can values do for me?

31. What's the proper role of the board in setting values?

32. What's the best way to establish values—a small group at the top or a widespread process throughout the company?

33. Today we talk about religious values, ethical values, family values, and core corporate values. Is there a common relationship among these types of values?

1. What if the boss doesn't "walk the talk"? (Or, as sometimes asked, what if your values clash with the boss's ideas?)

This boss question is a perennial. "I want to do it, but my boss won't let me." The issue is stark and very real for many people. To work toward an answer, look first at the role of values in an organization.

When values are absolute, the question is significant. However, values in a company are not absolutes. First and last, values are *operational* qualities. Once inside a company, absolute values such as Truth and Perfection shed their philosophical and ethical raiment. They put on mundane work clothes like Quality and Customer Service.

A few companies strive successfully for a higher level of abstraction. ServiceMaster defined Quality as Truth. This course is rare and risky. Most companies find keeping values and definitions at operational level is challenge enough. At the operational level, values can merge comfortably with the company's goals. They can become truly company values.

The boss question grows out of an ancient human weakness. We enjoy holding others, particularly superiors, to a higher standard. However, accurate evaluations of team leaders must always consider the context of the company, its personality and its values. Either from top to bottom or bottom to top, holding people accountable for abstractions is a waste of energy and time.

Author Raymond Chandler once described his literary hero as "the best man in his world and a good enough man in any world."[1] His definition shrewdly allowed for context. Context always matters in looking at others. The issue is not whether the team leader is Trustworthy, Honest, Brave, Clean, and Reverent. The issue is whether the team leader is consistent within the corporate personality and its values. We hope for leaders who are good in any world. We should expect only leaders who are among the best in their world.

Understanding that corporate values are not absolute and

that leaders operate only in a context leads to the third element of the boss question—the team member. Both team leaders and team members operate within the same context—the corporate personality. Within that context both are servants with differing roles.

This does not mean that the team member meekly submits to the autocratic authority of the boss. The boss also submits his work to a higher framework—the corporate personality. The boss's legitimate authority grows from her contribution to the corporate personality. Ideally, team leaders and members become extensions and expansion of that personality in human form.

When the team leader is operating within these limits, she is owed support and allegiance. This approach narrows the scope for disagreements. The issue is no longer the team member's egotistic preference for her ideas versus those of the team leader. As long as the leader's actions stay within the context of the organization's values and personality, team members should follow direction.

There is a time-tested principle behind this. In the absence of compelling reasons, the lower should always submit to the higher. Although many resist this idea, it is the value of values. We instinctively believe the individual should support the family, that the state should yield its will to the nation. We shower scorn on the individualistic athlete who ignores the needs of the team.

This principle works well as long as the team leader stays within the limits of the corporate personality. This leaves ample room for team members to elevate their performance on values. Even when they raise their values performance higher than the leader's, there is little cause for disagreement. Leader and team member move toward the same direction although at a different pace. Neither should worry if team members outperform the leader. Competition to excel in values can only benefit leaders, team members, and company.

There are always cases where the leader is clearly and consistently out of bounds. Team members should stop following any leader heading into a swamp of illegal or dishonest activities. If such actions are embedded in the corporate personality, find another job, no matter what the price.

Sometimes a team leader acts independently of the limits set by a basically healthy corporate personality. In that case, team members must risk appealing to higher levels. In a functional company, such appeals produce action. Only a dysfunctional company continually condones or ignores behavior inconsistent with its personality. Frequent lapses of will weaken personalities that once were strong. The only choice then is to get out as quickly as possible.

In summary, judge the boss as you would like to be judged. Avoid high abstractions in favor of operational values. Allow for the context of the corporate personality where you both work. If the boss is seriously and consistently out of bounds, take action to remove him or yourself. Otherwise (which is almost always the case), follow his direction. Don't automatically translate any failure to live up to your high ideals as a failure to walk the talk on values.

With these issues resolved, shift your attention from the boss. Work on elevating values in your own work. You will strengthen the corporate personality, yourself, and probably your boss. After all, there is no higher compliment than a boss who imitates you.

2. Any hope for values after a downsizing?

Conventional wisdom holds that downsizing dooms a values effort. People grow cynical. Leaders forfeit the benefit of any doubt. Downsizing dramatizes management's lack of feeling. Sensitive managers succumb to survivor guilt. No one has faith in "soft" initiatives.

Surprisingly, however, the downsizing environment is wide open for rediscovering values. Success provides nowhere near as fertile ground. An unbroken string of victories leads to complacency. "Who needs it? We're doing great as we are." Adversity, on the other hand, breeds humility and, among the strong, determination.

Except on Wall Street, downsizing is commonly understood as a corporate defeat. The casualty and missing-in-action lists are painfully visible. Few leaders brag about downsizing, at least in public. Their words are apologetic. They promise to do better, to get back to the organization's roots, to pay more attention to the basics. "One benefit," they invariably commit, "is that we will get decision making back where it belongs—closer to the customer." This is the language of values renewal.

As a company expands, success dilutes its original values. The qualities that gave rise to "the way we do things around here" can begin to fade. Rote actions replace innovation. Routine substitutes for excitement. The original qualities are not lost, however. They are still locked in the company's genetic code. They are the seeds of renewal.

If values dilute in expansion, they should logically strengthen in downsizing. That requires a commitment to rediscover Core Values. A financial leg alone is not enough to support downsizing. That makes downsizing little more than a start-and-stop mechanism to compensate for sloppy leadership. Tied to values renewal, however, downsizing opens the way for true corporate revitalization.

Jack Welch took over a lethargic General Electric Company in 1981. In the next decade, he reduced employment by 200,000 through restructuring, attrition, and disposition of units. Well before downsizing ended, he successfully launched an ambitious values effort throughout the company. In his usual succinct fashion, Welch explained his strategy: "You've got to be hard to be soft."[2]

3. Aren't all other values a subset of Quality? How do you fit other values programs with a Total Quality Management program?

Excellence was the headline word of the 1980s. Quality is the headline word of the 1990s. Any set of values can be grouped under either word. Any grouping of values carries benefits and liabilities.

Quality, the current favorite, consists of a package of values at many levels. Quality cascades into Precision, Safety, Speed, Customer Service, Punctuality, Development of People, plus a half-dozen more. All of these are also stand-alone values.

Quality programs grew out of the quantitative side of the ledger. First came systems to measure defects at the end of the manufacturing line. Later, statistical process control streamlined the process. Such leaders of the Quality movement as W. Edwards Deming and Joseph Juran highlighted the necessity of a humanistic ingredient in Quality.

Today, the best Total Quality Management processes effectively blend quantitative and qualitative techniques. They marry statistical process control with humanistic change strategies. The aim is to cascade a single value and its many component values throughout a company. The success record, like those of all values processes, is mixed. Where there is commitment and clarity, there can be significant results. Where management follows a fad, the programs waste energy and money.

Grouping values under one heading focuses a unit on a single target. If the leader lends personal weight to that target, the chances of success are high. A single target communicates easily. It reduces the tension created by separate-but-equal values. Of course, it quickly becomes apparent that the single target is really multifaceted. The framework for the Malcolm Baldrige Award for Quality sets five criteria. Among these are everyday values such as Customer Satisfaction, Employee Involvement, and Continuous Improvement.

Thus Total Quality is about far more than just Quality. It is, in fact, a system designed to introduce or expand a whole range of desirable values within a company. In that, it makes a great contribution.

However, when Total Quality keeps attention focused narrowly on one value, it limits the search for other values. Zealots proclaim Total Quality as the sole and ultimate value for any company at any time. It isn't. A company can have satisfactory quality by incurring huge cost overruns, or by bullying its people. "That's not Total Quality," the zealots protest. Then they define Total Quality more expansively. Of course, they are right. However, to be right, they first must introduce and give equal weight to other values.

It is better to start with the company rather than a preordained "ultimate" value. Find out what the company needs to progress. Identify the strengths and weaknesses of its five components. Then decide which values will be most effective in energizing the weakest components. Elevate those values throughout the company. One of those values may well be Quality. Then again, it may not be. If you pick one value, recognize from the beginning that it will quickly lead you to others.

Companies already deep within Total Quality should stick with it. The system will produce results whenever it is followed sincerely and energetically. However, see Total Quality not as an end but as a path that should open wider, disclosing new values at every juncture. This will add dynamism and continual renewal to any process.

See your company or department as a network of values to be elevated, a continual process of strengthening and renewal. That vision has one additional advantage. You will be able to incorporate the next headline word into your system with ease and continuity.

4. **We are already working on TQM, diversity programs, and three benchmarking projects. Now we want to elevate another value. How do we coordinate these efforts and set priorities?**

Behind the priorities question lies a deeper issue: Why has management introduced a variety of projects? As a piecemeal attack on problems or as parts of a central strategy? When the people working on the programs don't understand the priorities, management must explain. Leaders need an overall strategy for change efforts. They need to communicate it. Otherwise, they waste three valuable assets—time, money, and the enthusiasm of their best people.

Management sets up priority conflicts by keeping projects alive too long. Many projects should die an early death. Some are failed experiments. Some are false starts that can be replaced by a better idea. When management introduces a new project or process, it should review existing efforts and clear the way for the new.

In dealing with remaining priorities, managers should stay focused on the company, not the programs. The test of an effective performance improvement program is whether it is *in tune* with the company. Does it support the company's general movement forward? When focused on the company, competing managers usually can settle conflicts.

When managers lose this wider focus, turf wars can block progress. It takes work to push any improvement process through a company. People commit to "their" process. They see another process as a competitor rather than an ally. Management often breeds disharmony by showering praise and high expectations first on one process and then on another.

Implementation is often at the heart of priority conflicts. Management launches initiatives with little appreciation of the resources that will be needed to see the work through. One management group assigned a team to benchmark characteristics of successful cultures. The team spent weeks visiting, interviewing, and analyzing a dozen companies. Management received its report warmly. However, management had no commitment or plan to introduce its suggestions. Except as development for team members, the effort was wasted.

5. Why spend all this time defining values? Why not just do it?

Business leaders are action oriented. They get ahead based on their capacity to act. "I've got it. Let's go." This energy is one of their strongest contributions to society.

Values seems a simple concept. Values-driven companies don't spend much time talking about values. They just do it. "If we study what they do, why can't we then just do it too?" Companies that have tried that approach have quickly discovered an important truth. Copying what you see on the surface in values-driven companies does not ensure you will get to where they are. The surface shows only what they do now. It does not reveal all they have done to get there.

A familiar example explains why pure imitation alone won't work. For 40 years, countries have tried to get to the root of a simple word—development. At the end of World War II, all Westernized countries except the United States had collapsed economically. Within a decade all of them, including those who lost that war, had returned to economic health. The United States had reached economic levels unsurpassed by the empires of the past.

Around the globe, nations set out on the path to development. As late as the 1970s, it seemed simple. Imitate what you liked from the West. Ignore what clashed with your sensitivities. Above all, just do it.

Today, we know better. Successful development is preceded by policies that favor it. It requires a political and social climate that fosters work. Development needs networks of organizations interlocking at all levels of society. These networks form the social, commercial, administrative, and educational infrastructures that sustain development. Based on these assets, a society creates a culture of development. That culture releases a flood of human energy. Individual initiative supports the whole effort. Society learns to value both production and purchase.

Watching how a person functions in a developed country or company can teach valuable lessons. It is inspirational. It opens the mind to the possibility of similar success. However, the lesson and inspiration cannot be transplanted wholesale to a company or culture not yet ready. In the 1970s, planners from the Soviet Union visited my office in Brussels. Their mission was to adapt the best of Western management methods into the Soviet system. As we now know, the mission was doomed from the start. The Soviet system lacked the policies, climate, and infrastructure for a culture of development.

Many of today's benchmarking teams are on a similar wild-goose chase. You can watch Xerox practice quality. You can study customer service at 3M or Disney. Watching what people do is industrial tourism. It takes months, not days, to trace how the networks link together to form infrastructures. By the time you understand how it works at Xerox, 3M, or Disney, you know you are not ready to import techniques into your company.

Does this mean the developing country or the developing company is condemned to repeat the past? Must it take 100 years to produce another 3M? Fortunately, no. The United States has compressed into three centuries the development that took Europe a millennium. Several Asian countries made the leap in a few decades. Northwestern Mutual took a century to build a values-driven culture. AT&T Universal Card did it in three years.

Conceptually, the evolutionary process works like this:

- **A compelling social atmosphere generates a pressure to work.** Current research tells us two things about the role of fathers in successful families. They are present, and they work. In effect, successful fathers generate a pressure to work that is imitated by their children. Focused leaders play the same role in a business. The social atmosphere in a developing country must favor productive work before development can take hold.

- **Work requires and creates an organization with inbuilt systems.** Basic or complex, work requires a system. The farmer rotates his crops with a system. The executive creates a system to launch a new product. In repetitive work the systems are built into the work. Over time, a network of repetitive systems requires and creates an organization.

- **For an organization to grow, it must develop organizational skills (systems) and the skills of the individuals within it.** Sustained growth requires systems and skills. Evolving organizations develop both. Creating a product requires physical and mental skills. Managing people needs a system as well as psychological skills.

- **An organization's values shape its systems and skills.** Market-driven values will create one type of systems and skills. A survival-driven company in the same industry will evolve in another direction. Core Values provide the energy that keeps systems and skills moving toward a culture of development.

Values are the drivers of accomplishment. By values we mean that which people accept as valuable. The values effort is intended to make the people in a company more conscious of the importance of certain qualitative characteristics in their work. It aims to encourage a conscious effort to upgrade work behavior in conformity with people's definition of the values. The entire process is an act of generating awareness, raising expectations, elevating consciousness. It is essentially a mental process that translates into new external behavior.

This process involves many inner steps. The first stage of the process focuses on enhancing understanding, acceptance, internalization, and ownership of the values among all employees.

Asking people to identify, define, and discuss the values stimulates their thinking. It encourages ownership, giving people a sense of participation and choice in the process. Taking the time to work on this stage thoroughly immensely enhances acceptance, commitment, and enthusiasm.

The direct question is: Why not just do it? There is an equally direct answer. If you just do it, it probably won't work. It will certainly take longer.

6. Senior management announced our values with fanfare. The next week they took a conspicuous action contrary to the values. Why should we support the values program now?

As Jack Welch would say: "Face reality as it is, not as it was or as you wish it were." Senior management is double-talking. That's not your issue. Your issue is how conscientiously you will carry out a legitimate, even honorable, directive. To be conscientious means to identify with your conscience, not the behavior of others.

If your conscience says management's behavior is illegal or immoral, leave. If management's behavior is merely wrong-headed, conscientiously follow the directive. Dragging your feet because of management's inconsistency weakens your own will. Also, you miss all the opportunities inherent in elevating values in your work.

Again and again I have emphasized the importance of sincere commitment at the top. The reality is that sometimes it isn't there. Your values "program" may fail for that lack. That doesn't excuse you from following a legitimate instruction.

In this, follow the example of effective civil servants. Conscientiousness is one of their Core Values. When political administrations change, they execute new mandates that are the opposite of yesterday's policies. Their duty is to implement, not create.

When values are handed down to you, your duty—and your

opportunity—is to implement them in your work. You will never lose by this. On the contrary, you grow more in an adverse climate than when fully supported from above.

7. **Even in my values-driven company, many people come to work for the paycheck. Isn't it hypocrisy to get people to mouth platitudes they don't believe in?**

Certainly. But then we live in a hypocritical world. We believe marriage is till death us do part. We used those words in nearly 2.4 million U.S. marriages in 1994. Yet that same year, nearly 1.2 million marriages ended in divorce. We say employees are our most important asset. Yet American Management Association member surveys show nearly 3.5 million jobs were lost through downsizing since 1989.

Living compromises our ideals. This is so common that we hardly notice—except, of course, in others. The gaps between what we profess and what we do grow from the same root cause. The cherished ideals in our minds have not yet seeped down to the practical, physical reality of our lives. When the ideal fully enters the physical level, we live it. The power of values-driven people goes far beyond their words. We see their values in physical action.

In a company, values start at the top and seep down. The values-driven company has evolved further than the average company. Its distinction is that most people profess the values and act on them. However, there are bound to be people who do not yet believe in the values. The key issue is not what they believe. What matters is how they act. Nonbelievers often follow the values because "that's the way we work around here." In time, consistent behavior will shape their beliefs. If not, they are likely to leave.

At the highest level, employees identify with the values. They translate them into behavior off the job. Du Pont has espoused the value of safety for nearly 200 years. Long-time Du Pont employees are careful drivers and keep their homes safe.

8. How do you make values work when you face a suspicious labor union?

Labor's suspicions must be analyzed. They must be faced honestly. Employees' doubts may indicate the company has few values beyond survival. In that case, stick with market-driven values. They are more likely to make sense in terms of job preservation. Ford and Chrysler gained wide union support for Quality by linking it to market survival.

Perhaps previous initiatives masked a hidden downsizing plan. If so, management must put its credibility on the line. Issue a clear statement separating the values initiative from downsizing. If you can't or won't do that, expect a long and difficult haul.

Go easy on rushing to measure values too early. "People who work for me are not stupid," one company president told me. "None of them will help me fashion a stick that I can then use to bash them on the head." It is unlikely people in your company are that stupid either.

9. Can values be effective in a civil-service atmosphere?

For most of the 20th century we thought government was the answer. At the end of the century we think government is the problem. Naive optimism has betrayed us in both attitudes. Government cannot solve 21st-century problems by getting bigger or smaller. Big government had little impact on crime rates. Small government won't make much difference either. Government is neither the answer nor the problem. It is a key element in an evolving process.

The next cycle is clear. We need larger economic units—common markets, multinational corporations, financial and telecommunications systems. Simultaneously, political units are shrinking. Through war, revolution, or democratic process, political power is shifting to smaller units—states, local school boards, political subdivisions of great nations, religious/nationalist groups.

These parallel trends are already clear in business. Every day global corporations extend their economic reach. Simultaneously, the same corporations begin delegating real power to self-directed work teams. Government must expand to act as global referee, police officer, and infrastructure builder. To promote economic and political stability, it must relinquish power to smaller entities. Both trends are accelerating. Together, they manage to cheer and confound the advocates of big government and small government alike.

This is the world of 21st-century civil service. The huge, leaden bureaucracies are disappearing or evolving. What will stay constant is the context of civil-service work. For the military, victory is the goal. For corporations, victory is survival and growth, winning over competition. For the civil service, there is no victory except service.

This opens a great arena for values within civil service. Many bureaucracies perform today like survival-driven companies. They carry out work routinely. People get cost-of-living raises. They concentrate on not making mistakes. Now everything is changing. Such a moment opens the way to move to the next level. For the civil service, the transition should be to a true service-driven organization. Such an evolution opens the door to a host of subvalues like Accuracy, Promptness, Courtesy.

In the next decade, government will downsize many agencies. To increase their chances of survival, both agencies and individuals need to upgrade their values, particularly Service, as quickly as possible. Beyond the current upheavals, civil service will acquire a new style. A higher standard of service is sure to be a standard of that new style. People planning to remain or enter the civil service should work on that value today.

10. Aren't these values programs just a lot of work for consultants? If you live by the Golden Rule, isn't the rest just obvious common sense?

There's nothing common about common sense. When were you last in a meeting where emotion-drenched people talked drivel? If it's been more than four weeks, you work in an exceptional company. Few people can consistently control their emotions. That's why intelligence is no guarantee of common sense. Any company with in-depth common sense is a sure winner in the marketplace.

Most companies don't follow the Golden Rule or any rule that's even close. Both common sense and values would abound in any company that did. Most companies are organized in a way that destroys values, pays no attention to valid rules, and defies common sense.

Obvious common sense is often the best prescription. Want to stay healthy? Give up tobacco, alcohol, and caffeine; cut back on sweets and meat. Exercise regularly and get to bed by 10 P.M. The prescription hasn't changed in at least 50 years. It's obvious common sense. The hard part is developing the will and system to do it.

Obvious common sense is often the best prescription in business too. The customer is important. The product has to work right. We should respect the people who work here. That prescription hasn't changed in 50 years either. It's also obvious common sense. The hard part is developing the will and system to do it.

Core Values provide a proven way to develop that will and system.

11. Does it take a charismatic leader to get values off the ground in a company?

Someone asked former U.S. Secretary of State Henry Kissinger whether charisma exists. "Oh, yes," he replied. "When you were in a room with Charles de Gaulle, all eyes were on de Gaulle. When you were in a room with Mao, all eyes were on Mao." However, he added, "Charisma is not the same thing as judgment."

Any leader can implement values. That leader must commit to the values. She must exercise her will to overcome resistance. She must follow a systematic approach. Charisma is an optional extra. Over time, success with values creates charisma.

12. How can you recruit for values?

My mother sat in a crowded waiting room together with a dozen job seekers. After 10 minutes the receptionist left the room. A few seconds later the phone rang. The job candidates ignored the ringing, looking uneasily at one another. The phone rang again and again. Finally, my mother answered the phone.

"What's your name?" demanded the voice on the line. After my mother identified herself, the caller told her to come into the boss's office. "I wanted to see who would answer the phone," he told her before hiring her for the scarce job.

Not an elegant technique. No doubt the attitudinal tests of ServiceMaster get answers less crudely. Still, that boss needed initiative and a service mentality in his next hire. He found a way to get them.

Few companies do as good a job today. In a credential-conscious society, resumes and job interviews focus on the what of achievement rather than the how of attitudes. Later, in those painful disciplinary and firing interviews, attitude is usually the core of the problem.

"It's hard to judge attitudes," executives complain. That's true. However, when a clear sense of values informs the hiring process, attitude-oriented questions rise naturally. The most successful recruiters understand the values and technical capabilities they want. The least successful concentrate on technical capacities alone.

Values-driven companies are inhospitable to those who don't share their beliefs. People "fire themselves," Jane Gandee of ServiceMaster told me. I hear that often when I visit companies with strong values. While it's better to fire yourself than be fired, there is pain behind any firing.

Clarity about values is a powerful before-the-fact control. People who share your values will quickly see themselves as successful employees. A sense of coming home often persuades people to choose a job with smaller salary and benefits.

13. Is it in keeping with the idea of values to test potential new hires on their personal beliefs and attitudes? Yet how can you hire for values if you don't?

The only proof of effectiveness in recruiting and selection is a quality hire. Individual definitions differ. However, there is one constant. A quality hire is still performing effectively in the same company two to three years later. Quality hiring has at least three prerequisites:

1. The right work atmosphere in the company.
2. Executives with high recruiting skills.
3. An organization that can beneficially absorb the recruits.

Companies often try to upgrade their work atmosphere through hiring. To a limited extent, this works. Replacing an unskilled head of finance with someone better qualified will improve the quality of financial data. However, hiring a disciplined foreman to work under a disorganized head of production will lead to trouble. Hiring cannot substitute for creating the right work atmosphere. Consistent attempts to make it do so will lead to rapid turnover and high expense.

A few people are naturally gifted recruiters. For the rest, it's a skill to be mastered. There are essentially three issues to be addressed. Does the candidate have the necessary knowledge and skills? Has the candidate demonstrated the strength of will necessary to succeed here? Does the candidate have the values we want in this job?

At the top level, values become the most critical of all. In recent years, all U.S. presidents have encountered difficulty getting congressional approval for some of their senior appointees. All the nominees had the necessary knowledge and will. Their nominations failed because of a difference in the values espoused by the administration and the congress.

Within the context of quality hiring, testing for beliefs and values makes good sense. It is fair and appropriate. During the process, the company has revealed its values clearly. Both Disney and ServiceMaster use videos early in recruiting to introduce the company and its values.

Values-driven companies take the time and effort to define and implement their values. Their strength grows from the personal identification of employees with those values. They know from experience there will be problems for both employee and company when values don't mesh. It is in the interest of both company and candidate to get that issue straight as quickly as possible. Carefully designed instruments can uncover major gaps in beliefs, attitudes, and values. Used in the context of quality hiring, such instruments are an aid to job seeker and employer.

14. Isn't making a profit the ultimate value for any business?

On the surface, yes. Look deeper, however, and the issue is more complex. Even more basic than this year's profit is survival of the business. To ensure survival, we put limits on this year's profit. We train people. We invest in equipment. We elevate product quality. How we choose to ensure survival by limiting profit defines our values. It's more accurate to say that ultimate value is sustained profit. And that's a measure of our performance on all values.

15. How do you make your financial compensation system more responsive to values without losing focus on financial results?

Financial compensation should be based on productivity. The greater the department or individual's productivity, the higher the compensation. In theory, that's how it should work. In practice, most compensation systems don't focus on productivity at all. Either the company believes productivity can't be measured accurately, or, where it's measured, it can't be enforced as a compensation guideline. Instead, market rate still reigns as the all-purpose guideline for compensation.

Today, however, many companies are wrestling with new systems of compensation. Teams create an opportunity for innovation. It's pointless to reward teams on a market rate. Who gains by rewarding all teams equally? Seniority makes little sense in team compensation. The driving force behind self-directed teams is to improve productivity. In any rational system, the most productive teams will receive the highest compensation.

As innovations like this take hold, they expose the linkage between productivity and values. Begin measuring a team's productivity and you immediately must go beyond measuring its output. Values are not just a cause or source of results, they are a component of the results we invariably seek. Measurement must focus on a host of factors, all of them linked to values. What is the team's defect rate (Quality)? How well does the team adhere to schedule (Speed)? How efficient are team members in using the latest technology (Development of People)?

Every team measured on productivity will become a center of values. Self-directed teams will recruit, train, and reward for the operating qualities they need to maintain and enhance performance. Their commitment to the specific values the company needs will be reinforced by the most powerful lever of all—pay.

As traditional compensation systems evolve, values-driven systems will emerge naturally. Even companies with market-based systems will eventually see the necessity of introducing values-based criteria. There is no faster way to link pay with productivity.

16. How do you reconcile conflicting values?

Values never conflict. Values are powers of harmony and cannot come into collision. A lubricant cannot generate friction. This talk of conflict baffles many values-driven companies: "Customer Service versus Respect for our people? We have to do both. What's the problem?"

To be sure, there are often conflicts between a new value and older methods. Perhaps the old mode was "get it out, we'll fix it later." Attempts to elevate Quality will certainly generate clashes in that environment. Conflicts also arise between the new values and older systems. Compensation, discussed under the previous question, is a common example.

That said, many people will continue to worry about the danger of conflicts. "At the end of the day, in final analysis, I want everybody to know absolutely which is our most important value." Fair enough. There are two ways to resolve this issue.

You can always lift apparently conflicting values to a level of abstraction where they unite. Manufacturing executives uncomfortable with a perceived conflict between Speed and Safety can find a common home under Quality.

The second choice is to rank values. In practice, such rankings are artificial. Values selected with an eye to a company's needs always support one another. However, ranking values simplifies communication within a large company. What is lost is a healthy dialogue on reconciling apparent conflicts. Disney World offers a successful example. Its four values—Safety, Courtesy, Show, and Efficiency—are clearly ranked for everyone. This works for Disney. Simplicity and clarity are important advantages for a company that must train thousands of part-time workers each year.

17. What are the highest values? Is this absolute or situational?

High or low is never the issue. What matters is which values are best suited for this company at this time. Values are suitable when they strengthen the corporate personality. They are unsuitable when they lack relevance.

Too high a value can break a poorly developed organization. A survival-driven company may view the customer as a means, not an end. It attempts to fool the customer with misleading claims. Such a company should not adopt Customer Delight as a value. The gap between performance and ideal is too great. Employees will view the new value with cynicism. Customers will see it as hypocrisy. The distance between ideal and reality will create negativity at every level.

For such a company, Customer Satisfaction is a far better choice. The gap between performance and ideal is narrow enough to create a challenge. Employees can support management's new resolve. Customers will appreciate small but visible changes. Reinforced, the corporate personality will acquire stronger will for further improvement.

18. In my company people with poor values, or even no values, succeed all the time. Why?

Success is an interaction between the individual and the situation. When an individual takes a job, she normally has insufficient knowledge and will for the tasks at hand. This is the challenge of work. Growth arises from the expansion of knowledge and will to the level required. When there is an overflow of knowledge and will, the individual is ready to rise further.

At this point, the situation comes into play. People with few or no values, once they acquire sufficient knowledge and will, will rise in a valueless company. Sustained success requires staying in tune with the corporate personality.

The reverse is also true. The person *who actually practices* considerably higher values than her company can temporarily be at a disadvantage. However, if she continues to grow in knowledge, will, and values, opportunities are likely to come her way.

Success depends on being in harmony with yourself and your environment. Change is in order when either is consistently out of sync.

19. If I investigated any company you cite as values driven, I would certainly find some abused and unhappy employees, ignored customers, or other failures of business values. How do you account for these discrepancies?

Values-driven companies consist of fallible human beings, not saints. Set high standards and you will lose people along the way. The issue is not whether incidents of values failure happen—they do and they will. The real issue is whether they are a normal part of business, whether they are openly tolerated. Do those who consistently abuse employees or ignore customers still get promoted based on numerical results?

The companies identified as values-driven in this book have consistently better-than-average records of defining and sticking with their values. A major leadership change can reverse that record tomorrow.

A values-driven company does not automatically qualify as a good guy. GE's problems with its financial services subsidiary Kidder Peabody are well known. *Fortune* headlined its story on that debacle "Jack Welch's Nightmare on Wall Street."[3] Intel shipped a faulty pentium chip and then initially stonewalled customers about problems. Yet both companies have strong values and work at them.

Strict adherence to values does not guarantee paradise on earth. As American Steel & Wire's Tom Tyrrell described his values-driven company: "This is a steel plant. It's cold in the winter. It's hot in the summer. People don't . . . skip through the plant singing 'How Wonderful Life Is.'"

Values won't save your soul, but they will make your department or company more productive. Units that are more productive increase their profits. Units that are more profitable perform better than competitors. Better performance leads to accelerated growth. Accelerated growth opens opportunities for the company and the people in it.

That may not be the path to heaven, but it's a better deal than most here below.

20. What is the best values-implementation model?

Values implementation follows the form of strategic planning. Like planning, it asks and answers three basic questions: Where are we? Where do we want to go? How will we get there?

Begin by studying the organization's five components (Chapter 6). Where are the components out of alignment? How do different components reflect the same basic weaknesses?

Choose values on the level where you are. Choose values that are the opposite of your current weaknesses. If your study shows a widespread lack of punctuality, choose Speed. If internal and external customers are dissatisfied, choose Customer Service. If people are demoralized, choose Respect for Each Other. If people don't have necessary skills, choose Development of People.

Commit to and define your values. Communicate them. Train for them. Set standards. Elevate the values in your processes. Recognize and reward for your values.

Survey again. Find new weaknesses. Identify values to offset those weaknesses. Begin again.

Ask the same questions each time you choose a new value. If we elevate this value even a small bit, will it move us forward? If we make a major effort, will it change the dynamics of our business? Those are the values that are worth pursuing.

This is the simplest model. I presently know of none better.

21. **How do you handle a key individual in a group (not the boss) who won't buy into an effort to upgrade values?**

A few people are too stupid to see any advantage in values. "Who needs to improve relations with customers? We treat them OK now." Most are smart enough to disguise such lame ideas with legitimate-sounding objections. However, no skill in answering objections will close this sale. This customer sees no benefit in buying.

More intelligent resisters grasp the advantages but are unconvinced change will occur. Often these are among the strongest people in a unit. They are confident enough of themselves and their skills to disagree openly with the latest management initiative.

Your task is to win over the intelligent resisters while working around the stupid ones.

Start by assuming all resisters are intelligent but unconvinced. You persuade people by entering their door. If your idea has merit, they eventually come out your door. For intelligent resisters, the door is their problem. What's causing big problems for this individual or group? How will elevating a value alleviate these problems? Get them to help you think through these questions. If you can't find a link between the value and their problems, question the validity of that value. Any relevant value should add something to the work of every individual in a company.

All except the most closed minds eventually see relevance in a correctly selected value. While establishing the utility of the value, begin showing commitment. How well are you and the other enthusiasts in the group supporting the value in your behavior? Don't expect intelligent resisters to move faster than your example suggests.

First, explain utility. Then show real change. Most intelligent people will join such an honest effort. Once convinced, strong resisters often become powerful advocates. Their visible change adds fuel to the effort. Reduced to an insignificant minority, the remaining resisters grow silent or leave. Either way, they no longer influence your success.

22. What are signs a values process is working in an organization?

Any common cause directs people away from bickering. One sign values are taking hold is a drop in gossip levels. Excessive gossip suggests a lack of values. Energy that should be focused on responsibilities to others, on competing in the market, is turned inward.

A change in the pace of work is a second sign of values in action. In values-driven organizations, work moves forward briskly. Initially, there is a common complaint: "We spend so much time working on values we can't get our work done." The same phenomenon occurs in introducing any change in human or corporate personality. To get more energy for work, we start exercising. Initially, exercise takes time away from a burdened schedule. Although we make progress in exercise, there is no crossover to our work. Things actually get worse.

Then one day we can accomplish more in less time. We have absorbed the exercise schedule while reaching a higher level of efficiency. The energy released by exercise flows naturally into the work schedule.

An attitude of continuous improvement is a third index of the presence of values. Values are guiding stars, pointing to a direction but never reached. A greater commitment to values unleashes a stream of positive dissatisfaction. Values march to the balanced drumbeat of two insistent questions: How are we doing? How can we do better?

Finally, evidence of effective values shows up in the financial results. When values work properly, they generate positive results. Often the results do not seem to be directly linked to values. A customer places an unexpected order. A new product suddenly takes off. A troubled acquisition rights itself. Competitors drop a potentially damaging lawsuit. The company is suddenly on a winning streak. Track each event back to its root cause, and you will find an elevated value or a changed attitude.

Serious attention to values creates an exhilarating work environment. Try to judge the level of energy in the next five businesses you walk into. If you attune yourself, you can actually feel the force of the corporate personality. Match your sense of the organization's commitment to values with its energy level. With practice, the correlation will be immediate and accurate.

What are the signs of values in action? Speed, efficiency, and zest are three reliable indicators in any business.

23. How do you identify training and development needs arising from values?

Values release energy. Learning new skills converts that energy into human development. Once a group commits to Core Values, members quickly discover development needs in at least four areas:

- **Knowledge** must be upgraded to support any value. Elevating Customer Service requires better knowledge of products. Commitment to Safety demands more information about OSHA regulations.
- **Physical skills** are values made visible. If Speed is the value, shop workers must accelerate production while maintaining Quality. Office workers must upgrade their skills in moving paper. Before Quality can have any real meaning, workers must know how to read and write.
- **Interpersonal skills** support any value. Implementing Teamwork requires effective listening skills. Pursuit of Diversity means elevating empathy. Continuous improvement on any value requires the ability to give and receive honest feedback.
- **Management's capacity** must expand. Leading through values requires new understanding and skill. Managers need to understand the values and be able to define them at their level. They need to set and monitor standards for values. That's a skill not commonly available today. Once values take hold, rewards and recognition will change. Managers must learn how to work the new system.

People thrive on learning new skills. Remember when you last learned a new computer program. Recall the surge of energy and feeling of mastery. However small and fleeting, that surge of energy built confidence for the next challenge. We all love learning. It's a game that never tires us.

People committed to values always find something new to

learn. When do you know enough about the customer? Who has all the skills to continually upgrade Quality? If Teamwork can reach perfection, why do Superbowl champions take time to practice?

Learning and development tie values to individual aspiration. The more people learn, the higher their aspiration. Properly supported, this combination of learning and values creates a perpetual engine of growth and personal satisfaction.

How do you identify training needs arising from values? Simply ask what it will take to implement and maintain this value. The list of required learning will be in front of you.

24. We staff people are convinced. How do we persuade line people to take action?

These staff people may subscribe to values, but their commitment is not yet visible. Otherwise, the line operators would be eager to learn what changed staff attitudes. Too many staff departments view their sole values job as teaching others. The old motto about the shoemaker's children going barefoot often applies here. A staff department that hopes to have an impact with values needs to begin work at home. If the new value is Customer Service, the staff should first raise its level of service twice the amount it advocates for others. After that, less persuasion will be necessary.

25. How can values help when external change is destroying your market?

A shrinking market takes a heavy toll from survival-centered companies. They disappear first. As the dynamics of the market changes, the market-driven company can easily lose its bearings. A second-tier supplier totally devoted to serving a first-tier company will buckle with its customer. A mature values-driven company has developed more balanced strength to respond and react.

Markets shrink, evolve, but seldom suddenly disappear. Survival depends on the strength and flexibility to regroup and move in a new direction. The values-driven company with strength in all components is far better equipped than its competitors to weather the storm.

26. **We are a division with an effective values process in place. We've been working on this for five years. Now, corporate has published its four values and wants us to implement them. What are we supposed to do? Throw away five years of work?**

Accept the principle that values never collide. Accept the principle that the lower should conform to the higher. Keeping those principles in mind, look at corporate's values and your own. Any conflict will be minor. Your task is to reconcile values, not rework them. Accept the corporate values as your own.

Often you can use your values as definitions of the corporate values. Where one of your values is not included in the corporate mix, consider keeping it as an extra. Few corporate centers object to divisions having an additional value. However, they rightly expect conformity with the overriding Core Values.

This question arises frequently when big corporations adopt formal values. Their most dynamic subsidiaries are invariably ahead of them. Management often spends too much time fussing over how to handle this supposed problem. It is really not open to debate.

The center must insist on uniformity around its values. Failure to do so strips values of a potent advantage. To compete, the modern corporation must delegate power to local subsidiaries. Successful delegation requires before-the-fact control. The best instruments we have for before-the-fact control are a clear mission, current policies, effective planning and budgeting, and universally supported values.

The division with values sees problems where few exist. Remembering the struggle to communicate values at every level, division executives see confusion and difficulty ahead. Actually this division will communicate and implement the new values faster and easier than divisions working on values for the first time. Any organization that has successfully implemented values can add new values at any time. The process and skills are in place. The objection is usually centered in the ego. Take it as a compliment that corporate is trying to catch up, and move ahead.

27. What's the best approach when two companies with strong values merge?

In theory, mergers or acquisitions should add strength to the surviving organization. At least one of the survivor's five components should expand or develop. Mergers can bring economies of scale by uniting markets. Acquisitions can fill out gaps in product lines. Sometimes one partner gains capital from the other for expansion. The prospect of combining technologies brings others together. Some of the most thoughtful unions aim for greater depth in human resources.

This is the appeal of mergers and acquisitions. Too often that appeal is more romantic than real. Like the supermarket tabloids, the business press regularly chronicles the glittering marriages followed by messy divorces of mergers supposedly made in heaven. The quantitative logic seemed impeccable. The numbers crunched to perfection. Market synergy was assured. However, it didn't work out.

Clashes of values are a root cause of many divorces, human or corporate. Due diligence is required on the financials of a merger or acquisition. What would constitute due diligence on the qualitative side? A few suggestions:

- How harmonious are the market-driven values of both partners? How do they treat dissatisfied customers? Is the emphasis in their training primarily customer-focused or profit-focused?

- What physical values are most important to each partner? Safety? Cleanliness? Systematic functioning?
- What do the two organization structures reveal about their organizational values? A flat organization with empowered people? A highly disciplined staff in a clear hierarchy?
- How are people treated? As ends in themselves, strictly as means, or something in between? What do the respective policies reveal about attitudes toward the value of development of people? What about promotion from within? Evaluations? Discipline?

It is unusual when such issues are probed prior to a merger or acquisition. Yet where there are serious gaps in the values represented by these issues, trouble is sure to follow. Paraphrasing the old saying about marriage: merge in haste, repent at leisure.

Values-driven companies are more likely to investigate such issues. During its rapid expansion in the middle 1980s, Service-Master expanded its due-diligence process to include extensive interviews with employees in the companies to be acquired.

28. Is there a difference between values in a for-profit and those in a not-for-profit organization?

In principle, there is no difference. Values elevate performance in both. Frances Hesselbein, CEO of the Peter Drucker Foundation, identifies three pillars for success in the nonprofit field. Nonprofits should be "Mission focused, values-based, and demographics driven." Hesselbein established the foundation in 1990 to promote management excellence in what she calls the "social service sector." Named for management author Peter F. Drucker, the foundation each year identifies the most innovative social service, nonprofit organizations in the United States.

Each of Hesselbein's three pillars supports the others. The bottom line for a nonprofit, as Peter Drucker notes, "is changed lives." That gives every nonprofit a dangerously wide scope of activity. Trying to do too much diffuses effort, a common weakness for nonprofit boards and staffs alike. An effective Mission narrows that focus. "A compelling Mission describes your reasons for being," Hesselbein says.

Today leaders, workers, and donors all want to know more than just Mission. They want "to understand the values that drive the organization," Hesselbein says. Values also attract volunteers. People want to give time to organizations that match principles and practice. Before they can do that, leaders must specifically identify their values. Mission and values provide the framework for reviewing demographic changes that uncover new needs. In turn, accurate knowledge of demographic change can signal it's time to update the Mission or add a new value.

While the principles are the same in for-profits and non-profits, practice can differ. Most social-sector organizations espouse high psychological values in their missions. They serve the disadvantaged. They teach people with disabilities. They help people with addictions. They work to improve the physical environment. Too many nonprofit leaders believe these high purposes give them a pass on other, more mundane values. For that reason, nonprofits usually need greater focus on physical and organizational values. Are their operations efficient? Are they clean? Are they fast enough in response?

David M. Cooney, a retired U.S. Navy admiral, became president and CEO of Goodwill Industries of America, Inc., in 1981. Goodwill is one of the world's largest employers of people with disabilities. When Cooney retired from Goodwill in 1995, the organization was serving 147,000 clients, compared with about 30,000 when he arrived. Work in its 184 member centers was generating $1 billion annually, compared with $230 million in 1981. In addition, by 1995 the organization was providing employment services or training to people in 54 international markets. This expansion grew from many causes. However, one indisputable contributor was the value of Systematic Functioning that Cooney brought with him from his navy years.

When Cooney arrived he found a staff of dedicated people. However, "I think they made up what they were going to do that day when they came to work," he says. From the beginning, Cooney insisted people clean up their offices. He mandated that they dress professionally. He promised executives in the member centers that national would answer every letter and phone call. He created a tight control system to keep track of correspondence.

He introduced detailed questionnaires giving member executives a regular chance to rate the work of his corporate office team and identify priorities for new services. Every corporate staff member visiting a local Goodwill writes a report used in the organization's annual planning. Without that, says Cooney, "you are only getting half your dollar's worth" for each visit. He extended Goodwill's planning cycle to seven years, with wide participation in annual updates. Cooney clarified evaluations and pay scales. He introduced career path training. He wanted his organization judged "on our productivity instead of our personalities."

He expected and met resistance. He sat with groups of employees to discuss the importance of systems and procedures. He sold the concept that better organization makes work more effective and less stressful. He insisted "there are no pleasant surprises." Not surprisingly, there were resisters. "This guy wants to do everything the military way," was a common complaint. Says Cooney: "They blamed their own rejection of Systematic Functioning on my previous employment instead of their own inability to change. Those who persisted in that attitude shortly left. They either left voluntarily or they left with an invitation, although that was a very small number."

After the first months, morale improved. People saw the benefits. Neater offices increased productivity and lowered stress. Better budgeting gave them advance information on what they could spend. Hiring and training became more systematic. With more competitive salaries, people stayed. It became worthwhile to train them.

Cooney created a list of troubled Goodwills, organizations that needed special help from the national office. When he started, the list numbered 25 or 30. By the time he retired, there were only "the troubled 10." Most satisfying of all, the 10 names now changed periodically, where before they had remained the same.

At no time did Goodwill lose sight of its Mission— "to achieve the full participation in society of people with disabilities and other special needs. . . ." However, before Cooney arrived, many at Goodwill believed that laudable ambition was a dispensation from physical values such as Cleanliness and organizational values such as Systematic Functioning. Cooney corrected that and launched the organization on a new path of growth.

While Goodwill was rising, other nonprofits, notably United Way, were losing their luster. When a nonprofit falters, it is seldom because of unworthy goals. Decline more usually stems from a lack of attention to basic physical or organizational values. For this reason, every nonprofit CEO should explore the power of basic values to increase productivity and growth.

29. How do values differ from social responsibility and business ethics?

Corporate values as discussed in this book refer to operational qualities of a business. Social responsibility extends a company's responsibility to shareholders to other constituencies. Ethics are personal codes of behavior. All attempt to broaden business decisions beyond the short term. However, confusion among them lessens their utility.

Values support many of the goals of social responsibility. Most values-driven companies eventually reach out to other constituencies. They espouse customer and people-oriented values. H. B. Fuller Company specifically puts the interests of customers and employees ahead of shareholders. It specifically identifies a commitment to the communities where it works. In doing so, it elevates social responsibility to a commitment to specific values.

Ethics apply in every situation. To its champions, social responsibility is equally universal. Effective values are more precisely focused. They always relate to what will make this specific business a success at this specific time. They require no sanction other than common sense.

Ethical employees are an asset for any company. Companies are wise to foster training and practices that encourage employees to behave in an ethical fashion. However, human history does not offer strong support for the ideal of an ethical organization. This would imply a whole organization dedicated to specific personal ethical values. Groups united in ethical or religious beliefs sometimes temporarily achieve this lofty aim. However, as they extend their boundaries, they usually meet unbridgeable gaps between practice and belief. ServiceMaster openly encourages employees to "honor God in all we do." However, it wisely does not carry that principle into individual ethics. It relies instead on values like serving customers and on a quantified goal of growing profitably.

Many people believe that a rigorous code of ethics ought to guarantee success in the marketplace. As Dr. Samuel Johnson said in another context, this is a "triumph of hope over experience." Balancing values within the five components is challenge enough. It is also a surer formula for business success.

30. Where I work, you don't get promoted because you have the right values. You get promoted because you have the right results. What can values do for me?

Values can improve your results. The question is what are the values where you work? Are there are any values beyond survival? If people get promoted for results at any price, you work for a survival-driven company. In such an environment, pick any value that you believe will improve the company's success. Customer Service is always a promising choice. All pioneering acts, all development initiatives start with an individual, never the crowd, whether that individual is CEO or an individual contributor. Individuals set new standards that challenge companies to grow out of their narrowness. Pursuit of values many levels beyond current practice may not be realistic. However, raising the standard to the next higher level should improve results for both the company and the individual.

31. What is the proper role of the board in setting values?

Boards should play an active role. Directors and trustees are the guardians of their organization's future. Values are enduring qualities on which the organization builds that future.

The board should begin by ensuring the staff has identified values. Some boards participate in the process. Others prefer to approve staff recommendations. Either approach works, assuming the board becomes actively engaged.

After the board approves the values, it should monitor progress. The board should charge a specific committee, usually Strategic Planning, to conduct periodic reviews. Developing objectives to upgrade performance on values should become a routine part of strategic planning.

The board also should define how the organization's values apply to its own work. How will Core Values shape board decisions and activities? Any board should periodically assess its own performance. The board of a values-driven organization will always include its values in that assessment.

32. What's the best way to establish values—a small group at the top or a widespread process throughout the company?

The wider the participation, the better. You want values-driven decisions throughout your organization. Give people some ownership in the process. Early involvement enhances support for implementation later. That said, values will work their magic even when established by a small group at the top. Many CEOs have successfully mandated values on their own.

Begin by gathering ideas throughout the organization. Don't ask about values directly. Ask, What's it like to work here? What should it be like to work here? Why is there a difference in your answers? What are your biggest problems? What causes those problems? Such questions will ensure the values you eventually select will resonate with reality.

Top management reviews the responses and creates a list of values. Which of these qualities will most help the company realize its aspirations and resolve its problems? It narrows the list to three or four and defines the finalists. No matter how pleased the top managers are with their work, they delay the ultimate decision and validate the tentative choices with focus groups, e-mail or both. What has been overlooked? What is unclear? How could we have phrased our definitions better? Top management then reviews and revises. Does the feedback suggest all selections miss the mark? If so, worry about management's grasp of operational reality. Are there few or even no suggestions for revisions? If so, worry about the openness within the company.

After a careful discussion, publish the revisions and begin implementation.

33. Today we talk about religious values, ethical values, family values, and core corporate values. Is there a common relationship among all these types of values?

All types of values have a unifying theme. To be values driven means consciously trying to live your life consistently with your values. Your values become visible when your inner and outer attitudes coalesce.

In any sphere, much talk about values is just words. Yet we all know people who try to live their religious, ethical, or family values every day. We understand these are not perfect people. What we admire is their consistent effort.

And we all know companies that try more than most to live their Core Values every day. They are not perfect either, but we admire their consistent effort. This book is an invitation to join them.

CHAPTER 20

THE LEADER WITH
A THOUSAND FACES

Leaders stand out by the impact they have on others. They rise through a capacity to envision inspiring goals. They pursue these goals with focus and enthusiam. They channel the energy of their followers through a visible commitment to common values. A final look at how leaders shape values and are shaped by them in return.

In *The Hero With a Thousand Faces,*[1] Joseph Campbell traced the central themes of mythic heroism. He identified commonalities across eras and cultures. Studies of leadership uncover similar commonalities. Leaders commit to a cause greater than self. The leader rallies discouraged followers to that cause. Adversity tests the leader. Mastering adversity expands the leader's personality. The leader sacrifices short-term gain to advance the cause.

Leadership is the visible pursuit of values. Not all our presidents have been true leaders. When we do think of a president as a leader, we honor his values. We celebrate Franklin Roosevelt's faith in freedom, Lincoln's determination to save the Union, Wilson's commitment to the rule of law, Truman's determination to protect Western civilization.

As politicians, they all tracked the numbers, the votes, the quantified results. Without successful numbers, they couldn't win elections. They never forgot the importance of those quantified results. On significant occasions, however, they went beyond the numbers. They acted on what they valued. In politics or business, that defines a leader.

A CAPACITY TO IGNITE ENTHUSIASM

Leaders stand out from managers by the impact they have on others. They rise through a capacity to ignite enthusiasm. They channel the energy of their followers by revealing their values. Jefferson defined liberty through the Declaration of Independence. Lincoln defined the issue of saving the Union in his debates with Stephen Douglas. Working in a practical field, political leaders strive to create the structures to support their values. For Wilson it was the League of Nations, for Truman the Marshall Plan.

Leaders in this book emerged through competence wedded to values. Jack Welch woke up GE through Speed, Simplicity, and Self-Confidence. Bill Popp distinguished Popp Telcom through Systematic Functioning. Walt Disney brought Safety, Courtesy, Show, and Efficiency to the traditional amusement park. In doing so, he created a company—indeed a whole industry—that attracts customers in the millions.

The business entrepreneur is an American mythic hero. True to this heroic archetype, Earl Bakken started a billion-dollar business in a Minneapolis garage. His six principles released energy that animates his company today. Denise Marie Fugo and Ralph DiOrio distinguished Sammy's by committing to World Class Food, Service, Management, and Ambiance. At American Steel & Wire, Tom Tyrrell brought a new value of Empowerment to an old industry.

Recuperating from an accident that nearly blinded him, Marion Wade realigned his work and his personal values. In months, he transformed himself from a survival-centered to a values-driven leader. The change was visible in him, his company, his company's results. ServiceMaster took off in an accelerated growth that continues a half-century later.

In launching companies, the imperative for these entrepreneurs was survival. Yet they moved past the survival-centered leadership that limits so many companies. They moved on to market-driven, even values-driven leadership. All earned respect not only for founding companies, but for the values they brought to work.

EXPANSION OF EXISTING VALUES

Other leaders gain respect by expanding existing values. Robert Haas inherited a tradition of care for workers at Levi Strauss & Company Building on that heritage, he embraced the 21st-century value of Diversity. Hal Rosenbluth added a people-first emphasis to Customer Service at his family's company. The company grew 7,500 percent in 15 years. Bill George elevated Earl Bakken's Quality value by seeking to increase it tenfold. Desi DeSimone took time-honored values at 3M and made them contemporary. James Burke energized the Johnson & Johnson Credo by challenging it. Tony Andersen inherited H. B. Fuller's Safety tradition and made it international.

Crisis makes values-driven leaders starkly visible. Don Schuenke tripled Northwestern Mutual's results in a period of sustained crisis. His simple strategy was to keep faith with Northwestern's values. Eric Benhamou reanimated 3Com by redefining its values. Ken Melrose brought Toro back from the brink through quantitative methods. He then led it to success by recommitment to Core Values. In the wake of the Tylenol recall, Jim Burke became a universally admired business leader. Yet, he insists the Credo challenge left him "no alternative."

Values-driven leaders work at every level of the organization. At Disney University, Valerie Oberle taught her staff to sprinkle "Pixie Dust" on thousands of cast members every year. At GE, Jim Baughman taught future leaders how to apply Speed, Simplicity, and Self-Confidence to their work. Jane Gandee reassures stressed customers that ServiceMaster of Alexandria will get there in 15 minutes. Faced with an appar-

271

ent conflict in Northwestern Mutual values, Gloria Venski transformed the structure of her division. The change honored three Northwestern values, using Teamwork to elevate Service while containing Costs.

Whatever their industry, wherever they work, values-driven leaders exhibit three common characteristics.

1. **They lead by example.** Quiet like Don Schuenke or exuberant like Jack Welch, the values-driven leader becomes a living embodiment of the company values. Over time, this link becomes seamless. Even close associates often believe the leader is expressing an inherent character trait. What the associates miss is the self-discipline and commitment behind every values-driven leader.

Above all, values-driven leadership is an act of will. "I don't think I can do this," Eric Benhamou confided to Debra Engel at a desperate moment at 3Com. "How can you tell someone they won't have a job tomorrow?" He went on to lead the company through a devastating layoff. "I am routinely available to you through e-mail," he told associates in announcing the layoff. "Informally, please feel free to stop and chat with me in the halls and the cafeteria." During downsizings, many executives hide in their offices. Overcome by grief and fear, they avoid the pain in the hallways. Benhamou emerged as a leader by dramatic acts of will in support of 3Com's values.

2. **They consistently champion the values.** Intel calls its values awards Role Model Advocates. Before accepting, you commit to speak out openly for all the values. Again, this requires will. Sitting in a crisis meeting, it's difficult to ask, "How do these decisions track with our values?" There is fear of ridicule. ("Get real. We haven't time for that stuff now.") There is fear of embarrassing others who have forgotten the values in the heat of the moment. Still, the values-driven leader honors the values. She overcomes fear to speak truth to power.

We define leaders by their capacity to inspire enthusiasm in others. Speaking out is the essence of values-driven leadership because it gives others the courage to follow. Speaking out also means openly recognizing performance on values in others.

3. **Their key decisions are values driven.** The caliber of the team defines the caliber of the leader. Who was hired? Who was promoted? Who was let go? Successful business leaders surround themselves with people with the knowledge, competencies, and experience to succeed in their business. They look for people with the will to act on their strengths.

The values-driven leader adds one more element, enriching the team with other values-driven people. The team balance among knowledge, will, and values reveals the leader's commitment to values even more than personal example and words.

Values impact performance through commitment. Values-driven people become leaders. Values-driven leaders communicate their values by example. They define values in the context of where they work. They set values standards, first for themselves and then for their team. They search for opportunities to link values and performance. Every opportunity is a chance to teach, recognize, or reinforce values. At first the effort is conscious. Over time, it becomes an unconscious habit.

From CEO to solo contributor, values energize work and enrich life. Although values-driven leaders have a thousand faces, their stories resonate with complementary themes. Values-driven leaders change the way we look at work. They uncover standards we didn't see. They create traditions that shape behavior. They transform routine into adventure, careers into voyages of self-discovery. Above all, they inspire others by revealing the power of a commonplace miracle called values.

Readers wishing further discussion of the ideas in this book may contact the author at Synthesis Consulting, Suite 532, 7873 Heritage Drive, Annandale, VA, 22003, or by e-mail at 74477.1223 @compuserve.com.

NOTES

Chapter 1

1. Robert Slater, *The New GE: How Jack Welch Revived an American Institution*, Homewood, Il.: Richard Irwin, 1993, p. 260.

2. William M. Carley, "GE Locomotive Unit, Long an Also-Ran, Overtakes Rival GM," *The Wall Street Journal*, September 3, 1993, p. 1.

3. Brian Dumaine, "How Managers Can Succeed Through Speed," *Fortune*, February 11, 1989, p. 54.

Chapter 2

1. Robert Howard, "Values Make the Company: An Interview with Robert Haas," *Harvard Business Review*, September–October 1990, pp. 133–144.

2. Noel M. Tichy and Stratford Sherman, *Control Your Destiny or Someone Else Will: How Jack Welch Is Making General Electric the World's Most Competitive Company*, New York: Currency Doubleday, 1993, p. 245.

3. Alan Towers, "Realizing the Benefits of a Good Name," the *New York Times*, June 16, 1991.

275

NOTES

4. Joseph Weber with John Carey, "A Big Company That Works: J&J's Ralph Larsen Gives His Units a Lot of Latitude—and They Produce," *BusinessWeek*, May 4, 1992, pp. 124–132.

Chapter 3

1. Carol J. Loomis, "Stars of the Service 500: Strict attention to costs and a passion for satisfying the customer have kept profits blazing at nine standout companies," *Fortune*, June 5, 1989, pp. 54–56.

Chapter 5

1. Patricia Jones and Larry Kahaner, *Say It and Live It: The 50 Corporate Mission Statements That Hit the Mark*, New York: Currency Doubleday, 1995, p. 44.

2. Ibid., p. 12.

3. Ibid., p. 44.

Chapter 6

1. The concept of the five components as engines for sustained growth was introduced in *The Vital Difference: Unleashing the Powers of Sustained Corporate Success*, by Frederick G. Harmon and Garry Jacobs, (AMACOM, 1985). Garry and I, together with Garry's consulting partner Robert Macfarlane, developed the concept further while working on assignments in the late 1980s. Garry and Bob discuss detailed applications in their book, *The Vital Corporation: How American Businesses Large and Small Double Profits in Two Years or Less*, (Prentice Hall, 1990).

2. "The Schwab Revolution: Billions are pouring into the discount brokerage, thanks to a radically new approach that's high tech, low cost, no pressure," *Business Week*, December 19, 1994, pp. 88–98.

Chapter 7

1. For additional details about Harvey Golub's values definition program at IDS, see my book, *The Executive Odyssey: Secrets for a Career Without Limits*, (New York: 1989).

2. Kerry Capell, "Reshaping IDS Financial Services: The largest financial planning firm in the country has embarked upon a campaign for change and self-criticism," *Financial Planning*, November 1992, pp. 23–26.

Chapter 8

1. Thomas J. Peters and Robert H. Waterman, Jr., *In Search of Excellence: Lessons from America's Best Run Companies*, New York: Harper & Row, 1982.

276

NOTES

Chapter 10

1. Thomas A. Stewart, "A New Way to Wake Up a Giant," *Fortune*, October 22, 1990, p. 91.

2. Paul H. O'Neill, speech before the New York Society of Security Analysts, Inc., April 18, 1995.

Chapter 11

1. Robert Howard, "Values Make the Company: An Interview with Robert Haas," ibid.

2. For more information about Dialogue, contact The Dialogue Group, 2310 Lake Forest Drive #342, Laguna Hills, California 92653.

3. For more information about Open Space Technology, contact Harrison Owen at H. H. Owen & Company, 7808 River Falls Drive, Potomac, MD 20854. Phone 301-469-9269.

Chapter 15

1. Robert Howard, "Values Make the Company: An Interview with Robert Haas," ibid, p. 141.

2. Hal F. Rosenbluth and Diane McFerrin Peters, *The Customer Comes Second and Other Secrets of Exceptional Service*, New York: William Morrow, 1992.

3. Hal Rosenbluth, "First Person: Tales from a Nonconformist Company," *Harvard Business Review*, July–August 1991, pp. 26–36.

4. Ibid.

5. Ibid.

6. Ibid.

Chapter 17

1. Don Clark, "Stunning Turnaround at 3Com," *San Francisco Chronicle*, November 30, 1992).

2. Ibid.

3. Ibid.

4. Ibid.

Chapter 18

1. Joseph Weber with John Carey, ibid.

Chapter 19

1. Raymond Chandler, "The Simple Art of Murder," New York: Vintage Books, 1988, p. 18.

2. Tichy and Sherman, ibid., p. 245.

3. Terence P. Pare, "Jack Welch's Nightmare on Wall Street: Like it or not, the scandals at Kidder Peabody were brought on by GE's management," *Fortune*, September 5, 1994, pp. 40–48.

Chapter 20

1. Joseph Campbell, *The Hero with a Thousand Faces*, Princeton, NJ: Princeton University Press, 1949.

INDEX